COLLECTIVE CONVICTION

Collective Conviction

The Story of Disaster Action

Anne Eyre and Pam Dix

Disaster Action

LIVERPOOL UNIVERSITY PRESS

First published 2014 by
Liverpool University Press
4 Cambridge Street
Liverpool L69 7ZU

British Library Cataloguing-in-Publication data
A British Library CIP record is available

ISBN 978-1-78138-123-6

Typeset by Carnegie Book Production, Lancaster
Printed and bound by CPI Group (UK) Ltd, Croydon CR0 4YY

© Disaster Action 2014
Correspondence address:
No. 4, 71 Upper Berkeley Street, London W1H 7DB.
www.disasteraction.org.uk
Registered Charity No: 1005728

DEDICATION

This book is dedicated to all those who have been affected by disaster and most especially to the memory of Maurice de Rohan AO OBE, founder of Disaster Action. His calm authority, warmth and experience enriched our lives. His skills in bringing together and getting the best out of people from diverse backgrounds in order to identify common goals were exceptional. His guiding hand is greatly missed.

CONTENTS

ACKNOWLEDGEMENTS

The authors are indebted to Sophie Tarassenko, whose judicious editing helped to shape the final text.

The key to Disaster Action's success lies in the unwavering support of individuals who since the foundation of the organisation have often put their own personal needs and expectations in second place.

There are others whose understanding of and belief in the rights of survivors and the bereaved to be heard has been crucial to the influence Disaster Action has been able to bring to bear. We hope that those who have played their part will recognise their contribution. We are grateful to them. Some names do, however, stand out: Mick Free, Duncan McGarry and Moya Wood-Heath. Their thoughtful encouragement and unwavering support has been significant.

Without the contribution of our members there would have been no Disaster Action.

PHOTOGRAPHIC ACKNOWLEDGEMENTS

Disaster Action Launch Pamphlet, 1991
The pictures on the cover of the pamphlet are reproduced with the kind permission of:
Top row, left to right: *Guardian*, 1987; Express Newspapers/Express Syndication; © *The Times*, London, 08 07 1988
Middle row, left to right: *Guardian*, 1988; Mirrorpix; Telegraph Media Group, 1989
Bottom row, left to right: Mirrorpix; Express Newspapers/Express Syndication; © *The Times*, London, 22 10 1966
Aberfan © Michael Davies; Herald plaque and church, King's Cross, Lockerbie, *Marchioness*, Southall, Bali, 11 September, Tsunami, London bombings and Bethnal Green memorials © Alana Francis; Hillsborough memorial © Liverpool Football Club
UT 772 © Jérôme Carret/Familles de l'Attentat du DC10 d'UTA; UT 772 aerial photograph © Aviation sans Frontières & Sahara Conservation Fund; Maurice and Margaret de Rohan © Australian High Commission; Paul Foot © Private Eye; Anne Eyre with the late Lady Mary Soames © Peter Holland; Disaster Action 20th anniversary reception, pictures 19–32 © Wayne Pilgrim

INTRODUCTION

I joined Disaster Action in 1996, six years after surviving the Hillsborough football stadium disaster. I had heard of Disaster Action when it first formed in 1991 but at that time was working abroad. When I returned to Liverpool I found continuing support through counselling and support groups available through the Hillsborough Centre at Anfield and elsewhere.

By 1996 I had moved away from Liverpool and the natural support of friends and the community there, but there were still ongoing issues around the political and legal aftermath of Hillsborough and for me personally in dealing with the consequences of what had happened. In addressing these I developed a keen academic interest in events from the 1980s and began to gather reports and research papers examining the causes and consequences of these predictable and preventable tragedies. Refocusing my career as a sociologist, I began to specialise as a consultant in disaster prevention and management, with particular emphasis on the psychosocial aspects and addressing the needs of people.

Attending my first Disaster Action meeting was overwhelming. Words cannot describe the impact of sitting round a large table in someone's living room, being surrounded by the human faces and accounts of the disasters that before had been news headlines to me and other people's stories, and now feeling such a strong sense of belonging to this gathering of people. Most significantly, these new friends understood the pain and depth of my experience without my having to tell the whole story. It was – and still is each time we meet – very much a given, an implicit understanding and respect, as is the sense of mutual support, acceptance and validation of my feelings and experience as a survivor.

Since joining I have taken an active role in Disaster Action and seen its core values and messages become more embedded within emergency management as the field has become more professional. With the approach of the 20th anniversary of the disasters that led to its inception, new members were still joining our organisation from different tragedies. Disaster Action was evolving in response to a rapidly changing world and developing context of emergency planning and management. For those who remember the events that led to the founding of Disaster Action, and for those who were not alive then but who wish to understand our experiences and journey, the time seemed right to commit the story to print.

While no one involved in a disaster – directly or indirectly – is untouched, most do not choose to speak publicly or write about their personal experiences, or indeed join support groups. But some do. These accounts are clearly different from 'official' versions reconstructed by professional responders and public inquiries. They give real and powerful insight into what it feels like to be involved in disaster and highlight the fact that statistics cannot convey the depth and impact of such experiences.

Throughout this book, survivors and bereaved people – some of whom went on to be founder members of Disaster Action and others whose experiences are more recent – share their stories. We are also grateful for being able to include reflections and comments from some of the professional colleagues we have been privileged to work alongside over many years. In this sense the production of this book has been a collective effort and achievement and so we wish to thank and give credit to all contributors.

While preventing future disasters from happening has been one of the building blocks underpinning our aims from the outset, we know that absolute safety and security are impossible to achieve. Yet those charged with corporate governance in companies and organisations large and small should be enabled through our experiences to appreciate the significance of their responsibility, from an ethical as well as legal standpoint. And through reading this book those whose work is to assist people in the aftermath of extreme events should gain knowledge and understanding that they will be able to apply in helping others in the future.

Most important of all, those survivors and bereaved from disasters will, I hope, find some solace as well as guidance that will help them, through our sharing our challenging and difficult experiences of 28 disasters from a period of over 40 years.

This book is both a set of personal stories and the story of the birth and growth of a small but significant organisation. We hope that it will not only offer some insight into the direct personal experience of those whose lives have been shattered, and rebuilt, but also illuminate the life-changing consequences of some of the greatest tragedies of our age.

Dr Anne Eyre
March 2014

Within two years of the death of my brother Peter in the 1988 Pan Am 103 bombing, a number of those who had been bereaved in the disaster were invited to meet a group of people whose lives had been similarly torn apart by major tragedy – Aberfan, Manchester, Zeebrugge, King's Cross, Enniskillen, Piper Alpha, UT 772, the *Marchioness* and others. For all our differences we had much in common. A powerful desire to bring about change in regulation and the law, as well as in the prevailing perception of the helpless 'victim', brought and kept us together. There was a sense that we could – and should – *do* something to influence the unacceptable status quo.

Taking on the tasks that go with bringing about such change was hard, with such an acute sense of loss at my brother's death. The Lockerbie families were also in the early throes of our fight for justice (which continues). My two children were born within three years of Lockerbie, my son just two months before the launch of Disaster Action in 1991. With hindsight, being made redundant from Penguin Books in the spring of 1990 was fortuitous – if this had not happened it is hard to see how my role at Disaster Action could have evolved as it has.

Without the support and encouragement of my husband John Francis, carrying out this work would not have been possible. I also owe a debt of gratitude to my children Alana and Liam, who have never questioned my commitment to Disaster Action.

I do not subscribe to easy notions of how good can come out of adversity. Yet I have seen at first hand how people can resist, refuse to be overcome, can make a difference and help to create a more just and equitable world. I am proud to say that Disaster Action has been part of that movement.

Pam Dix
March 2014

CHAPTER 1

DECADE OF DISASTER – HOW IT ALL BEGAN

The 1980s are remembered for many things – the shooting of Pope John Paul II, Margaret Thatcher as the UK's first woman Prime Minister, the fatwa against Salman Rushdie following the publication of *The Satanic Verses*. For some it is also 'the decade of disaster'. Certain names and places can still conjure up images of death and destruction: 'Zeebrugge', 'Lockerbie', 'Hillsborough', '*Marchioness*'...

A number of disasters occurred between 1985 and 1989, each involving many deaths and injuries – physical and psychological – within relatively quick succession. At one point it seemed like each time the television news came on there would be another report of a sudden major tragedy. Each incident received much media coverage and interest, particularly in the first few days and weeks. In the case of the Bradford fire and Hillsborough football stadium crush they unfolded live on our television screens on a Saturday afternoon.

The fact that these tragic events involved ordinary (often young) people doing everyday things – travelling on public transport, going to a football match, doing a day's work, taking a holiday – heightened the national sense of shock and mourning. It also brought home to people in the broader community their own sense of mortality: 'It could have been me'. Those for whom it *was* them – *their* experiences as survivors and *their* loved ones – have unique personal stories to tell and common experiences to share, not only with each other but with all those interested in understanding the impact and consequences of these events on ordinary human beings.

THE MANCHESTER AIR CRASH, 1985

LINDSAY'S STORY

On 22 August 1985 my boyfriend, Charles Hickson, and I were among the 133 passengers who boarded the early morning British Airtours flight bound for Corfu. In the relaxed holiday atmosphere we were unaware that minutes later an event would occur which would change the lives of every person on that plane.

Seconds into the take-off as the plane was gathering speed along the runway, a rupture in one of the combustor cans in the port side engine severed a fuel pipe which resulted in a major fuel fire which spread alarmingly both on the aircraft and the surrounding runway.

The pilot immediately brought the plane to a standstill and the fire service was at the scene in a matter of seconds. Fulfilling the standard requirement for evacuation certification, half of the total six exits were available. The accident was survivable. Both Charles and myself were among the fortunate ones who did. However, 55 people died trying to escape.

The cause of the fatalities was restricted access to exits and lack of protection against toxic fumes. Those passengers had no space in which to move to the exits and no time in which to wait for the space. Of the 55 deaths, 48 were solely attributed to the inhalation of toxic fumes.[1]

The plight of families concerned and unable to find information about loved ones who might be involved in the Manchester air disaster illustrates the additional anxiety and trauma associated with the way disasters were managed in those days. In an interview with the *Lancashire Evening Post* published to mark the 20th anniversary of the disaster, William Beckett vividly recalled the hours and days after receiving a telephone call telling him and his wife that there had been a crash at Manchester Airport involving the flight to Corfu. They began the difficult process of trying to find out if their teenage daughter Sarah was still alive.

'We lived in significant hope that she was okay but we didn't hear anything from her or the authorities. We then started to phone round the hospitals, which took a long time. When we phoned the last hospital on the list and she wasn't there, of course we assumed she was dead.'

The family trauma was made worse as Sarah's death was not officially confirmed until five days later. Mr Beckett added: 'Up to that stage we had still lived in hope that were was some reason why she was still alive and hadn't been in touch.'

After the tragic news Mr Beckett said they managed to get through their loss with the help of friends and family: 'I don't know how you do cope. You are like a zombie and just sit there staring at the walls.'

A few months later Mr and Mrs Beckett became involved in the legal action against British Airways and Boeing. 'That was extremely traumatic,' he said. 'While we weren't wanting financial compensation we wanted them to admit they were wrong and they would never do that.'[2]

The survivors and the bereaved from the Manchester disaster met for the first time during the ten-day coroner's inquest at Manchester Town Hall. A few years later Mr Beckett joined with others to form the Survivors Campaign to Improve Safety in Airline Flight Equipment (SciSafe).

William Beckett and others from SciSafe went on to be founder members of Disaster Action.

After each major disaster of the 1980s, relatives, friends and survivors formed support groups to help those directly affected. The questions of how and why people had died and been injured and how similar disasters might be prevented in the future, drove those from different backgrounds, of all religious persuasions and none, to come together. Each group had its own focus – for Zeebrugge, ro-ro ferry safety, for Lockerbie, airline and airport security, for the *Marchioness*, a full inquest and riverboat safety. These groups worked tirelessly to cope with and campaign on issues relating to their own tragic circumstances, lobbying government and other interest groups.

The 'tunnel vision' described by Pam Dix whose brother Peter died in the bombing of Pan Am 103, when the focus is just on the single individual, gradually widened to include all the families, not only one.

Just how did the disparate individuals and groups affected by this series of preventable tragedies in the 1980s come together to form the umbrella association that was to be Disaster Action? The answer lies in the quality and nature of the individuals involved in the Zeebrugge disaster.

ZEEBRUGGE DISASTER, 1987: BRAVERY AND HORROR

Shortly after leaving Zeebrugge harbour in the early evening of 6 March 1987, water entered the car deck on the *Herald of Free Enterprise*, a Townsend Thoresen ferry, as the bow doors had been left open when she set sail. The ferry rolled over and capsized within minutes. One hundred and ninety-three passengers and crew died; there were hundreds of survivors.

Stephen Homewood, the ship's assistant purser, felt the ship wobble a bit, then go over:

'The furniture started to move. The bar was busy with people. I remember all the people on the starboard flying through the air and hitting glass windows on the port side. There was no time to phone the bridge. Water began to come through the glass. And then the lights failed. The emergency lights came on for a few seconds and then went out. Paul (the ship's cook) was nearest the door; he got out first and pulled me out.'

Homewood then began to lift people through a door overhead and to pass lifejackets out to passengers in the water.

'A diver went down in the water where a lot of lifejackets were floating. I tied people to the rope but some gave up and slipped back. Glenn Butler was there. He said he was all right. Later, when a diver reached him, he was dead. There was a diver in the water working tremendously hard, but needing assistance, especially in saving people's lives as there were people there without lifejackets and they were still alive. Some were hanging on to ropes. There was an accumulation of dead bodies at the base of the ladder and I am sure they were floating on top of them.'[3]

Even though he fell in the water himself, Homewood stayed on the wreck for six hours, going back to help people to safety. He was later awarded the Queen's Gallantry Medal.

Andrew Parker, an assistant finance manager at a City bank, was in the ship's café with his family.

'My daughter flew past me and crashed into the side of the corridor,' he said. In darkness he organised a group of passengers to climb along seats only to reach a six-foot wide space full of water. 'I jumped down and spread myself in the water. I arched my back and held on to the railings on the other side so people could use me as a stepping stone.' Safely across, the group reached another space full of water. The only escape was 15 feet above.

Someone outside half opened the double doors and dropped a

rope through the hole. As the rope hung, offering escape, two drunks forced their way to the front but fell into the water to perish. Everyone became more calm, particularly after seeing these two men fall in. Two hours later all of the group had climbed the rope to the precarious hull of the ship.'[4]

Andrew Parker was later awarded the George Medal for what he described as an 'act of practicality rather than bravery'.

Australian businessman and engineer Maurice de Rohan had settled in the UK in 1976 with his wife Margaret and family. The death of his daughter Alison and son-in-law Francis in the Zeebrugge disaster marked a turning point in his life. Together with his wife Margaret, Peter and Pam Spooner, and Joan and Alan Reynolds, all of whom had lost adult children in the disaster, he started the Herald Families Association. Joining with many other bereaved and survivors from that tragedy, a number of them went on to become stalwarts of the HFA. Their purpose was to secure justice and to create awareness of the need for higher standards of ferry safety. Their concerns were with the law and the prevention of disasters, but also with the practice of management and the governance of corporate bodies.

Maurice could not understand how the deaths of nearly 200 people could have happened with no one being accountable. Those in the media and others whose lives have not been touched by such tragedy often appear to believe that probing questions about how and why a disaster took place are born of a desire for revenge, to blame indiscriminately, from an obsessive inability to 'move on'. This was not the case for Maurice, nor for those who joined the organisation he went on to found. Natural justice demands that just as company directors and other senior officials rightly take credit in the good times, so too must they acknowledge and accept responsibility when things go tragically wrong. Lord Justice Sheen's public inquiry into the sinking of the *Herald* found that the company was guilty of 'the disease of sloppiness from top to bottom', yet that elusive justice and accountability could not be obtained.

In the words of Sophie Tarassenko, trustee and co-chair of Disaster Action, 'If a dry cleaner damaged your coat you would probably get an apology, and some compensation. If your family member died in a disaster you got pretty much nothing – certainly no apology, and virtually no compensation.'

Looking beyond the tragedy at Zeebrugge, Maurice could see the common concerns and connections across the events that continued to occur in the 1980s. This inspired him to reach out and invite others to come together to talk to each other. Maurice always maintained that he had the ability to surround himself with good people, and with no one was this more the case than Peter Spooner, who was to become a great friend and colleague. Maurice's flair was to inspire purpose and steadfast loyalty in those who worked with him, Peter's to put into words what many could not express – the profound sense of loss, pain and injustice that was to be harnessed for good, to influence those in a position to enact change in corporate attitudes and the laws governing corporate manslaughter.

Following an invitation from the Herald Families Association an informal meeting was held in autumn 1989, bringing together for the first time many of the separate disaster family and survivor groups. From all parts of the UK came those whose lives had been changed irrevocably. A church hall in St John's Wood, north London was the venue for the HFA meetings, and this site also saw the first meetings of the fledgling Disaster Action.

At these early meetings feelings ran high. All those in the room had their own personal sense of loss, pain and grief. Could such strong subjective feelings be harnessed in a productive way for the good of others in the future? Was there enough in common to reach the conclusion that a new organisation should be formed? After much passionate discussion over a period of several months the answer was reached: yes, on both counts.

A new and permanent organisation would emerge, which could bring a new sense of purpose and focus. It would address the issues and problems common to all, issues that had added immeasurably to the distress and frustration felt by the bereaved and survivors.

The origins of Disaster Action lie in the personal experiences of individuals. The first, the Aberfan coal tip disaster, happened 20 years before the decade of disaster that was to give rise to Disaster Action. The founding members included Chris Crocker, who as a young child had survived Aberfan. Twenty-five years after her personal experience, the value of sharing that experience and joining with others to work towards common goals was crystal clear. It is a telling illustration of the life-long impact that direct involvement in a disaster can have.

There were already official bodies and voluntary organisations working to improve matters. Yet each tended to concentrate on a specific area of disaster prevention or response, working in separate silos. The human aspects of that response barely registered with those whose job it was to investigate and restore 'normality' after disaster. People on the receiving end had experienced little coordination on a national or regional basis, and very little understanding of their point of view:

> In the aftermath of disaster, too many survivors and relatives have felt deserted because of a lack of qualified counselling, bewildered by press

harassment and further saddened by poor understanding. In many cases a total lack of information from official sources, complicated problems in claiming compensation and a lack of legal guidelines for the establishment and management of disaster funds, have all added pressure to an already intolerable situation.[5]

Those who attended the first meetings of Disaster Action felt strongly that they wanted to work to prevent others suffering as they had done. Difficult as this was, the founding members did not wish to remain rooted in the past, but to learn from it and to ensure that others learnt too, so there would be fewer disasters in the future. They wanted to work with the established disaster organisations, bringing people together in an effective momentum for change.

Much of the early debate focused on what the organisation should be called. The name 'Disaster Action' was chosen carefully. It recognises that the organisation came into being because members had all been directly affected by disasters and, more importantly, conveys a sense of moving forward in a positive, constructive way, with action resulting from those experiences.

The challenge was to find the best way to work together despite the personal traumas, personal differences and diverse circumstances of so many individuals. Maurice's considerable diplomatic skills were required in the early meetings, where he demonstrated an aptitude to harness experience to the good. Everyone was given the opportunity to contribute; everyone was valued equally. Yet decisions had to be made, and Maurice's talent also lay in reaching a point when the talking had to stop and action agreed.

For some of the first participants in the early meetings it was perhaps too soon after their disasters. Some did not remain connected. Over time, membership varied according to people's personal circumstances, their ways of coping, developments in the resolution (or lack of it) of their own particular disasters and degrees of interest in further collective engagement.

Maintaining the independence and autonomy of the organisation was a constant objective for Disaster Action. From the outset Maurice was clear that people wishing to participate should volunteer their time and that the organisation should think long and hard about any funding support. This principle reflected the determination that lack of funds would not deter the work that needed to be done.

At that time, supporting 'disaster victims' to come together was not a popular cause and there was little external support, or encouragement. If anything, the empowerment that came from a group of those with common purpose was seen as a possible threat to government and those with a vested interest in the status quo. People's desire to meet was satisfied by members finding ways to get together, securing a room for free, or meeting in someone's front room. It was also about political independence and freedom. Another key principle was self-determination and the wish not to be dependent on external help, particularly from those who might bring political pressure to bear. Disaster Action had to be free to set and work to its own agenda.

LAUNCHING THE CHARITY

On 30 October 1991 the public launch of Disaster Action took place, bringing together members from all the family and survivor support groups at Regent's College, Regent's Park in London. Invitations were extended to the national press and those organisations, individuals and government departments who might wish to cooperate with Disaster Action's aims. Some of those who attended did so because of their personal experience of other kinds of tragedy, such as Diana Lamplugh, whose daughter Suzy had disappeared at work as an estate agent in 1986. Diana, who died in 2011, and her husband Paul set up the Suzy Lamplugh Trust and was an assiduous campaigner on personal safety.

Moya Wood-Heath, then a Chief Inspector at the Metropolitan Police Service, was one attendee who was to play a significant part in bringing recognition of the importance of the messages of those directly affected by disaster. A highly valued associate of Disaster Action throughout her career as a police officer and then with the British Red Cross, Moya went on to become a trustee in 2007.

In his inaugural speech, Maurice highlighted Disaster Action's aim and two broad objectives as being supportive and preventive:

On the supportive side, Disaster Action wants to use the experience of its members to help those who may be affected by future disasters. ... one of our aims is to publish a suite of leaflets which can be made available to people after a disaster which may help them understand what they may go through over the coming weeks and to indicate where they can go for help and support. The leaflets will address issues such as trauma, counselling, legal services, compensation.

The preventive role for Disaster Action is to do whatever we can to ensure disasters do not occur and we see our efforts directed into two main areas.

Firstly, we want to encourage all organisations that have a duty of care for the safety of people (their customers and their employees) to accept that this responsibility resides with the people at the top. We would like to assist in the definition of what that responsibility means and how it can be properly discharged because we feel there is a lack of clarity in many boardrooms, and amongst senior management, on what this responsibility means.

Our aim therefore is to raise the level of debate on the subject of corporate responsibility. We see this theme as positive and beneficial, not only to the community at large, but also to organisations, as these matters are better understood.

Secondly, in parallel with action on corporate responsibility, Disaster Action also sees the need for change in the law as it relates to corporate manslaughter. We believe there needs to be a significant sanction against the corporate body that has been reckless or grossly negligent.

Disaster Action also feels there is a need to question matters of safety where there may be a risk to people's lives, particularly in the transportation field. We will do so whenever we believe there is such a need to question the actions of Government or business.

A number of those in the audience responded to confirm the view that there was a groundswell of concern in the country over the lack of safety standards and corporate responsibility among large companies, and welcomed Disaster Action's establishment. Others expressed their frustration with the legal system, the lack of coordinated response when disasters strike and the rivalry between different established action groups.

Membership of Disaster Action has always been open to anyone, regardless of nationality, who has been involved in a disaster in the UK, or who is from the UK and has been affected by a disaster anywhere in the world. An Executive Committee was established at the outset, originally consisting normally of nine members taking their appointment for a maximum of two years, with half of the committee standing down every year. The importance of appropriate governance in companies and other organisations had to be reflected in Disaster Action's own management structure. The first elected Executive Committee was as representative of the experience of the membership as possible, consisting of those affected by a number of different kinds of disaster.

Maurice's ability to find and inspire good people struck gold in Judy Cooper. A number of Judy's friends and colleagues had died on the

Marchioness and she became the Honorary Secretary/treasurer of the Marchioness Action Group, members of which credit her with keeping the group going through times of great strife and near despair. Iain Philpott, a survivor of the *Marchioness* whose partner Tamsin Cole died, suggested to Maurice that Judy should take on a pivotal role for Disaster Action. Her calm strength and organisational abilities made her a touchstone for that first Executive Committee. Apart from a brief period on sabbatical in her native Australia, when member Mary Campion took over the reins, Judy has been Secretary/director of the charity ever since.

Associate members were also invited at the beginning. Given the fluid and informal nature of membership (there are no subscriptions, for example) it has always been difficult to quantify the size of the organisation. This is further explained by the fact that by the nature of individuals' engagement with Disaster Action, its size has understandably tended to wax and wane over time.

One member has used the following analogy as an explanation of what Disaster Action is:

> It is a special kind of family. With any family come frustrations, common concerns and extremes of emotion both good and bad. We accept each other for what we are, the crankiness and the fragility as well as the warmth. There is the core group at the heart of it all. There are the slightly more distant 'family members' who turn up every so often and bring something with them, sometimes helpful sometimes not. There are those who just want to belong and hear what is happening. At the same time, Disaster Action judges no one who sees themselves as a survivor, or is bereaved. We offer what help we can, and expect nothing in return. Sometimes people join, sometimes we never hear from them again.

Sophie Tarassenko adds:

> I believe that one of the most important things Disaster Action has done is to remind each human being working within a large organisation that they must always treat the rest of us, 'the public', as fellow human beings, rather than 'units of passengers' or 'groups of whinging relatives'.

In June 1991 The Joseph Rowntree Charitable Trust (JRCT) generously agreed to allocate funds to Disaster Action from its corporate accountability programme. The connection with JRCT had arisen from a suggestion made by veteran campaigning journalist, the late Paul Foot, to the Herald Families Association.

JRCT Grant Manager Stephen Pittam writes:

The Trustees of JRCT were enormously impressed with the integrity and commitment of those involved. They felt that Disaster Action managed to combine the passion which came from the suffering that its members had endured with the practical 'nous' of doing something about it. It was the focus on prevention of future disasters that most interested JRCT. The Trustees assessed that the people who had been directly affected by failings in corporate culture could provide a valuable input to the corporate responsibility debate. They would probably achieve more than those working on corporate accountability issues from a more detached standpoint.

The guiding principles and purpose set out in the original constitution are still the bedrock for the organisation:

---

(1) To promote the safety of the public generally or of any section of the public and or members of the public, against disasters involving multiple deaths or injury or extensive destruction of buildings or property, where such disasters occur in public places and whether by land, water or air, and in particular for the above purposes to devise, research, carry out, make known, disseminate, advocate, explain and advance principles and methods for securing or furthering the prevention of and protection against accidents of all kinds likely to give rise to such disasters.

(2) To enlist and provide support, succour, guidance and assistance generally to those including dependants and families, who have been or may be affected by such disasters or may be so affected in the future.

Along with the donation of rent-free office space, the grant from the JRCT enabled the setting up of an office in Lamb Street, London, and the employment of Judy Cooper. Judy was joined by Donat Desmond, who having survived the 1989 Kegworth air crash in which his wife Marja died, was determined to spread Disaster Action's messages far and wide, not least in the health and safety community.

Disaster Action kept going by 'begging favours from all and sundry' (Donat's words) but needed to put the organisation on a firmer financial footing. Judy and Donat set about contacting trusts, companies and individuals over the following few months, asking for their financial support for the work. Apart from the support of advertising agencies Yellowhammer and DMB&B, the corporate response was limited. Finally, it became clear that as a self-supporting organisation based on principles of volunteer activity and cherishing its independence, Disaster Action's sustainability lay in its members' personal commitment.

For one member, that commitment had come in the aftermath of the death of her husband Ian.

PIPER ALPHA OIL PLATFORM EXPLOSION, JULY 1988

ANN'S STORY

Ian Gillanders was a pipe fitter on Piper Alpha. He had been taking a shower at the time of the first explosion. He had returned to his cabin, and was tidying his socks into a drawer when his roommate, Bob Ballantyne, found him. After convincing him to escape the two men ran to a lower level, but when they reached there they went in opposite directions. Bob climbed down a rope to a lower deck, while Ian went to the other end of the platform where he was caught in an explosion. Ann's was one of the families who suffered the additional trauma of their loved one's remains never being recovered.

'It sounds ridiculous to put things away in a drawer, but that was Ian as I remember him, having to make sure things were tidy before he left.

Not having been able to be with him when he died and not having had his remains returned, I'd really wanted to be ... where he'd been at the end, and on the first anniversary those who hadn't had the remains of their loved ones returned were taken out to the marker buoy and we had a service there, and that really did help.'[6]

Disaster Action was established out of a collective will to see a more just and safer Britain. The answers to how, and why, that collective will emerged can be found in the stories of disaster etched on the minds of all those affected by them.

NOTES

1 Lindsay Davies, in Disaster Action Newsletter, Issue 3, Autumn 1995, p. 2.
2 Interview in *Lancashire Evening Post*, 25 August 2005.
3 Stuart Crainer, *Zeebrugge: Learning from Disaster: Lessons in Corporate Responsibility* (Herald Families Association/Herald Charitable Trust, London, 1993) p. 11.
4 Crainer (1993, p. 14).
5 Disaster Action Newsletter, Issue 1, Spring 1992, p. 1.
6 'Piper Alpha - The families', STV 7 July 2008, http://news.stv.tv/scotland/30422-piper-alpha-the-families/.

CHAPTER 2

THE COMMON BOND

Self-help support and action groups provide a natural forum and focus for many people affected by collective tragedy. During the decade of disaster they enabled members to look back at what had occurred and in many cases to look forward in terms of dealing with the complex procedures associated with seeking help, as well as compensation, justice and accountability.

In the aftermath of their individual experiences, despite their differences in personality, background, education and interests, many of the bereaved and survivors formed strong bonds born of common adversity. There was solidarity and mutual support provided by others facing similar challenges thrown up by the management – or, rather, mismanagement – of their particular disaster. Often working collectively was a more effective way of seeking information and answers to questions about what had happened and why, and what could, should and would happen next.

Those affected by a disaster often form an extraordinary common bond. Group members say that only with others from 'their' disaster can they open up completely, without fear of judgement, about the most difficult aspects of their experience. The difference in response to each other partly lies in an acknowledgement and recognition of that common experience. Unlike other friends, who share your pain but wish you to feel better and get beyond it, friends from the disaster appreciate that your life has been altered forever, and that it is not possible to go back to the way you were before.

The examples on these pages illustrate the kinds of support groups that grew out of those disasters of the 1980s. Many of the accounts from the different support groups from this period were reproduced in Disaster Action's first newsletter, in 1992.[1]

Following any disaster, whatever its origin, there are many practical problems to overcome. An inquest and any criminal inquiry process can be easier to cope with if there is the support and understanding of others affected.

Sophie Tarassenko explains the origins of the group formed after the King's Cross fire.

KING'S CROSS FAMILIES ACTION GROUP

My brother Ivan, 25, was killed at King's Cross probably due to mistaken 'evacuation' from the Northern Line platform into the ticket hall, and I identified his body two days later. I was chair of the King's Cross Families Action group and became a founder member of Disaster Action.

A public inquiry headed by Desmond Fennell QC in 1988 found that safety management on the underground was 'appalling' and that staff were 'woefully equipped to deal with such an emergency'. Exits were locked and train drivers had no directions as to what to do; people were evacuated erroneously into the fire, losing their lives as a result. The Fennel report contained 157 recommendations, and on its publication two directors resigned.

Bereaved relatives did not meet until the inquest took place a year after the fire. It was only then that we discovered we had all suffered similarly, but in isolation, and that sharing information and acting as a group was incredibly powerful. We wanted to press for recognition by London Regional Transport that they had not taken the safety of their passengers seriously and had been too focused on making a profit. This, despite all the evidence to the contrary, was never once acknowledged.

The jury at the inquest, pressured by the coroner, returned a verdict of 'accidental death', implying no fault on their part. Nonetheless, we asked the Director of Public Prosecutions to press criminal charges of manslaughter, we pressed for London Regional Transport to accept civil liability and we, at the very least, expected the Railway Inspectorate to press charges against London Regional Transport for breach of Health and Safety Law.

None of this happened. Despite all the factual evidence contained in the Fennel report, the law failed to find that London Regional Transport and London Underground Ltd had played any part in the death of our loved ones. We obtained advice from a leading lawyer that there was a case to be made for corporate manslaughter, but to launch a private prosecution was far beyond our means. Minimal compensation was paid to the bereaved and injured, but without any acceptance of liability by those in charge of the underground.

The families' actions did, however, achieve a degree of public awareness, and changes took place not only in safety management on the underground but also in the way survivors and bereaved are dealt with in the aftermath of a disaster.

The process of seeking help from government services, voluntary agencies, the legal profession or insurance companies can seem fraught with difficulty. Support groups, in which people can offer each other concrete advice and suggestions about how to deal with specific issues, can be very helpful. A group can also be a forum for sharing information about matters of importance to everyone.

The personal views of individuals affected by different disasters give some insight into why disaster groups can help:

'You do have a common grief, therefore you feel no need to explain your pain or suffering, it is almost like having a shorthand in conversation and feelings.'

'As a group, we were heard by the government on issues such as memorial services. If we didn't have a group, decisions would have been made for us.'

'For some who grieve, to be involved in something positive, to have an agenda to follow (for example a memorial, or an intention never to let this happen again) helps, especially I think for men.'

'People bereaved by a horrific disaster – or afflicted by the shock of having survived one – are consumed by a mixture of grief and anger. These emotions are inescapable but quickly become destructive. The only remedy is to channel them into a constructive activity such as a support group.'

The experience within Disaster Action shows that the most harmonious groups are those that establish a clear purpose and aims. These may be very clear from the outset, or it may take longer for these to emerge from discussion at meetings and informal get-togethers. The Herald Families Association stands out as a group that enabled those who felt disenfranchised by their disaster to come together in a productive way.

Peter Spooner, who was to play a pivotal role in Disaster Action's work on corporate responsibility and whose son Martin died on the *Herald of Free*

Enterprise, reflected on the first five years' activities of the Herald Families Association. Peter died in July 2008, which was a great loss to all those who had the privilege of knowing him. He had stepped away from active work for Disaster Action in his latter years, explaining that he did not wish to die a bitter man. He was not to know then that his efforts were to lay the foundation for the eventual passing of the Corporate Manslaughter and Corporate Homicide Act 2007.

HERALD FAMILIES ASSOCIATION

Although now in its fifth year, the Herald Families Association is still very active. General meetings are held two or three times a year; the last on 15 December 1991 was well attended, despite atrocious weather.

The HFA's strength lies in the fact that from the start its No.1 objective has been to help members come to terms with their losses by making a positive contribution to the prevention of other disasters. As part of this 'group therapy' we are still actively campaigning on two issues.

The first of these is ro-ro ferry safety. Our association can take much of the credit for forcing the Department of Transport to concede that the 'damage stability' of existing ro-ros is unacceptably low and that they should be upgraded to the SOLAS 90 standard for new vessels.

The Department originally set a target date of 1 May 1993 for this work to be done. Since then it meekly acquiesced with a decision by the International Maritime Organisation that the upgrading should be done from 1994 to 1999 – the latter being 12 years after the *Herald of Free Enterprise* tragically demonstrated the tendency of ro-ros to capsize so rapidly that passengers do not have a reasonable chance of surviving a serious incident such as a collision in mid-Channel.

The HFA thinks this is wrong. We have already set out that view to the Secretary General of the IMO, William O'Neil, and the Transport Secretary Malcolm Rifkind, and are now urging the Transport Secretary to take action.

Our other major cause is corporate responsibility for the safety of employees, customers and the general public. This, of course, takes us well beyond the disaster that led to the formation of the HFA.

Our concerns are still being vigorously promoted from academic and professional platforms. During the second half of 1991 we have presented at least four papers – to a conference organised by the Disaster Prevention & Limitation Unit at Bradford University; the Crisis Management Working Party of the European Group of Public Administration at The Hague; to a workshop arranged by the Emergency Planning Information Centre in London; and to a Law Society meeting.

On a broader front we recently cooperated in the production of a 20-minute item on the ferry safety issue, which gained pride of place in a Channel 4 'Checkout' programme. This gave HFA member Andrew Parker GM (George Medal) an opportunity to put vital questions to varied parties.

Meanwhile the huge volume of information we have collected is now being assembled into three publications by professional authors. The first will examine the need for legal reform to deal with 'crimes of violence' by corporations, both private and public; the second will analyse the management failings revealed by a selection of past disasters; and the third will look at the many lessons to be learnt from the Herald tragedy and its aftermath.[2]

There are a number of different options for the structure of family and survivor groups in terms of membership, legal status and management. Some groups have set up unincorporated associations, while a few have chosen to apply for charitable status.

Whatever the nature of the group, committee members need to be chosen and decisions taken about who will carry out key roles such as arranging meetings, taking notes and looking after the accounts. UK Families Flight 103 is a group in which the same coordinator and treasurer, Jean and Barrie Berkley, have continued in these roles since late 1989.

In March of that year, a number of those bereaved in the bombing of Pan Am 103 came together from all round the UK to meet each other for the first time at a hotel in London. The families were only able to do so because one person had been sent a list of contact details for the next of kin in the UK, anonymously, by someone who must have understood how important meeting each other would be. It was an emotional and painful occasion. Mothers, fathers, siblings and partners shared their stories of those who had been killed, considering what such a dramatically altered future would now hold, above all wanting answers to the questions of how and why it had happened. Pam Dix described in 1992 just what it was to be part of such a group.

UK FAMILIES FLIGHT 103

My brother Peter, a 35-year-old management consultant was one of the 270 people killed in the bombing of Pan Am 103. The lives of our family changed dramatically in the most appalling way possible when we learned for certain that Peter was aboard the plane.

The disaster resulted in the biggest murder inquiry ever held in this country, an inquiry that has still reached no conclusion. It has involved police forces and security agencies from the UK, USA and Germany, and clearly has complex political ramifications.

In the aftermath of the disaster relatives and friends of the dead felt the necessity to come together as a group. UK Families Flight 103 was formed in March 1989. Meetings are held on a monthly basis in different parts of the country. About twenty people usually attend, although our newsletters are sent to over 70 families and friends of those killed in the disaster.

Our two main aims are to provide mutual emotional support and friendship, and to press for an independent inquiry into the disaster and aviation security in general.

Initially much of the anger, frustration and hurt that we felt were channelled inwards, and towards each other. As far as possible we have turned that hurt into a driving force for change in airline and airport security systems, and to seek the truth surrounding the events that led to the bombing of Flight 103. We have also lent support to those affected by air disasters that have occurred since Lockerbie.

Having had a Fatal Accident Inquiry in Dumfries that lasted four months, we are now concentrating our efforts on getting the independent inquiry. As for most, if not all, of the family groups in Disaster Action, these efforts have been hindered at every turn by the various authorities involved.

Those bereaved by the disaster have taken a wrongful death action against Pan Am, but over three years later this case has not yet been brought to court.

Lockerbie itself remains to me a place of pilgrimage, a place which is in some extraordinary way the most special and most peaceful place in the world.[3]

Twenty-five years after the bombing the families continue to meet as a group for mutual support and to discuss the unresolved issues. The civil litigation against Pan Am went ahead in the United States, with the company found to have been wilfully negligent. The criminal investigation continued, and the two accused Libyans were tried for the murders in a special court convened in The Hague in 1999; one was found innocent and the other, Abdelbaset al-Megrahi, convicted and imprisoned in Scotland. Released on compassionate grounds because of illness in August 2009 in controversial circumstances, Megrahi was permitted to return to his home country of Libya, where he died in 2012, protesting his innocence but having given up the appeal process to leave prison. At the time of writing in 2014, the criminal case remains active, although the chaotic situation in Libya and the wider Middle East make it difficult to see how a just resolution can be achieved.

It may take some time for individuals to feel that they can take on specific roles and responsibilities within a group, not least when the experience is new to them. Some groups, such as UK Families Flight 103, have found it helpful to rotate most of these roles so that people do not have a constant time-consuming commitment. At the same time, if one or two people can take on a core position this will create a consistent and stable focus for a group.

Groups often choose to distribute a newsletter, occasionally or regularly, and/or to set up a website; some find it helpful to run smaller, regional subgroups where people can get to know each other better and focus on the issues they have most in common.

Good communication channels between members are important and telephone-based meetings or email forums may make this possible if members live far apart or may not wish to attend all meetings. The area of communications is one in which there have been major changes since the early formation of the groups that were to make up Disaster Action. In the late 1980s having a mobile phone was extremely unusual. Now it is the norm. Exchanging information through email and the setting up of e-forum discussion groups as a development of social networking websites means that disaster groups can be in speedy and indeed constant communication with each other.

In our experience the dynamics of every group are different and differing views may emerge on how long individuals wish personally to remain part of a group. Some groups continue for many years, while others disband after they fulfil a specific purpose. The HFA members felt that they had found a natural point of conclusion in the mid-1990s. Then with the publication of the report into the sinking of the ferry *Estonia* in the Baltic Sea with the loss of over 900 people showing that the work on ro-ro ferry safety was incomplete, the group continued until the tenth anniversary of Zeebrugge.

A number of the survivors and bereaved from the sinking of the

Marchioness riverboat in August 1989 formed the Marchioness Action Group. Amongst the founding members were Iain Philpott, a survivor whose partner Tamsin Cole died, Eileen Dallaglio, whose daughter Francesca died and Margaret Lockwood-Croft, whose son Shaun died. These three individuals were to play a significant role in pressing for a full inquiry into the traumatic event and its aftermath.

MARCHIONESS ACTION GROUP

Sunday 20th August 1989 was just another hot summer's evening and a clear night with a full moon. The brightly lit pleasure boat *Marchioness*, full of young people enjoying themselves at a party began its trip on the River Thames.

Shortly after the journey began, it ended in disaster when the *Bowbelle* dredger struck and sank the *Marchioness* killing 51 young people, including my only son Shaun. This preventable tragedy devastated the lives of the families, the survivors and their friends, leaving a permanent void.

Despite the efforts of the Marchioness Action Group, a full and open inquiry and an inquest continue to be denied, although disturbing new evidence came to light in Channel 4's 'Dispatches' programme broadcast on 8th December. On the following afternoon, an Early Day Motion in the House of Commons called on the government to reconsider their decision not to hold a public inquiry into our disaster like those held at King's Cross and Clapham.

We firmly believe that in the interest of public safety this new evidence must be evaluated in a public forum because our tragedy could be somebody else's tomorrow.[4]

The work of the Marchioness Action Group was to continue through and beyond the full inquest and public inquiry that they finally succeeded in achieving over a decade after the disaster. The recommendations in Lord Justice Clarke's *Inquiry Report into the Identification of Victims Following a Major Transportation Accident* have had a highly significant impact on the way in which individuals are treated following disasters. Without the commitment of the *Marchioness* survivors and bereaved, however, the public inquiry would not have taken place and these telling recommendations would not have been made.

This is one example of the power of support groups to be heard and make a real contribution to the welfare of all who may find themselves caught up in a similar tragedy in the future. The Marchioness Action Group continued to be active around the reform of the coroners' courts and the inquest process in the build up to the Coroners and Justice Act 2009 and around the improvement of safety on the River Thames. The Royal National Lifeboat Institution established the first lifeboat service on the Thames in 2002, the first time specifically covering a river rather than estuarial waters. The Marchioness Action Group had campaigned for this since 1990 and the Group continued to fund raise for these boats.

Other groups have focused on the creation of lasting physical memorials to those who have died, such as the memorial garden in Grosvenor Square, London, dedicated to the memory of those who died in the 11 September attacks in the United States, and the 2004 Indian Ocean Tsunami memorial at the Natural History Museum, also in London. Collective action to achieve permanent reminders has often been driven by the wish to establish formal and physical recognition by society of the experience of those who die in disasters, and those who are left behind. The group behind the Stairway to Heaven Memorial Trust for the Bethnal Green disaster of the Second World War is an example of this.

STAIRWAY TO HEAVEN MEMORIAL TRUST

On 3rd March 1943, following the sounding of the air raid sirens in Bethnal Green, the local population began to move towards the underground (the station was not in operation at this time and was being used as an air raid shelter). As they descended the stairs in the rain and poor light, a woman slipped, thus creating a blockage at the entrance to the tube. After hearing the unexpected and terrifying salvo of rockets fired by British Forces in Victoria Park the crowd surged forward, crushing the people. One hundred and seventy-three children, women and men died in the stair void. Many more were injured and one East London family lost six members. It was the worst civilian disaster of the Second World War.

Two young architects regularly used the underground station to go to work and noticed the small commemorative plaque above the stairs where the tragedy occurred and decided to find out more. Harry Patticas and Jens Borstlemann wanted to create a fitting memorial to the 173 people who died that evening. They were strongly supported by those directly affected by the disaster such as Alf Morris, a survivor of the disaster who continued to campaign tirelessly for a lasting memorial to those who died. 'I owe it to the people who died to make sure this permanent memorial is erected. Something should have been put up years ago.'

The Stairway to Heaven Memorial Trust charity was set up on 30th March 2007 and registered with a committee of 5 people. They were Alf Morris (Chairman); Sandra Brind (secretary) whose grandmother and cousin were killed and her mother and aunt injured in the tragedy; Derek Spicer (fund-raising coordinator) whose sister and brother were killed; Lee Scotting (accountant) and Rev. Alan Green (pastoral advisor), vicar of St. John's Church, Bethnal Green, next door to the underground station (the Church was used as a mortuary at the time of the tragedy). Over 1,700 signatures were obtained on a petition for the memorial to go ahead and the difficult task of fundraising approximately £500,000 to design and erect the memorial began.

The group was driven on by the determination to remember those killed and injured in the disaster, as well as the members of the emergency services, wardens, clergy and hospital staff who helped the injured. Within five years the Group had achieved full planning permission and two thirds of the funding needed. Part of the memorial was built in time to create a landmark at an important junction on the London Olympic Route, 2012.[5]

Within a few months of the sinking of the MV *Derbyshire* in which their son Paul died along with 43 others from the UK, Vivienne and Des King were lobbying government for a full inquiry into what had caused the disaster. Answers to their questions about what had happened were not forthcoming. It was only four years later on a visit to Liverpool that Vivienne met a number of the widows of the young men who had died, and so the Derbyshire Families Association was born out of collective sorrow and a conviction that the truth was more complex than the official suggestion that bad weather alone sank the ship.

MV *DERBYSHIRE* FAMILIES ASSOCIATION

In 1980 when the MV *Derbyshire* foundered on the Pacific Ocean with the loss of all 44 people on board, there was no concept of the need for disaster counselling for the bereaved relatives. The Sailors' Societies of all denominations gave much comfort to some of the families in the early days, but for many there was not even contact with other families bereaved by the tragedy; and after the memorial service in Liverpool Cathedral no further information as to the possible cause of the disaster.

All the families' news came from the media. The ship, having been caught in Typhoon 'Orchid', had not arrived at its destination. Searching planes had sighted an oil slick near her last reported position but that was all. Not until 1986, when the efforts of some of the families who for years had been calling for a public inquiry into the loss was reported in the media, did the families start to come together and learn of more recent information.

When the Formal Board of Inquiry, held from late 1987 to early 1988, ended it concluded (in the absence of other available evidence) that the ship was probably overwhelmed by the forces of nature. By then, more contacts had been made among relatives, and their need to talk with others who had suffered similarly and could understand and share their continuing grief, brought about the MV *Derbyshire* Families Association.

Meetings were held in Liverpool and the first Memorial Service arranged by the Association was held in the Lady Chapel of Liverpool Cathedral in September 1989.

On the 10th anniversary of the tragedy, a Service of Remembrance and Dedication was held, again in Liverpool, but this time at Liverpool Parish Church, Our Lady and St Nicholas. Known as the Seamen's Church, it stands at the Pier Head within sight of those sailing out of Liverpool. The Maritime Book of Remembrance dedicated that day was presented by the Association. It contains the names of all those lost on *Derbyshire* and will in future be made available to anyone wishing to enter the names of those lost at sea. Where there is no known grave-site for a loved one, the Memorial Book, we hope, will fill a need. During each memorial service held in Liverpool parish church the book will stand opened at the page commemorating those in whose names it was placed.[6]

Inevitably, individuals will respond to a disaster in different ways and have both common and unique needs. It is not always easy and passions may run high. While any group will need to have a core set of agreed aims, there are still likely to be different priorities for individuals at different times. Recognising and accepting these differences, rather than seeing them as a problem, can help a group evolve over time and focus when appropriate on the need for a common group response to key issues and concerns.

Differences between family members such as parents, partners and siblings of those who have died or been injured in a disaster are, unfortunately, not uncommon in Disaster Action's experience. These differences may spill over into a group. Or perhaps only one family member will become involved in a group, leaving the others feeling that too much time and energy is being expended on group activities instead of simply mourning the family's loss or trying to get beyond it.

The resistance of the authorities to the formation of such groups has gradually given way to a much greater appreciation of the need and the benefits for those affected to come together. After the 9/11 attacks in the United States and the 2004 Indian Ocean Tsunami, some funding was made available by the British Red Cross to enable the groups that emerged to get off the ground. Chapter 9 sheds more light on this, and on the ways in which Disaster Action has been able to contribute to this shift in understanding and consequent support.

Representatives from the groups of the 1980s, as well as individual survivors and bereaved people, went on to form, join and develop Disaster Action. This umbrella group was to become the platform for addressing the common issues and concerns beyond individual support and action groups, such as changing the law on corporate accountability, campaigning for a health and safety climate in which disasters were less likely to occur and improving the way in which people were treated in the aftermath of a disaster.

NOTES

1 Disaster Action Newsletter, Issue 1, Spring 1992.
2 Peter Spooner, in Disaster Action Newsletter, Issue 1, Spring 1992, p. 2.
3 Pam Dix, in Disaster Action Newsletter, Issue 1, Spring 1992, p. 3.
4 Margaret Lockwood-Croft, in Disaster Action Newsletter, Issue 2, Autumn 1993, p. 3.
5 'Stairway to Heaven Memorial Trust' http://www.stairwaytoheavenmemorial.org/index.html.
6 Vivienne King, in Disaster Action Newsletter, Issue 1, Spring 1992, p. 7.

CHAPTER 3

ACCOUNTABILITY, SUPPORT, PREVENTION

For the October 1991 launch, Disaster Action published a pamphlet setting out the organisation's origins and purpose.[1] The descriptions of the disasters that follow are stark, a shocking reminder of the human consequences that lie behind the bare facts. The issues common to all of them – a lack of responsibility and little understanding of the needs and priorities of those directly affected – gave rise to the three principle objectives, accountability, support, prevention, that continue to underpin the charity's activities.

The words in this pamphlet were written only a short time after the disasters of the 1980s. They capture a moment in time in the history of the organisation, when the experiences were still raw and fresh in the minds of those affected.

As we go about our daily life, we never stop to think that we're actually putting it in the hands of others.

We assume planes are airworthy.

We take it for granted that rail signalling equipment is properly maintained.

We expect staff to be trained in live evacuation procedures.

We can't imagine how profit motives could come before public safety.

Disaster Action is a charity formed by a group of people who thought that way too. Until we felt the pain of losing loved ones, in disasters.

Our committee is made up of individuals and representatives from all the family groups set up after recent tragedies.

As an umbrella group for these grass roots organisations, we're well aware of the dreadful common thread running through these disasters.

They weren't Acts of God.

They needn't have happened.

Preventing future disasters is the main aim of Disaster Action.

We don't want anyone else to go through what we've been through.

Zeebrugge. 6th March 1987. The cross-channel ferry, The *Herald of Free Enterprise*, capsized as it left Zeebrugge harbour. 193 passengers and crew died. The ferry had put to sea with its car deck doors wide open. However, the reason so many died is that the ferry capsized and sank in just 90 seconds.

Disaster Action was astonished when the charge of manslaughter against Townsend Thoresen, its principal directors, the captain and members of the crew was thrown out of court. This followed a public inquiry that unambiguously condemned the company as "infected from top to bottom with the disease of sloppiness".

We are determined to lobby for the law to be changed, to provide a legal framework in which failure to ensure reasonable safety measures becomes a serious criminal offence.

We also call for the application of SOLAS 90 regulations to all ferries using UK ports within 3 years, to reduce the risk of rapid capsize, and for safety to be made a priority in the ship-building plans of the future.

King's Cross. 18th November 1987. An escalator caught fire at King's Cross underground station. This developed into a violent flashover in the ticket hall. 31 people were killed, and a dozen seriously burnt.

The Government Inquiry revealed a management culture where it appeared that safety was the last consideration. Little or no cleaning of escalator areas allowed a layer of debris to catch fire. Sprinkler systems didn't work. Exits were locked. Emergency procedures weren't followed due to poor staff training.

Disaster Action is incredulous that London Regional Transport and London Underground were never made answerable in any responsibility for the disaster. We believe that accountability at law must be established if safety is to be a top priority for large corporations. We condemn London Underground's recent cutbacks in staff and cleaning, and the continuing lack of proper emergency procedures.

Nearly 4 years after King's Cross, only 8 recommendations out of 26 of the Fennell Report have been implemented.

Piper Alpha. 6th July 1988. An oil rig platform operated by the American company Occidental in the North Sea was destroyed by a massive series of explosions, which killed 167 men. There were only 62 survivors.

Disaster Action urges the Health & Safety Executive to speed up the implementation of the 106 recommendations of the Cullen Report into the disaster.

We regret that the Lord Advocate has decided that there will be no criminal proceedings arising out of the disaster, despite the fact that Occidental management were severely criticised in the Public Inquiry Report.

Clapham. 12th December 1988. A packed commuter train collided with a stationary train at Clapham Junction. 36 people died and more than 120 were injured.

Disaster Action believes that the signal wiring fault blamed for the tragedy is a symptom of a nationwide malaise within British Rail.

British Rail has kept very old rolling-stock in service and cut down the overall numbers of rolling-stock. The result is appalling overcrowding at peak times and less time for staff to carry out maintenance and safety checks.

We plead with the Department of Transport to review its plans to discuss subsidies to British Rail.

Lockerbie. 21st December 1988. A terrorist bomb exploded in the luggage hold of a Pan Am jumbo jet 31,000 feet above Lockerbie, Scotland. All 259 passengers and crew died. 11 people in Lockerbie were also killed.

Disaster Action insists that more must be done to prevent terrorist bombs finding their target. In the case of Lockerbie, specific and credible threats against American passenger jets were ignored by the airlines and Ministry officials.

Disaster Action believes that it should be obligatory for airlines to provide adequate levels of security, and we call upon the Government to enforce this obligation. We regret that no case for criminal negligence has been brought against Pan Am by the Public Prosecutor, and believe that the law should be strengthened so that prosecutions are brought.

Where the appropriate authorities receive warnings of terrorist threats it should be obligatory to communicate such warnings to passengers as a matter of urgency, and afford them the opportunity of declining the flights, unless they are satisfied that adequate precautions have been taken.

Hillsborough. 15th April 1989. At the FA Cup semi-final between Liverpool and Nottingham Forest, 96 people were crushed to death in the crowd and more than 700 were injured.

Disaster Action encourages the process of upgrading antiquated football grounds, as recommended by the Taylor Report.

We also believe that our whole approach to the policing of sports events should be continually reviewed and that medical facilities in stadia must be updated to provide good medical care in the event of a major accident.

We echo these conclusions from the Taylor Report, published after the Government Inquiry. "It is a matter of regret that at the hearing and in their submissions the South Yorkshire Police were not prepared to concede they were in any respect at fault for what occurred"..."Such an unrealistic approach gives cause for anxiety as to whether lessons have been learnt. It would have been more seemly and encouraging for the future if responsibility had been faced."

Marchioness. 20th August 1989. The Thames passenger launch, *Marchioness*, sank following a collision with the sand-dredger *Bowbelle*. 51 passengers drowned.

Disaster Action awaits with interest the outcome of a private prosecution for corporate manslaughter against South Coast Shipping, owners of the *Bowbelle*, and four employees of the company.

Meanwhile we urge the Department of Transport to hasten the implementation of the 27 safety recommendations made in the Marine Accident Investigation Branch report, particularly as there have been previous incidents involving sand-dredgers and passenger vessels on the Thames.

As failings in design and visibility were given as the fundamental cause of the disaster, we believe that it is complacent to allow a further 5 years for these recommendations to be carried out.

Disaster	Action
Aberfan. 21st October 1966. A waste coal tip slid down a Welsh mountainside, partially engulfing two schools and neighbouring houses below. The mass of black slurry moved several hundred yards killing 116 children and 28 adults.	Disaster Action believes that this disaster was apparently avoidable as the inquiry subsequently found. There had been several warnings that the tips were becoming unstable. Disaster Action believes that failure to act upon such warnings should give rise to serious consequences under criminal law.
The *Derbyshire*, September 1980. 44 lives were lost when the cargo vessel *Derbyshire* went down in the China Sea.	Disaster Action regrets that it took seven years for a full inquiry to take place and then only when it became known that five of the *Derbyshire*'s sister-ships had developed significant structural defects. All the plans (including the modified plans) for these ships should have been approved by Lloyds. We ask for a review of marine planning approval procedure, and for a statutory duty upon ship-owners to give priority to safety, coupled with criminal sanctions for failure to do so. We also call upon the shipbuilders of the *Derbyshire* to accept responsibility for the tragedy.
Bradford. 11th May 1985. Fire swept through a wooden football stadium stand. In a matter of seconds the stand was engulfed in flames and 56 spectators lost their lives.	Disaster Action deplores the fact that sloppy safety measures at the ground allowed inflammable rubbish to accumulate under the stand. We also regret that the 300 people injured in the fire, along with relatives of the victims, did not receive proper counselling and support.

Manchester. 22nd August 1985. 54 people were killed when a Boeing 737 burst into flames at Manchester International Airport.	Disaster Action applauds the magnificent efforts of the emergency services, but we demand that the Civil Aviation Authority brings about the mandatory implementation of smokehoods. We also urge the CAA to look again at evacuation procedures given the fact that front passenger doors and an over-wing exit are the only means of escape from a smoke filled jet airliner.
Enniskillen. 8th November 1987. 11 people were murdered and many injured when a terrorist bomb exploded near the Cenotaph at Enniskillen on Remembrance Sunday.	Disaster Action aims to provide support and guidance to individuals and groups touched by disasters, including acts of terrorism. In the case of Enniskillen no family group was formed, and apart from initiatives in the schools, victims were left to cope on their own for many months before meetings were arranged to share experiences. The lack of meaningful consultation with the bereaved by the trustees of the appeal fund regarding a memorial has added to the distress of relatives.
Jupiter. 21st October 1988. 4 lives were lost when the Greek cruise liner *Jupiter* sank in Piraeus harbour, 40 minutes after a collision involving an Italian vessel.	Disaster Action calls upon insurers to recognise that such incidents cause demonstrable post-traumatic stress to survivors. (Almost 500 British school children were on board the *Jupiter*. Some were seriously injured.) We ask the international community to institute a convention regarding the procedure of official inquiries. We also insist that the International Maritime Organisation set up by the United Nations should publicise and act on recommendations made.

Kegworth. 8th January 1989. 47 people died when a British Midland Boeing 737-400 crashed on a motorway embankment.	The Air Accident Investigation Branch report stated that the cause of the disaster was a combination of poor cockpit instrumentation, inadequate pilot training and a design flaw in the plane's engines. A vital warning instrument had no device to catch the pilots' attention, the pilots had received no flight-simulator training on a 737–400, and the engine design flaw had never been tested at altitude. Disaster Action is aghast at this fatal catalogue of errors.
UTA. 19th September 1989. 170 lives were lost over Niger, West Africa, when a DC-10 belonging to the French airline UTA was brought down by a terrorist bomb.	Disaster Action is appalled at the lack of concern of the British and French authorities and the hopeless state of international law regulating air travel. We feel that the initial attitudes of the consular department of the British Foreign Office was particularly irre-sponsible. The F.O. adopted a casual, amateur approach to the victim identifi-cation process and the return of victims' luggage.
Towyn. 26th February 1990. The sea-wall at Towyn, North Wales, collapsed and 3,000 homes were flooded with sewage-polluted water for four days. The emergency re-building programme which followed was the largest seen in the UK for fifty years.	Disaster Action petitions the Department of the Environment to institute an active policy of flood-risk assessment in vulner-able areas, to avoid such disasters again.

Accountability.

Many of the companies and transport bodies responsible for the disasters described in the previous pages have not faced any criminal charges. Attempts by relatives of the victims to bring companies and individuals to court have been thwarted, we believe, because of defects in the criminal justice system. Disaster Action will be calling for a new legislative structure of corporate criminal offences and sanctions.

While we accept that most companies will listen to the voice of reason, we know from painful experience that others will only be deterred by the threat of severe penalties, including imprisonment. For example almost 4 years after the King's Cross disaster, it has recently been revealed that 18 recommendations of the Fennel Inquiry have still not been implemented by the authorities. This would not have been the case if criminal prosecutions had resulted.

Support.

Our personal experience of disasters has taught us that the immediate aftermath is often made more painful by professionals and institutions who are insensitive and unsympathetic to the rights and needs of bereaved families and survivors. Disaster Action will be calling for substantial changes in their response.

Providing support and guidance to individuals and groups touched by tragedy is another of our aims. We will advise people of the best way to form support groups and how best to deal with the bureaucratic and legal hurdles they have to confront. We will also help to put them in contact with experts experienced in dealing with disasters.

Prevention.

After every disaster, a minister or public figure declares gravely "This must never happen again."

Inquiries may be held, committees may deliberate, recommendations are produced, yet still the disasters continue.

Disaster Action aims to break the cycle of tragedy and misery. Once and for all, we intend to learn the lessons of recent disasters and campaign for fundamental changes in the law and in business attitudes.

We will be seeking major reforms in the law to impose stringent duties towards public safety on companies and their senior officers. We also want greater public access to information concerning safety.

We believe that these changes will encourage a new corporate culture.

One where safety comes first.

Disaster Action members were not prepared to accept the lack of resolution common to their experiences as described here, however different the disasters had been in their cause and origin. We were galvanised by the injustice we faced. How we set about translating these desperate moments in time into societal change truly began to evolve over the decade that was to follow, the 1990s.

NOTES

1 Disaster Action, Launch Pamphlet, 1991.

CHAPTER 4

COMMUNICATING THE MESSAGES

From the outset, it was clear that Disaster Action would succeed in its aims and objectives only if we managed to reach and influence those in a position to take forward the initiatives that our experiences had shown to be so vital. For members whose lives were already full with work and family commitments, it was often demanding but essential to participate in that movement for change.

In the months leading up to the formal launch of the organisation, members were invited to contribute to numerous conferences, seminars, training events and exercises. We found ourselves sharing platforms with lawyers, civil servants, business leaders, police officers. At those early events there was much emphasis on disaster management, corporate responsibility and the litigation that inevitably follows in the wake of disaster, involvement in which had added so much to the distress of those on the receiving end.

For the first time, individuals with experience of the consequences of disaster had the opportunity to share that experience. The events and topics members were involved in discussing during 1991 illustrate the agendas of key institutions and authorities at that time and the contribution Disaster Action members were able to make to topical debates. They included:

- A series of seminars on 'Campaigning and the Courts' organised by the London School of Economics and Political Science, April–June 1991. Maurice de Rohan was a guest speaker at the first seminar on 'Disaster Litigation'. Members Sophie Tarassenko, Peter Spooner, Margaret de

Rohan and Judy Cooper attended three other seminars themed around 'Private Prosecution', 'Lobbying Courts' and 'Networking and Strategy'.

- In May 1991 the Research Institute for the Study of Conflict and Terrorism held a seminar on 'Victims of Terrorism: Needs and Provisions'. Martin Cadman and Jim Swire attended for Disaster Action. Martin Cadman reported that most speakers felt that the needs of victims were the same whatever the cause. Good legal advice was given by a solicitor seeking compensation for victims and relatives and a plea was made by the police for straightforward and readily available plans and guidance on disaster management, which would cut down on confusion and sloppiness in the post-disaster response.

- In the same month Aileen Quinton spoke about her personal perspective on disasters at North Yorkshire County Council social services department. Aileen's mother was killed in the November 1987 Enniskillen bombing and she had much to offer the seminar, which focused on 'Disasters – A Caring Response'.

- In July 1991 the Permanent People's Tribunal on Industrial Hazards and Human Rights held a conference at which a number of members spoke. Martin Cadman presented for Disaster Action, while Sophie Tarassenko spoke for the King's Cross Action Group and Iain Philpott on behalf of the Marchioness Action Group. The panel of judges concluded that there is 'clear evidence of gross violations by companies of individual rights, community rights and rights of people'.

- Fifty delegates at the 1991 CBI (Confederation of British Industry) Conference attended a meeting held by the Law Society at which Peter Spooner and two well-known lawyers spoke about corporate accountability. Roger Pannone, deputy vice-president of the Law Society argued that the most effective way to deter companies from exposing people to unnecessary hazards would be to introduce a system of punitive damages. Both speakers, whose firms had often found themselves on opposite sides in disaster cases, praised the objectives of Disaster Action.

In 1992, Chief Inspector Moya Wood-Heath of the Metropolitan Police Service invited Iain Philpott to speak on a course at the national police training college at Bramshill, Hampshire. Moya was then developing the MODACE (management of disasters and civil emergencies course) for the college. This was a watershed moment for the police, rather more used to command and control of an incident than considering the human implications of their actions and decisions.

Some months later Pam Dix was the second speaker from Disaster Action at a MODACE course: 'Arriving at this magnificent mansion in the

Hampshire countryside, it seemed impossible to believe that finally I was to have the opportunity to talk about what had happened to my brother, to my family, to me, in such a forum.'

Being faced with a silent semi-circle of uniformed police officers was daunting. Reassurance came from Moya, who quietly said, 'They are more nervous of you than you are of them.' For many of the police officers on that and subsequent occasions, it was the first time they had had the opportunity to hear and understand the views of those on the receiving end of a disaster.

Thus began a long and much valued association with the college and so many of the officers who have passed through its doors from all over the country. We had little idea then of the degree to which our words were to have an impact. In February 2009, Pamela met Glen Chalk, a former Dorset police officer who had been on one of those early courses. His words speak volumes about the way in which Disaster Action's perspective was to influence how in the future others would be treated following disaster:

I would go so far to say that the afternoon and evening that you spent with us at Bramshill in the early 90s was perhaps one of the most impactive training inputs I have ever had. I know others on the course were similarly impressed with your honesty, frankness and the way you put the victim's perspective across. Personally, after 28 years police service, I have always found those courses and training inputs based on practice and personal experience to be the best.

Later in my career, I found myself in charge of the Dorset Police Traffic Section at a time when we were rolling out ACPO's Road Death Investigation Manual, which itself has a large emphasis on the needs and attitudes of victims of fatal and serious RTCs (Road Traffic Collisions). By victims in the case of fatal crashes, I of course mean the loved ones of the deceased.

A lot of this shift of focus from the offender to the victim has helped to influence government in drafting legislation and sentencing guidelines. The work of road policing family liaison officers has been critical in this aspect, as has the very close links we've been able to forge with organisations such as RoadPeace, Brake, MADD (Mothers Against Drink Drivers) and other support groups and individuals.

I only mention this, as the presentation that you provided us all those years ago was always at the forefront of my thinking and in fact the bedrock when considering our approach to cater for the important needs and requirements of the victims and their loved ones.

Now, as coordinator for the Bournemouth, Dorset and Poole Local Resilience Forum, the lessons learnt in my previous role, underpinned by your presentation and experiences, have served me well in respect of matters such as Humanitarian Assistance plans and in particular, considering Mass Fatality plans ... All grim but unfortunately, as you know only too well, necessary stuff.

I consider myself ... fortunate (if that is not an inappropriate word in the circumstances) to have received your input at Bramshill all those years ago, that has helped me put the victim's perspective at the forefront of all considerations. No amount of reading and research could provide the weight and impact of your words – which I still remember so vividly and am so grateful and feel privileged to have received.

Yet there was also resistance to hearing the challenging and difficult experiences that Disaster Action members continued to visit the college to share. Indeed, sometimes there was outright hostility. One such occasion came in autumn 1999, when the pressure that the police often feel under boiled over. Many of the officers on the course were angry at having to listen to what they heard as unjustified criticism about past disasters that they could now do nothing about; the seminar had to be brought to a close. Our purpose, however, was not to offer criticism for its own sake, but to engage in meaningful discussion about how the lessons of that past could be applied to the future. On that occasion, one delegate on the course, Shaun Sawyer of the Metropolitan Police, made it clear that he had heard our messages. Sawyer was to bring much care, compassion and expertise to his role as the Senior Investigating Officer at the Ladbroke Grove rail crash only a few weeks later.

The connection with Bramshill resulted in police and other emergency services asking Disaster Action speakers to their own regions to speak to their colleagues. Gradually, almost imperceptibly, more widespread change in cultural attitudes, putting listening and understanding at the heart of the response, took place, which Glen Chalk and Shaun Sawyer were to demonstrate.

The opportunity to be involved in the training programmes of the police and other agencies was welcomed by Disaster Action, since an important aspect of our work continued to be getting across to those responsible for managing disasters what it feels like to be on the receiving end. Delegate evaluations and feedback over the years have consistently reinforced the feeling that Disaster Action's contribution has been amongst the most valuable because it reflects actual experience rather than theory.

Although every speaker for Disaster Action uses his or her own experience as the basis for a presentation, key universal messages remain the same, including the point that good lines of communication with relatives and survivors are essential.

> The main purpose is to get the audience to see disaster from a human perspective. Many of us feel that however terrible the disaster that changed our lives, what happened to us in the aftermath has made living with it harder instead of easier. By looking at the way things have been done in the past there is a chance of doing it better in the future, and organisations like the police are making a genuine effort to understand the point of view of those directly affected.[1]

Gradually it began to be clear that Disaster Action's input on training courses and conference programmes was having a direct effect on some policies and procedures, including those relating to matters such as identifying the dead and access to disaster sites. Senior Investigating Officer for the Ladbroke Grove rail disaster Shaun Sawyer put into place particularly supportive protocols for assisting bereaved families, which clearly reflected the impact Pam Dix's words had had on him.

As course leader for the MODACE course in 1997, Superintendent Andy Tyrrell wrote the following about Disaster Action's contribution over the preceding years:

> Disaster Action have spoken to at least 750 senior police officers at Bramshill alone, and the input has become an integral part of the course. At some time during the course someone will inevitably say 'we have the problem of managing relatives and survivors'. The DA presentation gives the officers the opportunity to consider the issues from a different perspective, and lets them see that if this aspect of a disaster is handled inappropriately, then to relatives and the survivors the police add to – and become – part of their problem.
>
> Over the years, speakers with experience of events such as Lockerbie, King's Cross and the *Marchioness* have shared that experience – at times at some personal cost. Frequently participants talk privately to the presenter after the session has formally ended. At the end of the course participants invariably value this input highly, considering it a unique chance to gain a different perspective. I am aware of many examples of officers returning to their forces and implementing changes to their contingency plans and training programmes, in some instances inviting Disaster Action speakers to talk to their officers.
>
> The Police Staff College is grateful for the continuing involvement of Disaster Action in this aspect of our training, which can only be to

the benefit of those whose lives may unfortunately be affected by future disasters.[2]

Other organisations have also given testimony to the value of Disaster Action presentations and other contributions. Moya Wood-Heath, who on leaving the Metropolitan Police Service became national emergency planning manager for the British Red Cross (and, in 2007, a trustee for Disaster Action) commented:

> Disaster Action's particular strength has been to alert us to the expectations of people involved in major incidents, and it has particularly done this by speaking at our organised conferences, and in providing us with information both through its leaflets and more generally. This has been invaluable in developing our training and clarifying what our contribution can be, for our recent emergencies have included transport incidents, building evacuations, floods and the Omagh bomb.[3]

As the world of emergency planning and management began to reflect on the needs of people, awareness grew of the important role and positive contribution Disaster Action could make in humanising policies and procedures. Some progressive and open-minded organisations began to invite Disaster Action to make representations and sit on working parties seeking to understand and draw on the experiences of those on the receiving end of disaster response. This was significant progress.

Such invitations offered Disaster Action a valuable opportunity to influence change and development at national levels. In 1997 we commented on a Home Office working party report investigating and seeking to improve the role of inquiries and inquests following disasters.[4] We also contributed to guidelines produced in 1998 by the Emergency Planning Society, which focused on good practice in addressing the human aspects of disaster.[5] And in 1999 Disaster Action made a submission to Lord Justice Clarke's Public Inquiry into the Identification of Victims following Major Transport Accidents.[6] As stated earlier, without the concerted and sustained efforts of the survivors and bereaved from the sinking of the *Marchioness* on the Thames in 1989 this inquiry would never have taken place. The recommendations by Lord Clarke on how people should be treated after disaster have played a huge part in influencing how responders plan for and respond to the human aspects of disaster.

In the late 1990s, as the emergency planning community began to turn its attention to new risks associated with IT concerns around the turn of the century (the 'Millennium Bug') and the threats and consequences of the changing forms and scale of terrorism, Disaster Action's advisory and consultative role became more consolidated. Further examples of these activities are detailed in Chapter 11.

In the first months and years of the organisation's development it became clear that with very limited resources in terms of finances and personnel, Disaster Action would have to rely on the services of committed professionals to realise its goals. Fortunately Yellowhammer Advertising shared our beliefs and was generously prepared to donate time and expertise during the period of Disaster Action's creation and establishment. They helped to formulate a coherent communications strategy, which contributed to creating awareness and an impact essential to the success of the early days.

The 'human interest' angle brought media interest and attention to Disaster Action from the very start. As well as extensive media coverage of the launch, television documentaries in the first year focused on themes such as corporate manslaughter; for example, two documentaries by Thames TV's 'This Week' (November 1991) and the BBC's 'Panorama' (January 1992) resulted in a number of new contacts for Disaster Action.

In 1995 Pam Dix took on the role of Press and Public Relations Officer in response to the need to keep the media informed of the organisation's work on corporate responsibility and other activities. Over the years the organisation has been approached on many occasions for interviews, comment and analysis of members' own and subsequent disasters.

Members also wrote articles for publication in the news media, academic publications and practitioner journals. Examples of these publications and further information about Disaster Action's relationship with the media are included in Chapter 10.

In October 2001 Disaster Action established a website, created, maintained and hosted by Steve Bradley of Chambers Technology Support, for whose time and expertise Disaster Action is very grateful. The website has proved to be an important medium for communicating our existence, purpose and main messages. The role of the website was to grow and develop as Disaster Action extended its influence and activities throughout the new century. The attacks in the United States on 11 September 2001 underlined the necessity for such a means to communicate with those on the receiving end of disaster as well as the wider community.

WHEN DISASTER STRIKES

In keeping with one of our primary objectives – offering information and support to other survivors and bereaved – a key activity was the production of a series of leaflets, entitled 'When Disaster Strikes'. Three leaflets were published in 1993: one for relatives and friends in the immediate aftermath, another for survivors in the aftermath and the third on injury and death overseas. Pam Dix, who coordinated the research with members of Disaster Action and various professional bodies commented at the time:

> The leaflets are aimed primarily at those directly affected, offering them the kind of information and informal assistance that we would have liked to have had available after King's Cross, Lockerbie, Hillsborough and all the other disasters that have brought us together. The two words that may sum up the ethos of the leaflets are *informed choice*: choice to exercise the right to take their own decisions about what may happen to them and to the injured or dead member of the family.[7]

The leaflets focus on the general response of organisations such as the police, coroner and others as part of disaster management and how those needing help may find it, guiding survivors and bereaved through the inevitable and often apparently insensitive processes and procedures that follow in the aftermath.

From the earliest days the leaflets were also intended to be of help to professionals such as the police, counsellors and social workers in their approach to issues such as communication, identification of the dead, support for survivors and bereaved and the role played by the media. Through the leaflets we hoped to overcome the preconceptions that many people have about disasters and their human consequences, by offering the benefit of our lived experience.

Producing the early leaflets was not without its challenges. It often involved revisiting painful personal experiences, including those arising from inadequacies in the systems that failed to provide the sorts of information we now sought to provide through these resources, which were aimed at filling gaps in knowledge and understanding.

> The work has not been easy, and has taken not only a lot of time but a great deal of emotional effort too. Getting the content and the tone right has been very difficult ... Yet if we succeeded in making the aftermath of one single disaster more comprehensible and bearable than it might otherwise have been to those yet to be affected then all the effort will have been worth it.[8]

When new titles are in draft, the text is sent to the relevant body or government department – such as the police, local authority, Foreign & Commonwealth Office (FCO) or Home Office – for comment on any factual statements that reflect their activities, in order to ensure accuracy. Doing this also engages the support of planners and responders for the leaflets.

In time, the leaflets were uploaded onto Disaster Action's website and are freely available for anyone to download, use and distribute. Following feedback from members and others associated with Disaster Action more leaflets have been produced from 2005 onwards, covering areas such as setting up support groups, personal reflections on disaster, disaster victim identification, legal representation and the inquest process. Comment from newer members of the organisation has shown the usefulness of the leaflets in times of crisis. As one member put it: 'Disaster Action (leaflets) were especially good because (they made) more specific reference to the issues involved with disasters – they are full of specific practical advice.'

The experience of people affected by disasters as they continue to occur informs the revision and publication of new leaflets in the series, which form a significant contribution to the way in which Disaster Action evolves as an organisation. One example relates to the July 2005 Sharm El Sheikh bombings. Trevor Lakin, whose son Jeremy had been killed at Sharm El Sheikh, felt strongly that people with family and friends missing after an overseas disaster should have immediate access to information and support concerning visiting the relevant country. Working in conjunction with Trevor, we developed a new leaflet entitled *Overseas Disasters: the Immediate Aftermath*, broadening out from his individual experience to create a generic leaflet intended to be relevant to those affected by any form of overseas incident.

---

23 JULY 2005

This date will be forever in my mind. Just four days before our 32nd wedding anniversary. The date our eldest son was killed by a suicide bomber.

Jeremy 'Jez' Lakin, 28 years old and on holiday in Sharm El Sheikh with his girlfriend, Annalie Vickers, enjoying their last night before flying home.

We (my wife Jill and I) heard about the bombings on the national television news on Saturday 23 July 2005. We could not contact Jeremy either through the hotel or his mobile phone. His girlfriend's parents couldn't contact her either. A parent's worse nightmare. We all (the four parents) got on the first available flight to Sharm El Sheikh on Sunday 24 July. It was the first time we had met! We travelled with the hope of finding them alive but injured.

The authorities did not 'find' Jeremy until Thursday 28 July 2005 and we had the task of identifying our gorgeous beautiful son to the satisfaction of the Egyptian authorities. This we did and Jeremy was released into the care of the British authorities. Jez did not arrive close to our home until the 18 August 2005!

We had arrived back in England on Sunday 30 July and drove home to share our loss with the two younger brothers of Jez but it was not until mid August that we heard about Disaster Action. A Red Cross representative told us. I looked at the website and read it a few times but I found most things difficult to understand in those days.

I contacted DA to ask what they could do but really didn't know what I was looking for. By then I had already started writing a check-list to help others in the future and agreed with DA that they should host it. This is now part of the DA literature. Had I known about DA before flying to Egypt I could have read their website and been better prepared for the difficulties we encountered. The British government who don't accept non-British identification procedures and many more small but very irritating things that we found adding to our trauma.

My experience was shared with DA and used to help them respond to various requests for information both in this country and Europe. They could judge how much progress, or lack of, had been made since the last event and push for more. They knew who was who so could contact the right people to get things done.

Personally I think that DA should be the front line support for those who find themselves in a similar position to us. They are independent and not beholden to a government paymaster or political pressure. They have experienced the situation for themselves; they know what is needed and why and through that experience ask the right questions of the relevant authorities.

I feel that if you can give something then do so and through DA I feel that I have been able to contribute a little bit because at the end of the day an individual is up against a faceless bureaucratic body both here in the UK and even more so overseas. In my mind DA know who hides where.

After much lobbying, and many meetings, Trevor and others affected by overseas terrorism succeeded in getting the British Government to change the law so that British victims of terrorism – no matter where in the world they are affected – now receive financial support via the Criminal Injuries Compensation Scheme. The law was passed on 27 November 2012.

In autumn 2008, we produced four new leaflets and revised the existing titles in the series. We publicised these to local authority practitioners through the Cabinet Office. This meant that every emergency planner in the country would have the opportunity of either being reminded about Disaster Action or newly introduced to the organisation and the extensive resources we were providing. The work of updating, revising and adding to the series continued in order to keep the information current. The experience of members such as Henry Luce, injured in the 2006 Dahab bombing while on holiday with his wife Therese, showed that the existing leaflet on surviving disaster needed to be supplemented by one that took physical injury into account.

The full text of the leaflets in 'When Disaster Strikes' available at the time of writing in 2014 together with the 'Guidance for Responders' leaflets described below can be found in Appendix 3.

GUIDANCE FOR RESPONDERS

Over time we began to develop information and advice for policy makers and practitioners. We felt we had a contribution to make to emergency planners and responders, government officials, health professionals and others who needed to understand from those with first-hand experience what the issues for survivors and bereaved are, and how to deal with them.

The first in this 'Guidance for Responders' series was a code of practice on working with survivors and the bereaved. This code addresses issues around privacy, confidentiality and anonymity, and has been adopted by organisations such as the Association of Train Operating Companies (ATOC), with the encouragement of Peter Lovegrove of ATOC, a long-term supporter of our work. A section of the Disaster Action website is devoted to providing this and other such resources for responders.

Every leaflet has its roots in the experience of our members. The leaflet on enabling the development of support groups is intended to show that a careful balance is required on the part of responders in order to *facilitate* self-determination rather than take over. It can be difficult for those who wish to support others to step back sufficiently from what can be a 'need to be needed' approach that ends up disempowering rather than enabling families and survivors.

TELEPHONE SUPPORT

For many years a telephone presence and resource has been a key activity within Disaster Action. Though staffed on a part-time basis since the beginning, the office has continued to handle calls on a regular basis not only from the media and professionals seeking information, advice and guidance, but most importantly from those directly involved in and affected by disasters.

In 1992 Disaster Action extended its support for the first time beyond its core membership to those newly bereaved from the PK268 crash in Kathmandu, Nepal in September of that year. Members were invited to speak to groups of families in Manchester and London. The Foreign & Commonwealth Office was instrumental in Disaster Action making contact with the families. Testament to the difference we were able to make lies in the cards and family news still being sent to Pam Dix over 20 years later by a man whose wife had been killed in the crash.

At that time Disaster Action was also in contact with families affected by a rail disaster in Alabama and an air crash in Vietnam, as well as by a coach crash on the M2 and the M40 school minibus crash, in which 12 school children and their teacher died.

The telephone service continued, the phone still being staffed on a part-time basis and based at the home office of Pam Dix, who became Executive Director in 2003. Callers' needs vary from wanting to talk to someone who shares their experience to seeking advice on matters such as the return of personal property, where to turn for legal help and how to deal with the practical and emotional needs created by the disaster. Some people develop an ongoing relationship with Disaster Action members and others do not want further contact. While it can be challenging offering telephone support to those who may be distraught and highly vulnerable, members find it very satisfying to offer some much-valued assistance, assistance that at this time is not replicated by any other organisation.

Margaret Lockwood-Croft reflected on the sense of privilege at being able to assist in answering calls following the screening of a Carlton TV series 'The Day I Nearly Died', which portrayed survivors' stories of disaster. At the same time, the experiences recounted on the phone were deeply saddening:

> I was dismayed to learn of the secondary delayed deaths that occurred following a disaster. Survivors that in the end did not survive. I listened to the stories from the bereaved of how their relatives who had survived a disaster changed, became ill, or had a heart attack, dying two to three years after their tragedy even though there was no history of illness in the family.[9]

Jackie Tancred (nee Hale), who also helped staff the telephone line in the early years of Disaster Action, wrote the following:

March 6 1987 changed the life of many people when the *Herald of Free Enterprise* capsized off Zeebrugge. At the time I was working as a secretary for Maurice de Rohan who lost his daughter Alison and son-in-law Francis in the disaster.

The Herald Families Association was formed with Maurice as Chairman and I was kept busy in the office as calls from the media and relatives came flooding in. Unused to speaking with people affected by tragedy thoughts such as 'What could I say to give comfort?' crept into my mind. I also wanted to do more for those involved but was unsure what. The difficulty became increased when Maurice became Chairman of Disaster Action.

It was not until I was asked by Judy Cooper to help man the telephone helpline for the Carlton TV programme 'The Day I Nearly Died' did the realisation come upon me. Some years had gone past from these disasters but calls from people showed that they were still feeling the effects – this now has a name: Post-Traumatic Stress Disorder.

Over the next months I researched post-traumatic stress and discovered that counselling played a valuable part in recovery. I had been told by friends and colleagues that I was a good listener and counselling felt right for me. I proceeded to investigate every counselling course available and eventually decided to do my training with the Westminster Pastoral Foundation.

Ten years on I am now in my second year of a three-year training course and whilst that terrible day will not be forgotten, I hope in my small way to make a difference to others in honour of those lives that were lost.[10]

Although Disaster Action was not set up or resourced as a frontline responder, when a disaster occurs the organisation continues to expect calls in the short- and longer-term aftermath and continues to offer availability to callers and others seeking advice and information. When programmes concerning disasters are shown on the BBC, for example, Disaster Action is often referred to as a responder for potential callers on the BBC Action/information line.

In the aftermath and in the longer term following collective tragedy, the police, local authorities and others such as the FCO Consular Directorate officials also pass on Disaster Action's contact details to those who find themselves on the receiving end.

NOTES

1 Pam Dix, in Disaster Action Newsletter, Issue 3, Autumn 1995, p. 1.
2 Andy Tyrrell, in Disaster Action Newsletter, Issue 4, Spring/Summer 1997, p. 4.
3 Moya Wood-Heath, in Disaster Action Newsletter, Spring/Summer 1999, p. 2.
4 Home Office, *The Report of the Disasters and Inquests Working Group*, Constitutional and Community Policy Directorate (Home Office, London, 1997).
5 Emergency Planning Society, *Responding to Disaster: The Human Aspects* (Emergency Planning Society, 1998).
6 Anthony Clarke, *Public inquiry into the identification of victims following major transport accidents report of Lord Justice Clarke*, Cm. 5012, TSO (The Stationery Office, 2001).
7 Pam Dix, in Disaster Action Newsletter, Issue 2, Autumn 1993, p. 2.
8 Dix (1993, p. 2).
9 Margaret Lockwood-Croft, in Disaster Action Newsletter, Issue 3, Autumn 1995, p. 2.
10 Jackie Hale, in Disaster Action Newsletter, Issue 4, Spring/Summer 1997, p. 2.

CHAPTER 5

NEEDS AND RIGHTS

Disaster Action exists because people come together with like experience with the understanding that they know their lives have changed, with the knowledge that emergency planning is not all that it could be and that the human dimension of emergency planning, certainly in the past, has been missing... we try to supply it. And because of the nature of our experience we have credibility.

This comment was made by one of our members in 1998. In all our work, Disaster Action members have sought to raise awareness and understanding of what it feels like to be directly affected by disaster and the practical implications in terms of addressing people's needs. While there will always be differences due to individual circumstances and personalities, there are common needs and wishes among survivors and bereaved people. Considering these common needs prior to an emergency as well as retaining sufficient flexibility around individual difference is part of the key to an appropriate response.

Significantly, and in contrast to the early days of the organisation, these needs are increasingly being recognised as rights, with the result that emergency planners and responders have continued to look to Disaster Action for advice and guidance on how to address them in planning and responding to disaster. Inevitably over the years we have come to use some of the terminology common within this field. However, part of our job is to make people think about what lies behind ideas such as 'back to normality', 'closure' and 'the recovery phase', which can seem meaningless for those confronting personal catastrophe. This work has sometimes involved challenging, negotiating and reinterpreting language and meanings so that professionals and others may come to understand what concepts such as 'time' and 'change' may and should mean in relation to the disaster experience.

Below are some quotes from Disaster Action members who took part in a 2008 research project in which they reflected on their needs and experiences.[1] The research findings highlighted the common experiences and needs, and their links with universal human rights, which underpin Disaster Action's work.

INFORMATION

Alongside physical comfort and safety, the need for information is one of the most fundamental, urgent and significant needs of those involved in disasters.

'Information, information, information. And choice. Choice is at the heart of what we are looking at.'

Our experience tells us that in the immediate and short-term aftermath information needs relate to getting basic answers about: who, what, where, when and how the disaster happened. In particular, those who think loved ones are involved in the disaster need to have this confirmed, despite their sense of dread, as well as being offered opportunities to see the body and go to the scene of the disaster:

'... whether it really was my brother who had died. I was told by the coroner's officer that it 'probably' was him, and waiting for official identi-fication was torture. I needed to see for myself that it was him; until then I held on to the hope that it might be someone else a lot like him.'

They also refer to the real need to *search* for information after being involved in a disaster and why there can almost be an 'obsession' with reading and hearing everything available:

'Searching, searching ... You have a need to trawl through masses of stuff; you need everything but you (can) only take in 1 per cent.'

'After something happens you search, (you) need to understand why it happened, just searching.'

Those providing information should ensure it is clear and understandable:

'What I wanted was simple language on who is doing what and when, who I can talk to and what the process is.' Such 'searching' can also be poign-antly literal. When Pan Am 103 exploded over Lockerbie in December 1988, one woman who lived in south-west Scotland and whose son was on the plane picked flowers from her garden, got into her car and drove through the county searching for him. Similarly, those seeking missing family and friends after the 9/11 attacks in the US pinned up pictures and descriptions of their loved ones all over New York City.

In the longer term, information needs tend to focus on finding out why the disaster happened, whether it might happen again and learning lessons. As seen in the work of the family and survivor groups, this is often pursued through legal processes, public inquiries, inquests, criminal trials and civil prosecutions.

PHYSICAL, PRACTICAL AND EMOTIONAL SUPPORT

Our experiences have taught Disaster Action members that social, practical and emotional needs are very much linked, even though those providing support often distinguish between such needs (for example the distinctions made between providers of physical and emotional first aid).

Some of these differing but linked needs include:

Practical: '... someone to get us to the disaster site, put us up in a hotel and keep us informed about events as they unfolded.'

Physical: 'I was hospitalised for the first three weeks so my immediate needs were met by hospital staff and family.'

Emotional: 'People to understand, offer advice and take measures to reduce my symptoms.'

Financial: 'We worried about having to borrow money for the funeral.... We needed to know immediately that ... a disaster fund, or another organisation, would cover the expenses.'

Social: 'It would have been useful to have had access to people who had been through a similar experience.'

'Someone neutral to talk to about my emotions and an idea of any peer support groups being set up.'

Good emergency plans now include arrangements for outreaching and coordinating such support to those affected by disaster, but in the early days of Disaster Action (and sometimes still, depending on the nature and location of disasters), this was not understood, or offered. On the contrary, the authorities sometimes felt hostile to the very idea of support groups:

'My needs were intense but I received none, there was no offer of assistance.'

'I got NO support from my colleagues or managers.'

'No immediate help forthcoming.'

'I badly needed support from the Embassy and close friends.'

'I expected the police to come and inform us... but no one came to our house... no personal contact at all.'

'We got (information) one month after the event via the Red Cross. Until then nothing useful.'

The nature and value of such support continues to be stressed to Disaster Action by those affected by disasters and thus these core messages continue to be emphasised in all Disaster Action's outreach work and resources.

HONESTY, OPENNESS AND SENSITIVITY

Many of the early members of Disaster Action came together to seek information, answers and truths at a time when facts relating to disasters and the fate of their family members and friends were hidden, distorted or made unavailable.

'The impression that was given was that the police and coroner were far too busy to deal with any questions, and would not answer them anyway, as it was information for them to keep to themselves. We were too shocked and too upset and too shy to demand to see someone.'

Although there are now greater expectations and in some cases operational procedures based on the principles of openness, information sharing and involving family members, part of Disaster Action's role includes explaining why truth and sensitivity in the relaying and sharing of information is so important and preferable to well-intentioned but potentially harmful attempts to overprotect or prevent such access.

INFORMED CHOICES

Building on the above, information brings with it power, control and choice. In the past families were not granted such rights:

In the aftermath of Lockerbie ... relatives were not allowed to see the bodies, irrespective of their condition. We were later to find out that this decision was made by the procurator fiscal (who carries out the role of the coroner in Scotland). This arrangement went completely against many people's wishes, who felt that as relatives and friends it was their duty to see their dead; no information was given to the bereaved about their condition. People were not able to make an informed choice about whether or not to see a body ... this is one of many examples of how the bereaved were distressed and alienated by the supposed good intentions of those managing the disaster.[2]

Part of our work involves asking the questions: 'who is being protected and for whom is information sensitive?' in considering the value of informed choice in matters such as seeing the body, visiting disaster sites, the return of personal property and getting answers to questions about what has happened, as well as how and why.

The recommendations of the public inquires arising from the murder of teenager Stephen Lawrence in south London in 1993 and from the *Marchioness* disaster stress the rights of bereaved people to open and honest information and highlight the impact of work by individuals and families in campaigning for such changes in professional attitudes and public expectations. Building on the work of Disaster Action and others, national guidelines for police family liaison officers and others working with bereaved families now emphasise the importance of giving families informed choices.

TO BE TREATED AS INDIVIDUALS AND WITH RESPECT

This right relates to the humanitarian principle of impartiality and the right to be treated with respect on the basis of one's humanity and individuality:

'(The need) to be treated as individuals or a family unit, not collated together with everyone else who were strangers to us.'

This can be a difficult right to understand and achieve, especially in the particularly stressful circumstances of a large-scale disaster. Here responders as well as bereaved people and survivors can experience exasperation, exhaustion, anger and anxiety. However, in such situations professionals have often made inappropriate judgements and comments about so-called 'difficult individuals' or 'difficult families'. The challenge instead is to seek to understand, empathise and respond to the difficult *circumstances* that prevail and in relation to the differing circumstances of individuals affected. The point is illustrated by a quote from a member whose brother was killed in a mass-scale terrorist attack:

The waiting is incredibly difficult because it messes up the natural processes. It is not that our reaction is complicated, but that the *death itself* is complicated.[3]

Disaster Action members have also reflected on their experiences of a 'hierarchy of grief', the explicitly stated or implicit assumption that one or some individuals' grief is greater or more significant than others and that some are consequently more deserving of empathy or support. Countering this is the sense within the organisation that people may be *differently* rather than *worse* affected, and that all should feel welcome and worthy of support based on their humanity as opposed to the specific details of their disaster experience.

PRIVACY, ANONYMITY, CONFIDENTIALITY

Those on the receiving end of disasters (the dead as well as the living) often have their lives exposed and pored over, necessarily by investigators but also through media intrusion. Collective awareness of the destructive personal impact of this grew with members' treatment by the media and others, who have sometimes used the very private experience of grief and personal circumstances as public commodities and ways of selling a story. The experience of such intrusion and its effects is set out in Chapter 6 and is reflected in members' experiences:

> Some researchers do not seem to understand the difference between *anonymity* and *confidentiality*. With the media I have learnt that there is no such thing as confidentiality – nothing is ever 'off the record'. How can I know whether I can trust any other reporter or researcher any more?[4]

There are, of course, honourable exceptions within the media, and Disaster Action members have had particular reason to thank the late Paul Foot, who treated his most vulnerable interviewees with the greatest respect. In the leaflet *Interviews about Disaster Experience: Personal Reflections and Guidelines for Interviewers*, Disaster Action details the positive opportunities and negative experiences associated with being interviewed by researchers, journalists and others.

Information may also be inappropriately or insensitively shared in the form of images, photographs and exhibits within the context of training and conference presentations. Members have even been present at training events when intimate details about disaster victims as well as about a criminal investigation were shared with audiences where family members have not been given the information.

A balance needs to be struck in such environments between sharing information where it has benefit and doing so gratuitously and unnecessarily.

Disaster Action suggests that the following guiding questions should be asked: 'Why do I need to share this? How much information needs to be shared? In what ways and for who may sharing this information be harmful? How might that harm be prevented or mitigated?'

Disaster Action's submission to the 2011–12 Leveson Inquiry into the Culture, Practice and Ethics of the Press (see Chapter 10) provided an opportunity to share these messages with legislators and those in the media who are in a position to influence the experience of survivors and bereaved in the aftermath.

ACCOUNTABILITY AND CORPORATE RESPONSIBILITY

This builds on the right to safety and the right to health, as well as Disaster Action's very reason for being, namely to bring about a culture change in favour of more responsible and accountable behaviour among individuals and organisations, especially large-scale corporations.

When asked why or whether we have felt the need to blame others for disasters, Disaster Action makes the distinction between 'blame' (an emotive word often used in a negative way about the focus of disaster survivors and bereaved) and 'accountability' (a more objective term focusing on those with legal, financial, political and/or social responsibility for the health and safety of the community). Explaining this distinction is a challenge. Blame and revenge are alien to Disaster Action's work and ethos.

MEETING WITH OTHERS AFFECTED BY DISASTER

An instinctive wish, need and motivation to meet with others from the same or other disasters is shared not only by members of Disaster Action but by many others affected by traumatic events. They should be assisted in choosing (if they so wish) to meet to share experiences and support each other. Members of support groups offer examples of how coming together has helped them:

'You do have a common grief, therefore you feel no need to explain your pain or suffering, it is almost like having a shorthand in conversation and feelings.'

'As a group, we were heard by the government on issues such as memorial services. If we didn't have a group, decisions would have been made for us.'

'For some who grieve, to be involved in something positive, to have an agenda to follow (for example a memorial, or an intention never to let this happen again) helps, especially I think for men.'

The early constituent groups within Disaster Action were set up because of a passionate commitment to mutual support, getting answers to questions about the cause of a particular disaster and a desire to prevent such tragedies from happening to others. There was some satisfaction to be had from research findings in the 1990s and beyond proving that our instincts that a group would help were right.

Disaster Action's leaflet 'Setting up Family and/or Survivor Support Groups' provides information and advice on how to set such groups up – guidance that was not available in the late 1980s. The leaflet emphasises the value of planners and responders facilitating, supporting and promoting natural support networks and resources as well as professional ones. This includes an acknowledgment that the freedom and independence of self-help support groups may also have additional benefits in terms of power, autonomy and independence. Facilitating such groups in coming together – for example, offering to make practical arrangements for meetings, assisting with a venue, covering the costs – does not mean taking over, which diminishes the very purpose of facilitating such groups: to enhance and encourage self-determination.

'RECOVERING' IN ONE'S OWN TIME AND WAY

Awareness of this right has arisen for many bereaved people and survivors when family members, friends, professionals and others have sought to prescribe methods and timeframes for recovery. This includes the sometimes patronisingly expressed desire for individuals to find neat 'closure' or to 'move on' at arbitrarily prescribed paces. Even when well intentioned, this can be hurtful and disempowering: '...the feeling of "disapproval" by some family members and some staff who could not understand why we were affected so badly and for so long after the disaster'.

This view is echoed in the comment to a bereaved person after reading a newspaper article about the disaster some years later: 'It must bring it all back'; the answer was simple: 'Don't you understand? It never went away...'

Aileen Quinton, whose mother was killed in the 1987 Enniskillen bombing, has spoken about the inappropriateness of other people's 'grieve-by dates', producing a mock certificate entitling the bearer to feel '...absolutely miserable for as often and for as long as he/she feels the need. Furthermore he/she is under no obligation whatsoever to pay any attention to "Time will heal", "Life goes on", "You'll just have to...", "Isn't it about time you..." Or any similar unhelpful rubbish.'

Aileen also makes the distinction between what she calls 'good' and 'bad' victims, as portrayed in the media and by others, underlining the right not to feel pressured to respond or recover according to other people's prescriptions or agendas: 'A "good" victim forgives those responsible and is brave and inspiring. A "good" victim puts everyone else's needs – to forget about what happened and to think that the worst suffering is past – over their own need to ease the pain. A "bad" victim is the reverse. Guess which I am?'[5]

'SHOULDN'T THEY BE OVER IT BY NOW?'

Given the passage of time, a decade after the disasters that had brought us together Disaster Action members were sometimes asked 'Shouldn't you be over it by now?' Those outside were often surprised to find that we remained actively involved in post-disaster issues. What was keeping us going, and why?

In September 1999, Issue 5 of Disaster Action's Newsletter focused on the fact that a decade had passed since a number of the disasters that had led to the founding of the charity, the tenth anniversaries of the events that had changed our lives so dramatically. The editorial comments in the newsletter from Charles Norrie, whose brother Tony had been killed in the bombing of a French airliner over Niger in September 1989, offer some insight into the feelings members had at that time, and why questions around 'closure' still lacked meaning for so many of us:

> It is over a decade since the disasters that caused DA to come into being took place – tragedies that have been cruelly dismissed as a 'nasty blip in the accident rate' – as if they were an outbreak of minor illness that would go away of its own accord.
>
> Of course there has been change. Airline security is much tougher than it was ten years ago. Football stadiums have been transformed, as anyone who goes to a major ground will know. Ferry companies are slowly having stricter standards for operation and construction imposed on them.
>
> Some things haven't changed. DA's campaign for a corporate responsibility law has not yet been debated in parliament and individual family groups still campaign on their own issues. Both Pan Am 103 and the Marchioness Groups have yet to see public inquiries.[6]

AN EXAMPLE OF ENDINGS: THE FINAL MEETING OF THE HFA

The Herald Families Association (HFA) knew that, a decade after the sinking of the *Herald*, much had already been achieved in terms of international regulations – Safety of Life at Sea (SOLAS) – and the modifications made to increase the safety of ro-ro ferries – but they also recognised that more remained to be done. Cameras were now required on the bridge so that the captain could see for himself whether the bow doors had been shut, amongst other significant changes. Passenger lists had also been introduced so that each ship putting to sea would have a proper record of those on board. Perhaps it was time to 'call it a day' as far as the HFA was concerned. Perhaps their work could more effectively be done through Disaster Action, which had been set up as an umbrella organisation to carry on the campaign for greater corporate accountability.

However, the publication of the report into the sinking of the *Estonia* ferry in the Baltic Sea in September 1994, in which over 900 people lost their lives and whose bodies were never recovered, soon changed their collective opinion. The report found that the locks on the bow doors were very much under strength and could not withstand the turbulent weather that the *Estonia* had endured.

The HFA had already been very unimpressed by this story after the finding by the Department of Transport's Marine Safety Agency that 35 out of 107 British ferries had safety issues, following checks carried out after the *Estonia* sinking:

> Brian Mawhinney, the Secretary of State for Transport, who was visiting Dover to oversee the inspection of a P&O ferry, *the Pride of Calais*, said he was surprised at the high proportion of ships that needed attention but emphasised that there had been no danger to passengers. 'We want to ensure the ferry operators maintain these seals because people seeing small amounts of water coming into the ship could become concerned,' he said. He watched as the inner of the two bow doors was sprayed with a high-pressure hose to check whether water could get past the seals.[7]

The Herald Families Association final meeting was in September 1997. It took the form of a beautiful and uplifting church service held in St Mark's Church, St John's Wood, London, where all but the very first (which took place in Birmingham) of the HFA's meetings were held. It seemed an appropriate time and place. Paul Foot, the campaigning journalist and great friend of the HFA attended that service. He said afterwards that it brought a tear to the eye of 'this old atheist'. As photographed for this book, a commemorative plaque hangs on the wall of the church, paying tribute both to those who died, those who survived, and those loyal supporters and friends who carried on the work. The present vicar of St Mark's, and his wife, ensure that candles and flowers are kept on the table below the plaque.

REMEMBERING AND COMMEMORATING

The collective experiences of Disaster Action members over time have reinforced the importance and significance of actively remembering and commemorating the events associated with particular sites, days and dates. They have also borne witness to the political dimension of acts of remembrance and commemoration and the ways in which it is important to participate. In the past, insensitive organisation of such events has – wittingly or unwittingly – reinforced hierarchies of grief and a sense of marginalisation. One relative reflected on how memorial services could be

> '... appalling occasions because the most important people at them are the Prime Minister and/or the royal people, the local dignitary; they are the ones who get to sit in the front pew, who get to read a lesson or something like that. So my family chose absolutely not to go in the immediate aftermath.'

This right reflects the value of participating in the nature, timing and organisation of memorials and anniversary events, the form of which is likely to vary according to the specifics of particular events and the needs and desires of those affected. Disaster Action has advised governments and organisations on the value and importance of consulting with individuals and family and survivor groups about the events that are often organised by the state following disaster.

A moving example of the life-long consequences of disaster, and the need for remembering and recognition, is the campaign described in Chapter 2 of those affected by the 1943 Bethnal Green underground disaster to create a fitting memorial to the dead. Over 60 years later Sandra Scotting, whose grandmother and cousin died and mother survived, said this about joining Disaster Action:

Having been secretary of the Stairway to Heaven Memorial Trust for four years I was very surprised to meet Anne Eyre at one of our station collection days and discover that there is such a thing as Disaster Action. Discussing the Bethnal Green tube shelter disaster – the worst civilian disaster of the Second World War – with Anne made me realise that there is help available for people who have suffered trauma from tragic events. Having more contact with Pam Dix and the people in Disaster Action has been a revelation for me.

It's good to know that there are people I can turn to for support in what we are doing, like a big like-minded family really. Also, it is comforting to know that we are not alone and that there are other groups of people from tragedies all over the UK and around the world going through similar emotions and experiences as my family and our members.

In today's enlightened and open world their reactions are still the same sort of anger, grief, anxiety, disbelief, guilt and numbness as the survivors of our disaster from 1943. The only difference is that our survivors and relatives had to keep our disaster secret due to wartime restrictions and it remained so for at least 50 years. Many are unable to talk about it even now, but that is probably because they have bottled it up for so long.

I have always believed that having a memorial to our disaster is essential for our survivors and bereaved relatives. Outsiders have questioned the necessity for such a project. However, I know how hard our members are working to try to raise the money we need for the Stairway to Heaven Memorial to be completed and how important it is to them.

Being able to participate in Disaster Action meetings and gatherings has confirmed this need for memorials as I have been able to witness just how important it is for others involved in tragedies and how much it has helped them. It has reinforced my resolve to ensure our memorial is built as quickly as possible to help our members to focus their grief on, to help them to come to terms with their suffering. They have not been able to do that for 70 years so time is of the essence now. They are also comforted to know that their suffering and that of their loved ones will be honoured publicly for generations to come.

With the help, advice and support of Disaster Action members I feel better able to support our survivors and talk to them about their experiences and to help them to talk to others who have been through the same trauma as themselves. Talking about their experience to strangers has also been cathartic, much like talking to a counsellor, something that was not available to them during or even after the War. Knowing where to obtain that help is something that I am now able to pass on to those who need it. I wish I had known about it while my mother (a survivor) was alive, but at least I know I can help others in a similar situation now.

Looking back, some of the ways in which bereaved people and survivors were treated when Disaster Action began, in what were relatively recent times, seem a world away from the standards expected today. The identification of these rights has evolved since Disaster Action's foundation, alongside gradual changes in understanding and appreciating the importance of integrating such rights into emergency planning and response.

The rights of the bereaved are now enshrined in international instruments and law, an expectation that would have seemed highly unlikely to be met in the 1980s and earlier. The work of the International Committee of the Red Cross and more recently of the International Commission on Missing Persons and other non-governmental organisations has done a huge amount to influence and change society's expectations.

Through its involvement in discussions, campaigning and education, Disaster Action has helped to bring about many of these changes within the UK. However, ongoing examples of variable understanding and treatment of those affected by new disasters both within and beyond these shores ensure that Disaster Action does not become complacent. Each disaster sadly highlights further examples of the need to continue promoting the needs and rights of people in extreme situations of conflict and disaster.

The rights of the dead sit alongside the rights of the living, with the right to retain identity after death set out in the ICPO-Interpol General Assembly, 65th session, Resolution AGN/65/RES/13 (1996): '...for legal, religious, cultural and other reasons, human beings have **the right not to lose their identities after death...**'[8]

People who find themselves affected by disaster are unlikely to be aware of these rights, however, and will be dependent on the knowledge, experience and humanity of those in the responding agencies in protecting and promoting their interests.

NOTES

1 Anne Eyre, 'Public Information and Disasters: A Report of Consultation with People Directly Affected by Disasters and the Implications for the Crisis Support Team for Essex (CSTE)' (unpublished, 2008).

2 Pam Dix, 'Access to the Dead: The Role of Relatives in the Aftermath of Disaster' in *The Lancet*, 352 (26 September 1998) p. 1061.

3 Disaster Action leaflet, *Disaster Victim Identification: Relatives' Experiences* (Disaster Action, 2013).

4 Disaster Action leaflet, *Interviews about Disaster Experience: Personal Reflections and Guidelines for Interviewers* (Disaster Action, 2008).

5 Aileen Quinton, 'You don't always have to be brave', in the *Sunday Express* (23 August 1998).

6 Charles Norrie, in Disaster Action Newsletter, Issue 5, Spring/Summer 1999, p. 1.

7 Christian Wolmar, 'Defects found in a third of ferries in UK waters', in the *Independent* (8 November 1994) http://www.independent.co.uk/news/defects-found-in-a-third-of-ferries-in-uk-waters-1439791.html.

8 Interpol, http://www.interpol.int/About-INTERPOL/Structure-and-governance/General-Assembly-Resolutions/Resolutions-1990-to-1999/1996-AGN65.

CHAPTER 6

MAD, BAD OR SAD? PEOPLE'S TREATMENT AFTER DISASTER

In the years following their tragedies, the individuals, family and survivor support groups that make up the membership of Disaster Action actively fought to be heard and collectively campaigned for change. This resilience, passion and perseverance did not fit some traditional ideas and stereotypes about disaster 'victims'. At worst, survivors and bereaved were approached as psychiatric cases (and therefore interesting research subjects) and at best, as helpless individuals unable to cope or know what was in their best interests.

At the same time, a 'disaster victim support industry' began to emerge, with ever increasing numbers of 'experts' ready to step into the aftermath of disasters. It soon became clear that many of these experts had to be challenged in their understanding of the psychological impact of trauma.

In the 1950s in the United States, analyses of the psychological effects of disaster focused on the idea of a disaster syndrome, according to which it was believed that after disasters survivors are dazed and apathetic. Generalised stereotypes of haplessness and helplessness contrast with the reality that in the midst of disaster even those who are somewhat injured often pull together and quickly become involved in looking for other survivors. Seeking to debunk such distorted assumptions about human reactions after disaster, in 1970 sociologists Henry Quarantelli and Russell Dynes described other inappropriate images associated with the syndrome:

This image suggests that individuals panic and ... lose their concern for others.... They act irrationally in terms of their own self interest. Also, as the result of the disaster experience, it is suggested that people become hostile and take aggressive action toward others. Another facet of the image suggests that victims develop a 'disaster syndrome', a docile, childlike condition, and as a result must be 'cared for' by some protective organization, acting in a parental way.... At the community level, the image of a 'social jungle' prevails. People, hysterical and helpless, gradually shed the thin veneer of civilization and exploit others. It is said that looting is common and outside authority is perhaps necessary in order to inhibit these resurgent primitive urges. It is assumed that many will flee from the disaster area in mass panic, leaving the community stripped of its human and natural resources.[1]

Although later evidence and other disaster researchers have consistently sought to debunk myths about such behaviour, these stereotypes and beliefs have led to inappropriate responses. After the 1972 Buffalo Creek flooding disaster, psychiatrists, psychologists and pastors converged on the ravaged US valley and door-knocked on survivors' homes, introducing themselves as mental health experts and seeking to help survivors cope with the emotional havoc. Typical of later responses were the television news reports about the 1994 *Estonia* disaster in which over 900 people died, which confidently informed the public that psychiatrists and psychologists were at the port helping people come to terms with what had happened. The notion that in the immediate aftermath of such a devastating catastrophe the most significant and appropriate need is for psychiatric help is entirely divorced from reality. (By contrast, media coverage of the November 2013 Glasgow helicopter crash emphasised the lack of panic, and showed the assistance that survivors and others were able to offer each other in the immediate aftermath.)

The British response to disasters such as at Aberfan in 1966 was more reserved than after Buffalo Creek. Yet there have been many examples since then of counsellors and other well-meaning but self-appointed 'helpers' converging on those affected by disasters, such as after the 1988 Clapham rail crash. The image of the vulnerable, weak and apathetic victim, reinforced by media images, seems to have encouraged those 'needing to be needed' to offer therapy, counselling and impose other forms of (often uninvited, unwelcome and uncoordinated) support on those affected.

WHAT IT FEELS LIKE AFTERWARDS: PERSONAL VIEWS

Over time it began to be appreciated that what was needed was planned, well-coordinated and proactive support, offered by those appropriately trained and experienced to understand and address the particular circumstances and psychosocial consequences of disasters.

Part of Disaster Action's work includes giving presentations to those involved in such work as well as commenting on emergency plans and procedures focusing on these aspects. A leaflet highlighting personal reflections on the experience of disaster written by members after the 2005 London bombings illustrates the social impact of disasters.[2] The leaflet was painful to produce and may be painful to read, but the intention is to inform and help those who might go through similar reactions. The writers hoped it might also help friends and family members to understand the feelings of those close to them with personal experience of disaster.

All the contributors had their own unique experiences and focus on what it was like for them in the first days and months. At the same time, they acknowledge that there is a wide range of reactions and that others affected by disaster may or may not feel something similar. The full text of the leaflet can be found in Appendix 3, but this short observation speaks volumes about what can help rather than hinder: 'Those who helped us most did not try to "pigeonhole" us or dictate how we *should* feel.'

'SPACE TESTS' FOR SURVIVORS

After the Aberfan disaster it was clear that the traditional networks of support would struggle to cope, given the effects on the local community. Psychiatrists and psychologists were keen to come in from outside, but were largely distrusted by local services.

In 1996, Gaynor Madgwick, whose brother Carl and sister Marilyn died in the disaster she survived, produced a book reflecting on the aftermath for child survivors such as herself as well as their families and community in the tragedy, which killed almost a whole generation of children within the village:

> I had lots of money given to me and I went to lots of parties with my friends that were left. I guess it would take a very long time for my parents to be happy again. It was very hard for a normal eight-year-old-girl, full of happiness, doing all the everyday activities with my family, then suddenly, within 24 hours of my life, things would change forever, each member of

my family being deeply disturbed, and feelings that were very difficult to deal with.

Not wanting to wake up each morning to face another dismal day of misery and grief. How could anyone cope with this burden as a close family, every day was a struggle, each of us giving the hope we had left to make each others' lives worthwhile ... I missed out on my childhood. Most of my friends my age had died which left a wide gap ... But we all struggled along each day with hope that time would heal our pains.[3]

In 1966 the stigma associated with psychiatrists and psychiatric help was very strong. Gaynor goes on to reflect on the fear and stigma associated with asylums and mental illness, which would have been the focus for assessing and treating trauma at that time:

There was talk amongst the survivors that their parents had letters for each child that survived to see a psychiatrist. I was totally horrified to hear this from my friends. God, what would people think seeing in my eyes a SHRINK? I confronted my parents and told them bluntly there was no way I was going for these head tests and talks...

Some two weeks passed and my parents were taking me on a shopping trip to Ponty, or that's what I thought. I put my best clothes on and we were off on our journey. Half way there my mother told me we were going to see the psychiatrist. This was the only way she could get me to go. I was horrified, crying, and shouting, 'I am not going'. I felt that everyone around me thought I was mental.

...The head tests were like some space tests with wires jelled to my head with metal clips. Lights were shone right in front of me. It was as if I was in a trance. No one can imagine how I was feeling. The relevance of these tests was for brain damage during the disaster, and your state of mind.[4]

Gaynor goes on to report the deep effect the disaster had on her and the value in her experience of seeing a psychiatrist for a number of years. She also wrote – some 30 years later – of the ongoing effects of post traumatic stress on a number of people within her community, many of whom remained on medication.

UNDERSTANDING POST TRAUMATIC STRESS

In 1966, however, normal post traumatic stress reactions and post traumatic stress disorder (PTSD) were a long way off being defined or diagnosed. In their book, *Aberfan: Government and Disasters* Iain McLean and Martin

Johnes reported how although local services were inundated with offers of help in response to the depth of the trauma that the disaster had inflicted, the availability of trained professionals was limited and there were no agreed or proven methods. The early proactive outreach that might have reduced the extent and severity of chronic stress and trauma was not available.[5]

Focusing instead on the vulnerabilities and deficiencies of individuals and families remained a convenient if unintended way of focusing on 'fixing the victim' through psychology and psychiatry rather than on the social and political causes and consequences of disasters. These, along with the financial and legal aftermath, ensured that those affected by disasters from Aberfan onwards would experience the ripple effects of secondary traumatisation, often through the very systems set up to respond to disaster.

What was really needed was understanding and support given for the normal reactions to trauma and grief after disaster. Mary Campion, survivor of the 1988 *Jupiter* cruise ship disaster, reported on the help this would have given her and the schoolchildren after she accompanied them on that fateful school trip:

> It became obvious that expert counselling was needed to cope with post-traumatic stress, a term we did not even recognise or know. Parents, themselves still in shock, were saying they did not know how to help their child come to terms with what had happened. Two weeks after our return, worried by the effects on our group, I found Miss Cass at the Charet Clinic reassuring us that our reactions were normal. Those who had taken Schools Abroad's offer of counselling encouraged the others to use the service. Yet some families were reluctant to seek professional help.
>
> Again with hindsight, independent advice to all the group, their families and our teaching colleagues would have been invaluable. We simply needed to be reassured that our reactions were normal, that they could be recognised, that some could be helped by counselling and to know the process might take some time. We were completely unaware of the psychological impact of a disaster. We could never have guessed that of the hundreds of people on the *Jupiter* some would be unable to work, suffer depression, develop phobias or even consider or attempt suicide. Nor guessed that some people would be badly affected ten years after the event.[6]

MAD FOR COMPENSATION

The sorts of psychiatric assessments introduced after Aberfan and offered after subsequent disasters were intended not just to diagnose the effects of trauma but also partly for the purpose of assessing compensation claims. Disaster Action members were among those who found that, unfortunately, fulfilling the criteria for PTSD and compensation had negative consequences on their suitability for insurance and mortgages.

In some cases, the media and others have focused on portraying bereaved families and survivors and their demands for compensation as being about revenge and greed rather than restitution, recompense and necessary financial support in order to continue with lives damaged by disaster. One relative comments on the media's obsession with compensation and how she responded: 'All I was ever getting asked was "Why the money, it can't bring him back?"' Her response was: 'My brother's life was deemed to be worth less than a second-hand Ford Fiesta.'

Part of the frustration of going through the process of making compensation claims relates to the fact that in defending themselves, those responsible for disaster often regarded such claims as attempts to exaggerate the minimal effects and consequences of survivors' involvement.

Mary Campion comments on her experience of the nature and impact of such insensitivity:

> A few months after our return, the insurers of both vessels, the *Jupiter* and the *Adige*, had accepted liability for the accident. In January 1989 we received a copy of a letter offering £2000 compensation with comments that as no one had witnessed any loss of life, only four people had died, and two thirds of the passengers hadn't got their feet wet, no one should suffer guilt or trauma. This letter came like a beating, hard and brutal. All that we had experienced was assessed in offensive terms. 'Only four' people had died. The phrase was so cruel. The principle behind claiming compensation became even more important. How can organisations and individuals be made to review their procedures? Having to pay compensation seems to be the spur required.[7]

Being interviewed and completing questionnaires for the diagnosis of traumatic stress disorder or for other research and assessment purposes has also been described as traumatising and humiliating. Lasting up to two hours or more they can be exhausting and cause distress. Delays in their processing, producing evidence as substantiation (such as receipts for prescriptions, telephone calls and visits to hospitals) and defending disputed claims can cause additional frustration.

The difficulties of coming to terms with what we had experienced were compounded for some by the assessments by psychologists, and the consultations with solicitors. For some, their compensation claims would not be settled until almost eight years had passed. Surely there is a need to review litigation procedures following a disaster?[8]

BEING RESEARCH SUBJECTS

It was at this time and in this climate that a number of psychologists and psychiatrists including Stuart Turner and James Thompson in London carried out some studies looking at the psychological reactions to British disasters such as the King's Cross fire, Hillsborough and the *Marchioness*.[9]

The main tool for such research was questionnaires designed to measure indicators of psychological distress such as depression, anxiety and PTSD. These were distributed and analysed with an emphasis on the immediate impact and the benefits of short-term outreach mental health intervention programmes.

What has it been like to be such research subjects? Disaster Action is often approached by students, academic researchers and journalists for interviewees willing to talk about their personal experiences. Giving interviews has been a mixed experience, at best almost therapeutic and at worst intrusive and upsetting. In the apparent absence of guidelines for those interviewing people affected by disaster, in 2008 Disaster Action produced its own, as a 'When Disaster Strikes' leaflet, reflecting our experiences of being interviewed by researchers and others, with suggestions for prospective interviewers.[10]

On the positive side:

'It was nice to feel I could **make a difference** by helping to learn lessons. As a survivor I tell myself this is one way to notch off some of the enduring survivor guilt.'

'It's good to be acknowledged and have the **chance to talk** about what happened. Feeling valued by people who wish to hear your story and who are willing to listen can be helpful.'

But negatively:

'Having **no control** over how what I say will be made sense of, interpreted or used can be a big drawback. This matters because what may be just "data" or detail to a researcher is usually part of a sensitive, significant and emotionally loaded account for me.'

'I have been upset on occasions when journalists **rewrite my words** for their own agenda or put words in my mouth/make up quotes. Sometimes they do this without asking me and it is no longer my experience. I feel used and abused. I am also taken back to what it was like not to be in control in the disaster.'

'Some are not interested in seeing me as more than **just a "victim"** and don't want to hear about being a survivor or about positive recovery. I think this is one of the differences between a good researcher/journalist and a bad researcher/journalist. The bad one has already written the story before they meet you. The good one will want to reflect what is really there rather than prejudging and using you to reinforce what they already think.'

Disaster Action includes members who at various times have been labelled mad, bad and sad. They have contended with making sense of their own reactions to disaster as well as the bewilderment of family and friends around them. Individuals have been referred to as 'obsessive', 'hysterical', 'unhinged' and 'morbid' in continuing to be actively interested in disasters and discussing them years after the event. They have been stereotyped as being greedy, ungrateful and vengeful.

Throughout the 1990s and into this century, the efforts of Disaster Action's members have contributed to the growth in interest, empathy and the desire to make sense of disasters by learning from those with personal experience. This period witnessed great strides in the professional understanding of the effects of traumatic events, and attempts to address the psychological and social aspects of disaster began to result in improved coordination and integration of this aspect of emergency planning and response. More still needs to be done.

Survivor of the Ladbroke Grove rail crash on 5 October 1999 Helen Mitchell writes about the emotional and psychological impact the experience was to have on her life:

HELEN'S STORY

One cannot begin to imagine how a disaster can have such a profound effect on so many lives. 5 October 1999 was the day that changed many lives irrevocably. From the 572 people actually on the trains, 31 died, 415 were injured, some suffered horrendous burns and 126 were not physically injured. This number does not include bereaved parents, partners, sons and daughters, brothers and sisters, grandparents; many were devastated or affected on that day, also police and emergency workers and Sainsbury's staff who rushed to help.

As a survivor, I witnessed much on that day and was so profoundly lucky to have walked away without a scratch. After the crash we were allowed to go in the clothes we were standing in and made our way home whatever way we could. I started to walk home in the direction of the M4 not realising home was over 100 miles away. On finally getting home and seeing the crash on TV, one realised how lucky one was and it became a sort of mantra, it seemed right to not talk about what you had experienced as it seemed somehow ungrateful and disrespectful – you were alive, for God's sake.

Over a year later the memories came flooding back with remarkable clarity and it seemed as if I was going mad. After months of sleepless nights and flashbacks I felt profound guilt at being the one that survived; I had no close family or partner so it would not have mattered as much if I had been killed instead. There was also real anger at the reaction of the train organisations that had caused the accident and many of the survivors got together and focused on campaigning, trying too to help each other understand what was happening to them. I also left a job I loved as I could not perform anymore.

No real help was at hand, doctors brushed you off with Prozac or sleeping pills, recommended counsellors were not able to deal with the problem, so alcohol became a handy crutch to enter oblivion. It was only when a friend pointed me to a specialist in trauma counselling and I was told I had PTSD, that I realised my response was totally normal and with lots of exercise and the right help I managed to manage the triggers (the smell of burning, the Nokia call tone) that set off the flashbacks.

Life changed that day but now I live knowing that each day is precious and I owe it to the people that did not survive to make my life the best I can make it.

One member became a lay representative on the Guideline Development Group set up by the National Institute for Health and Care Excellence (NICE) to develop guidelines for the diagnosis and treatment of post traumatic stress disorder by the National Health Service;[11] another contributed his personal experience to the NICE guideline testimonies of those affected by PTSD. Yet another joined – in her own professional capacity – the board of directors of an international organisation certifying traumatic stress specialists. Three others have professional training, qualifications and experience as counsellors and psychotherapist respectively.

Jelena Watkins, who became a psychotherapist some years after the death of her brother Vladimir in the 9/11 attacks in New York, explains the challenges faced by those affected by such traumatic events:

> In a desperate attempt to deal with my pain I searched through endless psychotherapy papers and books and attended international psychotherapy conferences. I was disappointed to discover that therapists were primarily focusing on individual psychological responses to trauma and methods for healing from trauma. Missing from the conversations were the social and political dimensions of the traumatic experience, which were central to my own experience. Issues of justice and truth seeking had only limited space in the psychotherapy literature I came across. At times the exclusive focus on the intrapsychic causes and solutions to an individual's distress has created problems for survivors of, and those bereaved by, the terrorist attacks. Some felt that their justifiable anger with the sluggish political and legal processes was being pathologised.[12]

In Jelena's view, collective trauma and its effects have not been sufficiently well explored and consequently are not well understood. Her views and experience echo those who have felt judged for their continued involvement in aspects of disaster prevention and response described in this book.

The NICE Guideline on PTSD was published only a few months before the 7 July 2005 London bombings. For the first time following a disaster in the UK, a 'screen and treat' programme was set up to try to respond to the need for a coordinated, professional mental health response. Direct approaches to those affected were made by the mental health team via the police, to try to reach as many of those who had been affected as possible. A further source of information about the service was the 7 July Assistance Centre, which formed part of the overall humanitarian support offered to those affected by the bombings.

Despite the Guideline and recommendations concerning diagnosis and treatment of PTSD (and indeed other adverse reactions and mental health conditions) the experience of those who contact Disaster Action for support shows that even now it remains difficult for those affected by trauma to access the specialist care that they might benefit from. Unfortunately only 4 per cent of those who eventually took part in the London bombings mental health programme were referred by their GP, underlining these ongoing difficulties.[13]

The opportunity for Pam Dix to be part of the Royal College of

Psychiatrists working group on training for mental health professionals in disaster was clear recognition of the value of involving those on the receiving end.

In 2011 Disaster Action was invited by the Ministry of Justice to apply for funding and support under the newly created peer support fund. The fund came about following a report and recommendations by the first Victims Commissioner, Louise Casey, who clearly saw that the work done by small, dedicated charities with specific aims to support those affected by bereavement through manslaughter and murder was not sustainable without financial support and advice on capability building.

While wishing to ensure that our much cherished independence would not be compromised, the Disaster Action management team also recognised that such a grant would offer the charity not only a more sustainable future but recognition for the importance of our work in supporting those affected by all forms of disaster. Part of the success of this grant lies in the opportunity for Disaster Action to refer those who could benefit from counselling to ASSIST Trauma Care (for adults) and Winston's Wish (for young people and children).

Director of ASSIST Barbara Goodfellow writes about the importance of this opportunity for both ASSIST and Disaster Action:

> One of the very positive outcomes of the funding provided by the Ministry of Justice has been the bringing together of likeminded organisations seeking to help individuals and families in the aftermath of disaster. Partnership working in this area is extremely important in enabling the wide range of different needs experienced by victims to be successfully met. It has been a very great pleasure and privilege to work with Pam Dix and Disaster Action, which we have come to respect as a professional and caring organisation. Together we have been able to combine our different skills to help those in our society who have been caught up in horrific occurrences and for whom timely professional help is not always available, particularly once the initial publicity has died down. We very much hope that this partnership between Disaster Action and ASSIST Trauma Care will continue and that the Ministry of Justice will continue to recognise the need for this funding.

By 2011, Pam Dix was a co-opted member of the Board of the UK Psychological Trauma Society, sitting alongside clinicians. This provides a rare opportunity to focus the minds of the professionals on what it is like for those trying to access mental health services after trauma, and the perspective of a 'patient' or carer.

These developments reflect changing attitudes and the fact that the experiences and perspectives of those with direct personal experience are no longer to be dismissed, but are being respected and valued. We have come a long way.

NOTES

1 Enrico (Henry) L. Quarantelli and Russell Dynes, Article number 30, Editors' Introduction, University of Delaware, Disaster Research Center (1976) p. 2 (Reprinted from *American Behavioral Scientist*, 13, No. 3 (January–February 1970) pp. 325–30) http://udspace.udel.edu/bitstream/handle/19716/2348/Article%2030.pdf?sequence=1.

2 Disaster Action leaflet, *Reflections on Personal Experience of Disaster* (Disaster Action, 2008).

3 Gaynor Madgwick, *Aberfan: Struggling out of the Darkness: A Survivor's Story* (Valley and Vale/Zenith Media, 1996) pp. 41–43.

4 Madgwick (1996, pp. 45–46).

5 Iain McLean and Martin Johnes, *Aberfan: Government and Disasters* (Welsh Academic Press, Cardiff, 2000) p. 107.

6 Mary Campion, *Jupiter's Children* (Liverpool University Press, Liverpool, 1998) pp. 130–32.

7 Campion (1998, p. 134).

8 Campion (1998, p. 137).

9 Stuart Turner, James Thompson and Rachel Rosser, 'The King's Cross Fire: Planning a "Phase Two" Psychosocial Response', in *Disaster Management*, 2 (1989, pp. 31–37); Stuart Turner, James Thompson and Rachel Rosser, 'The King's Cross fire: Psychological Reactions', in the *Journal of Traumatic Stress*, 8 (1995, pp. 419–28); James Thompson, 'Theoretical Issues in Responses to Disasters'. *Journal of the Royal Society of Medicine*, 84 (January 1991, pp. 19–22); James Thompson 'Psychological Effects of the Marchioness Disaster on Survivors and Relatives', in the *European Journal of Psychiatry*, 9, (4) (1995, pp. 197–208).

10 Disaster Action leaflet, *Interviews about Disaster Experience: Personal Reflections and Guidelines for Interviewers* (Disaster Action, 2008).

11 National Institute for Health and Care Excellence (NICE), 'Post-traumatic stress disorder: The management of PTSD in adults and children in primary and secondary care', Guideline number 26 (The Royal College of Psychiatrists and The British Psychological Society, 2005) http://www.nice.org.uk/nice-media/pdf/CG026fullguideline.pdf.

12 Jelena Watkins, 'How I Became a Therapist', in *Therapy Today*, 24, (10) (December 2013) http://therapytoday.net/article/show/4035/.

13 C. R. Brewin, N. Fuchkan and Z. Huntley (2009), 'Evaluation of the NHS Trauma Response to the London Bombings' (MRD 12/98), *Final Report to the Department of Health Forensic Mental Health R & D Programme* (2009).

CHAPTER 7

INQUESTS, INQUIRIES AND INVESTIGATIONS

> We have to get people to understand that unless the inquiries are conducted properly, unless there are conclusions drawn, the families will not rest ... (Others) sometimes find it hard to understand why people continue to want answers to questions many years down the line ... you continue to want justice but that message can be a little hard to get across.[1]

In the years following the tragedies of the 1980s that originally brought us together, Disaster Action's constituent family and survivor support groups demanded to be listened to and given answers. They were driven by the fact that they were often left with inconsistent, incomplete or conflicting accounts of how, when and where their loved ones died. In some cases this reflected the way the disasters had unfolded, for example where there were no witnesses or where, because their loved ones' bodies were never recovered, it would never be possible to establish the exact nature, cause and moment of death.

In other instances, however, it seemed that key questions were being blocked, questions such as why these often predictable and preventable disasters had been neither prevented nor mitigated. On top of the grief and trauma associated with their losses, the failure to get answers to these questions caused untold added anxiety and misery for those who found themselves caught up in the personal, political and legal aftermath of disaster. At such a time it became natural for many to seek out and find comfort and a shared quest amongst others when the chance presented itself. In a number of cases this opportunity came when people gathered together for the inquests despite, it seemed, the wishes and interest of the authorities. Margaret de Rohan's experience after the Zeebrugge disaster illustrates this.

'THE HEART HAS ITS REASONS' – ATTENDING THE INQUEST AND THE FORMATION OF THE HFA

From the outset there seems to have been a deliberate policy to keep survivors and bereaved apart from each other, when the immediate setting-up of a self-help organisation – such as the HFA, which eventually came into being – would have been of great benefit to everyone. And the sooner, the better. Were the powers-that-be afraid of a class action against P & O, who had recently bought the company from Townsend Thoresen? Who knows, but of course the old 'Data Protection Act' (or some early form of it) was trotted out as justification. I don't buy that argument – there were other more sinister reasons no doubt of a commercial nature...

We – the bereaved and survivors – didn't want to make any trouble, we just wanted the comfort of talking to others who had been similarly affected. And that's human nature: in a time of tragedy those involved draw strength from each other.

Despite the machinations of those in authority, the HFA was eventually set up. It came out of a meeting held in Birmingham a week or two after the start of the inquest in Dover on 7 September 1987. That date was significant for me – it was the second anniversary of Alison and Francis's wedding. But I had a strong, strong, feeling that I should attend the opening day of the twice-re-scheduled inquest in Dover when I saw that it had finally been set for 7 September 1987. My heart recognised the significance of what Jung called 'synchronicity'. In other words, these two events – the opening of the inquest and their second wedding anniversary should not have been connected – yet they were. My heart realised that, and my brain/intellect followed where my heart led. I just knew that 'it was the right thing to do'.

On that day we met the nucleus of those who formed the HFA. We had many survivors too, within our ranks, for which we were very grateful. It was a comfort for me to learn that 6 March 1987 had been a mild day in Bruges, which was where Alison and Francis spent most of the day. 'People were walking around in shirt-sleeves', one survivor told me, and I gave thanks that their last day on earth had been spent in sunshine.

For many survivor and family support groups, the quest for information and accountability often became legitimately focused on the responding authorities and the way in which they conducted their affairs before, during and after the disasters occurred. Each disaster had resulted in a series of inquests, inquiries and investigations, many of which remained ongoing for years, yet still leaving untold the full story of what had happened. While such inquiries are necessary in order to conduct a thorough and comprehensive review of what happened, the timeframe, bureaucracy, arbitrary conduct and discretionary nature of decisions and procedures contributed to and prolonged the emotional trauma.

Indeed, the ups and downs of ongoing legal battles would leave many people feeling as victimised by and as angry at the systems of inquest and inquiry as they were at the fact of the deaths themselves: 'Many of us feel that however terrible the disaster that changed our lives, what happened to us in the aftermath has made living with it harder instead of easier.'[2]

In the long run, this led our members to focus not only on resolving our own disasters but on campaigning for and contributing to broader changes within the often antiquated and highly politicised systems of inquest and investigations themselves.

Sophie Tarassenko, founder member, co-chair and trustee of Disaster Action, whose brother Ivan died in the 1987 King's Cross underground fire, remembers vividly the experience of the bereaved meeting each other for the first time at the inquest almost a year after the disaster (as described in Chapter 2). The conduct of the inquest, which she described in a press interview as 'a farce', had a profound impact on Sophie, who was to work steadfastly with other Disaster Action members to influence and change the antiquated coronial system:

> The coroner was very dismissive of any questions raised by the relatives' lawyers. At one point, after a difficult question was raised by a family who were turned away for three weeks, before the coroner realised it was their son, after all, he screamed: 'They are MY bodies!' He referred to the dead only by numbers, not by their names. When a family objected to him calling their daughter (by her number) 'he', he looked at the photo of the body, to which the family did not have access, and said he might have made a mistake because she looked like a boy. Later he ordered the jury to return a verdict of accidental death. They had no choice.

Two Disaster Action members wrote about investigation processes and their impact on families. Anne Eyre published an article focusing on proactive responses among disaster survivors in the *Australasian Journal of Disaster and Trauma Studies*[3] while Pam Dix published an article in the *Guardian* explaining why the painful fight against cover-ups continued.

DISASTROUS WAY TO TREAT GRIEF

Zeebrugge, Lockerbie, the *Marchioness* – they may seem very different, yet after each major disaster in the UK survivors and bereaved are left trying to make sense of the fact that the deaths of their loved ones were preventable. Why do those whose lives are shattered by disaster then embark on campaigns to find out how and why those disasters happened? Are such campaigns merely the natural reaction of the grief-stricken, or the result of the inadequacies of the systems in which we put our trust and from which we expect answers?

In every case grief is compounded by the realisation that the system appears to exist not to protect the public, but to shore itself up, to maintain the status quo – even at the expense of the truth.

Indications of an impending cover-up are there straight after a disaster, with officials taking the view that any information they give out may be used in evidence against them. During an interview in Lockerbie on Christmas Day 1988, the police asked for my brother's seat number. A straightforward request – but one that resulted in our being accused of causing a ruckus by a high-ranking American Embassy official, because we could not understand Pan Am's refusal to provide this simple piece of information.

Witnesses to the sinking of the *Marchioness* being pressured in the immediate aftermath to agree with the police version of where the disaster had happened is another such example. And at the 1990–91 Lockerbie Fatal Accident Inquiry, a witness for the Crown Office gave false evidence about a doctor who worked at the crash site, evidence later retracted after the doctor appeared as a witness called by the relatives.

There have been no explanations about why any of these things happened. But the effect on the families is to strengthen their determination to find out whatever they can – and to make them deeply suspicious of those who present the official viewpoint.

There are exceptions. The Air Accident Investigation Branch welcomed any inquiries from those bereaved by the Pan Am 103 crash. And the police, recognising that the needs of relatives have not been directly addressed in the past now invite members of Disaster

Action to give regular presentations at Bramshill Police Staff College in Hampshire.

Although inquiries will take place after a disaster, a common goal for campaigning families is an independent inquiry, with full powers of investigation. This stems from the belief that attempts will be made to cover up and the fact that each form of inquiry has only a limited remit to look at specific aspects of a disaster – how and why the victims died, whether a technical fault led to the deaths – rather than at the whole picture.

Government departments appear satisfied with this limited approach, and it is sometimes only through the families' dedication to the truth that the full facts may emerge. The recent successful fight to reopen the inquest into the *Marchioness* disaster highlighted the fact that without the devoted and 'unhinged' relatives – as described by a coroner – there would never have been a full inquest. The verdict of unlawful killing vindicated their determination to fight on for a full independent inquiry.

As the families of victims of the *Herald of Free Enterprise* disaster at Zeebrugge learnt in their campaigning, there is much strength in numbers. It is much easier for the Government to fob off single individuals than family groups with a clear and determined purpose.

Disaster Action, an umbrella organisation whose members are all survivors or bereaved from a major disaster, was founded in 1991 by Maurice de Rohan, chairman of the Herald Families Association. Coming together and exchanging information makes it clear that each family group comes up against the same intransigence in the official agencies.

For Martin Cadman, whose son Bill was killed at Lockerbie, the reasons for such a campaign are crystal clear:

'It is for the sake of my son, who cannot speak for himself, for the supreme importance of knowing the truth about how and why he died – and to stop these things happening again. In a civilised society we give over powers to others, whom we have elected to work on our behalf. We expect, therefore, to be protected.'

Margaret Lockwood-Croft, whose son Shaun died on the *Marchioness*, says 'Anger drives you on, the anger of injustice. I could not accept that in the capital city, a stone's throw from the House of Commons, 51 people could drown in the night.'

It is time the Government realised they are losing the battle. A rigorous system by which disasters are automatically investigated must be introduced. And, in the meantime, those who have lost most through disaster will carry on their struggle for justice.[4]

In a further article commissioned by the *Guardian* three years later Pam Dix attempted to explain what motivates people to carry on trying to get to the bottom of what happened, with the examples of Stephen Lawrence's family, Lockerbie and Julie Ward, whose 1988 death in Kenya was only shown unequivocally to be murder through the untiring efforts of her father, at the inquest in 2004:

> People find it difficult to understand that when you are on the receiving end of such events, you take on the responsibility to ensure that others do not go through the same ordeal... When the truth has been withheld, you are exposed at one extreme to the platitudes of those who want to protect you and, at the other, to the worst hypotheses of the conspiracy theorists. The truth must be known – only then can we feel that we can 'move on'.[5]

To the relief of those affected by the 1997 Southall rail crash, a public inquiry *was* held, as Maureen Kavanagh recollects:

The public inquiry into Southall began on 20 September 1999, two years and a day after the crash. I spoke up for the inquiry to be televised and was delighted when the chair, Professor John Uff, ruled in my favour. The lawyers were not! Afterwards, one of dozens of lawyers attending for the rail industry asked which law firm I was from. I thought this hilarious, but the media gave me lots of attention, which helped with campaigning for improved safety.

The inquiry lasted four weeks and in the second week the Ladbroke Grove rail crash happened, resulting in our inquiry being delayed by three days. The helpline our group had set up helped many people from this new rail tragedy. We successfully resisted efforts on the part of the government to combine the rail safety issues arising from Southall and Ladbroke Grove – people power.

In his final report Professor Uff issued a total of 93 recommendations, 84 of which had been actioned by February 2002 – the others had had to be dealt with alongside recommendations from the inquiry into Ladbroke Grove, led by Lord Cullen.

In 2001, Anne Eyre wrote about the personal experience of travelling the long road of inquests, inquiries and ongoing investigations following disaster and the implications for Disaster Action in its awareness raising and campaigning work.

ON THE QUESTION OF 'CLOSURE' AND THE CONTINUING PURSUIT OF JUSTICE

On September 12th 2001, 24 hours after the terrorist attacks in the US, a journalist asked me whether the families would be able to put 'closure' on these events. Reeling from the absurd timing of such a question, I patiently tried to explain that most people were probably still in shock and referred to the years of political, legal and emotional processes disaster victims commonly endure following such tragedies. The question, though, reminds us of how important a role we must still play in Disaster Action in explaining what those without our experiences cannot easily understand or appreciate; namely the nature, intensity and persistent impact of sudden traumatic death and its consequences.

In relation to my own experience as a survivor from Hillsborough, we've finally come to the end of the legal road 12 years after the tragedy, a winding path which has featured along the way a dissatis-fying inquest verdict, thwarted attempts at a re-inquest, the resurrection and dismissal of evidence highlighting a police cover-up of statements on the day and, ultimately, a criminal trial for manslaughter and wilful neglect of a public duty. The latter, a private prosecution costing an estimated £4m in prosecution and defence costs, resulted in the clearing of Bernard Murray and the jury failing to reach a verdict on former Chief Superintendent David Duckenfield.

The experience of going to court, especially so many years after the disaster, was traumatic in itself for all concerned. For me, having to travel up and down to Leeds on my own was economically, physically and emotionally draining. I am neither a member of the Hillsborough Families Support Group nor the Justice Campaign, both groups being physically and symbolically juxtaposed within the courtroom.

Fortunately the court officials were very supportive when I rang up during the pre-trial anxiety and, sympathetic of the fact that I had never been to court before, confirmed that I would be able to observe proceedings and even reserved me a place to sit. However, the whole process of the trial, followed mainly through the media, was a difficult and exhausting experience.

As the evidence presented highlighted, much has changed since 1989. Perhaps in today's legal environment the Human Rights Act would be invoked against such senior officials failing so spectacularly in their public duty. More positively in terms of football, many of the sorts of 'shabby' conditions at grounds referred to in the trial, have been replaced by all-seater stadia and even some purpose-built stadia – both outcomes of the Taylor Report produced after Hillsborough. Safety at sports grounds is still problematic though, as domestic incidents and international tragedies such as the deaths in an overcrowded stadium in South Africa in April 2001 in frighteningly similar conditions to Hillsborough demonstrate.

Debates around such events and issues retrigger the campaigning instinct in me but also the emotional fatigue of feeling an obligation to do something and revisiting the disaster all over again.

I'm writing this around the time of the 30th anniversary of Bloody Sunday, a date marked by a drama-documentary written by Jimmy McGovern. It was based in part on his desire to highlight and give expression to the experiences and perspectives of the bereaved and survivors. He took a similar approach in his powerful fact-based drama about the Hillsborough inquest and inquiry. Watching the drama, the current inquiry and renewed debates about Bloody Sunday reminds me that many other tragedies also endure for people because of the cover-ups, political interests and inadequate investigatory procedures characterising the aftermath of disaster.

We need to keep up our educative and campaigning work, influencing and informing professionals before disaster as well as fighting for justice after. This is part of the humanising of disaster work for those whose professional interests may conflict with the moral requirement for compassion and fairness and a basic ability to understand things from the perspective of the bereaved. After the Hillsborough documentary drama in 1997, Westminster Coroner Paul Knapman described McGovern's work as a 'grave illustration of mischievousness', adding 'Perhaps the most malignant combination is grief stricken relatives, an on-going support group, high profile lawyers and a dedicated and ambitious television producer.' I agree that we could do without some of the lawyers and certain members of the media we've had to battle with over the years, but thank God for the ongoing commitment and pursuit of justice amongst relatives and support groups![6]

When writing that article Anne Eyre could not have known that 12 more years would pass before the Hillsborough Independent Panel, set up by the then Labour government to review the papers and evidence from Hillsborough, would result in a damning report about the handling of every aspect of the response. The report led to the overturning of the original inquest verdict, fresh police investigations and a new inquest in 2014. Without the determination of the families to achieve a just resolution following the orchestrated smear campaign that had suggested those who died were at fault, such an outcome would not have been possible.

WHAT HAS CHANGED?

During the first decade of the twenty-first century Disaster Action was among a number of interest groups that worked towards change in the coronial system that had so badly failed our members over many years. Having long argued for openness and transparency and the importance of treating families with dignity and respect, in 2007, as part of a Ministry of Justice consultation with stakeholder groups Disaster Action's submission concerning inquests included the following:

a) Coroners must always treat deaths individually. Wherever possible, the bereaved should be offered (even if this is turned down) as much information as possible (for an example of good practice, see the excellent work of the coroner's officer at the Paddington train crash inquest) about the *exact* circumstances of each individual death. This ideally should take place away from the public gaze, possibly a little in advance of the information being disclosed to the public.

b) Coroners should, where they believe the deaths could be avoided in future, make recommendations. It was deeply disappointing to the bereaved that this did not occur at the inquest into the deaths in the Upton Nervet rail crash.

c) All coroners must be trained to see the bereaved not as a nuisance but as the people who have most at stake in the legal process.

d) The verdict (or 'finding') is required to have no bearing on an individual's (or company's) criminal liability or the civil liability of anybody at all – therefore it should not make a statement about liability *or lack of it*. 'Unlawful killing', to the untrained, denotes liability. 'Accidental death' denotes exoneration from any guilt. Narrative verdicts may cause fewer misunderstandings.

A number of significant inquests – into the 2002 Bali bombings, the 2004 Indian Ocean tsunami, the 2005 London bombings and the 11 September attacks – were held while the calls for change were being made, and changes implemented. For Bob and Sandra Empson, an important issue was whether to attend the inquest and therefore hear details of the way in which their daughter Lucy had died. They found the pathologist's use of the word 'remains' very distressing, and the hopes that had been raised by the police that they would learn exactly where Lucy had been found were dashed when the information was not available at the inquest.

Edie Fassnidge, whose mother Sally and sister Alice died in the tsunami, reflects on the impact of the inquest:

Our experience was a mixed one. We were disappointed about the communication prior to the inquest as we were only informed about where and when it was taking place at a very late stage. There was also a lack of clarity regarding the content of the day and we weren't sure what to expect. However, we were happy to be told that there would be the opportunity to give a eulogy at some point during the day.

The inquest began with a physicist giving a presentation on the science behind the tsunami which we found informative and appropriate. We also found it interesting to hear from senior police officers on the search and recovery process and felt that this was handled sensitively. The individual coroner's verdicts were read out in list form with very little time dedicated to each person. Perhaps this is inevitable in a disaster with so many fatalities.

We were very pleased to be given a few minutes for me to give a eulogy and speak about my mother and for my sister's boyfriend to speak about her. Talking about them as individual people rather than just as tsunami victims was important.

We had an unfortunate experience during a refreshment break after the formal verdicts when a very senior police officer casually mentioned to me that at this stage it would be extremely unlikely that my sister's body would ever be recovered. This was the first indication that we should give up hope and it was distressing and incredibly disappointing to be given this news in such a manner, especially following the formal coroner's verdicts. It really didn't seem right that my sister's body wasn't given the same level of respect as all those that had been recovered.

In our experience, there were positives and negatives of having a mass inquest. We found it quite challenging at times when families expressed their anger at the authorities during the proceedings.

This gave an uncomfortable atmosphere and caused us additional stress. However, there was some comfort in being surrounded by other families who had experienced bereavement in such exceptional circumstances.

The differences between the King's Cross inquest in the late 1980s and the tsunami 20 years later can be seen in the opportunity for Edie's family to read a eulogy, but going through a mass inquest is clearly still a disturbing experience.

Julie Nicholson, whose daughter Jenny died at Edgware Road and who was later to become a member of Disaster Action, presents a revealing personal view of the inquest proceedings:

At the start of the inquests into the 7 July London suicide bombings of 2005, I was asked what I hoped for, what expectations I had. Given that I already knew so much surrounding the death of my daughter Jenny in that horror, it was a reasonable question. In one sense, there was not a lot more to learn about the manner of Jenny's death or the circumstances surrounding it, beyond what I already knew. However, much of the early information conveyed by police and coroner was absorbed in a state of shock and trauma.

Over the last five years I have amassed much information, many parts of the whole picture, but it is fragmentary: a bag of jigsaw pieces. My expectation was that the inquest would be an opportunity to gain a fuller picture, as all the constituent parts were collated, set out, scrutinised and put together in a cohesive way. Since July 2005, families have been prey to conspiracy theories, media reports and question marks over whether 7/7 might or could have been prevented.

There are collective and generic concerns as well as individual ones, unique to each family. My daughter did not survive the explosion. I've had the comparative consolation, poor as it is, that Jenny's life could not have been saved even had emergency teams and medical assistance reached her within minutes. There are other families who did not have that assurance. There were many questions to be asked formally relating to response times of emergency services, resources, communication and, not least, what may or may not have been known about the four suicide bombers.

It has taken over five years to reach this point and I have been acutely aware that this was probably the last opportunity to have the events of that awful day rigorously examined and assessed properly, and through appropriate judicial proceedings.

I have travelled regularly, often daily, to attend, dedicating the last five months to the business of the inquest, putting work and much of the routine of life on hold to attend to this one last thing.

Throughout proceedings, my overriding attitude has been one of pragmatism. All cannot be made whole; there will remain areas of fuzziness even though a clearer overall picture might evolve. Over this time, there have been those who have wondered why, questioning what good it can do or what I hope to gain?

Why would I put myself through the revisiting, re-engagement and trauma of all the horrific details? I feel I owe it to my daughter to do all I can to gather as much information, clarity and understanding of the whole event as is possible. Quite simply, I have been attending in honour of my daughter.

The inquest has been a gathering up, a re-collection of all the elements of the day, put under rigorous scrutiny by Lady Justice Hallett and her excellent team. I have listened carefully, even through the tedium and frustration of command procedures and protocols, trying to distil some sense and meaning. I have marvelled at the usage and abusage of the English language as it has been applied by various agencies to the jargon of manuals and phrases packed with acronyms. From my lay, possibly plebeian perspective, I continue to marvel at mobile phones that 'fell over'; 'fast win' outcomes; 'ICCSs', 'CBRNs', 'NCCs' and the like. Although deeply frustrating, the overabundance of acronyms at times had its ludicrous and humorous side.

Now the inquest has come to an end as far as the hearing of evidence is concerned, I am left with a sense of 'so be it'. It has been both moving and harrowing listening to the stories and testimonies of those people deeply affected by their experiences. Through courageous acts, bravery, pain and suffering, appalling injuries, fortitude and near-death experiences, humanity flowed through the courtroom like a river as people spoke of their experiences.

Dame Heather [Hallett] did not merely thank each of the witnesses for their contribution and help to the inquest, she thanked them uniquely and deeply. She has been superb in conducting these proceedings. I cannot speak highly enough of the way in which she has attended to everything and everyone. I do not believe the inquests could have been conducted with more humanity, rigour, attention to detail and professionalism than they have been.

From the outset, Dame Heather made it clear that she would be guided by the law. I believe that law and structure has served the inquest, the 52 who were killed and the nation in more ways than can be articulated here. Collectively, questions have been addressed. All interested parties have been given the opportunity to have a voice, whether through the support of legal teams or on their own behalf.

Sitting through proceedings, listening, has been a valuable process and brought me to a point where I believe I can leave the business side of my daughter's death in its rightful place. The rest can be safely and confidently left with Dame Heather and her team to conclude.

Some of Julie's words are a clear illustration of a compassionate attitude that those in the past have found wanting in the coroners' service.

The Coroners and Justice Act 2009 was passed following extensive consultation with numerous interested parties including Disaster Action, yet in 2013 consultations about implementation of the various reforms contained within the Act were still taking place.

We have highly valued our relationship with organisations such as the charity INQUEST, which offers advice to bereaved families with a focus on deaths in custody, sharing common values around 'truth, justice and accountability'.[7] Disaster Action linked up with INQUEST, the Royal British Legion and a number of other specialist charities on a successful campaign to retain the role of Chief Coroner, when the government had made up its mind to abolish the post before even the first appointment was made. This was a good example of where organisations with different focuses – deaths on military service, cot death, in custody or through mass fatality incidents – can come together with a common purpose that achieves a good outcome for all. The mutual benefits for different organisations through such association can be seen in the words of Deborah Coles, co-Director of INQUEST:

> Disaster Action has played a vital role in raising public and political awareness about the specific needs of those bereaved after a disaster. Having bereaved people and survivors as founders and at the centre of its work brings a drive and determination that has been a powerful influencing and authoritative voice. Disaster Action have been generous in their support of better treatment of ALL bereaved people, they have inspired INQUEST and share common values about the need for truth, justice and accountability following contentious deaths. We have been proud to work with them on a number of successful campaigns including the reform of the inquest system, post of Chief Coroner and the

Corporate Manslaughter and Corporate Homicide Act. The legacy of its founder Maurice de Rohan continues as we strive towards a safer world in which human lives matter more than the profits of corporations.

By March 2012, a new charter for those in contact with the coroners' service, and an explanation of that service, was published by the Ministry of Justice. Yet there is no doubt that while the reforms have been welcome, more needs to be done, not least in the matter of giving all those who need it easy access to information about the inquest system and how it will affect them. All those affected by deaths in disaster should have the right of access not only to information but to a *consistent* service, whatever part of the UK those deaths take place in.

Lucy Easthope, adviser to the Home Office on mass fatalities, notes the progress that has been made concerning coroners' training for major emergency inquests:

A profound development in recent years has been the unified and modernising approach taken by a cadre of coroners. There has been a particular emphasis on the processes used for identification after major incidents, and regular training, several times a year, ensures that lessons from recent events are identified.

Without the work of Disaster Action I doubt these changes would have happened and DA speakers are a regular, necessary feature at training events. Their words, the injustices suffered, repeated at the start of this chapter, stay with all those who attend these sessions. This work has been undertaken with governmental support from the Home Office, the Association of Chief Police Officers and the Ministry of Justice, after many years of lobbying by DA members.

Disaster Action's work relating to the work of the coroner is vital, particularly as an advocate for families, but also their role in explaining the challenging, novel coronial processes to families, through the 'When the Disaster Strikes' leaflet series.

In all the teaching and training that I do, I endeavour to impart to new planners the lessons Disaster Action has taught me since I was a law student in 1998. My first port of call is always their guidance for emergency responders on the Disaster Victim Identification process.

INQUIRIES AND INVESTIGATIONS

The words of Lord Justice Clarke (from the Thames Safety Inquiry Final Report into the sinking of the *Marchioness* pleasure boat) concerning the investigation of disasters are particularly relevant to Disaster Action, noting why such investigations should take place. Explaining the purpose of a public inquiry he stated:

> Both the public at large and those intimately concerned have a legitimate interest in ascertaining the truth of what occurred. To my mind that is an important purpose of such an inquiry, although another important purpose of any inquiry (whether public or not) is to enable lessons to be learned which will minimise, or even eradicate, the risk of a similar casualty happening in the future.[8]

In 2013 Disaster Action was invited to make a submission to the House of Lords select committee reviewing the Inquiries Act 2005. The opportunity to share our extensive experience of public inquiries (and the lack of them) and the decision-making process as to whether an inquiry will take place with legislators, was most welcome.

The decision whether to hold a public inquiry remains in the hands of government ministers. A minister who decides, in particular, not to set up an inquiry, or who decides to set up an inquiry with narrow terms of reference, may be perceived as acting out of political self-interest. The action, or lack of action, of such a minister can be judicially reviewed, but this can be so financially prohibitive that the interested parties, who are usually the victims of the disaster, will have no recourse. It has been shown that a campaign by family groups over many years, and through many changes of government, is the only way to achieve what should have occurred in the first place.

SCOTLAND

Since devolution, a difficulty concerning division of responsibility between the UK government and the devolved administrations has emerged. In the case of the 1988 Lockerbie bombing, successive foreign secretaries and other cabinet ministers have refused to order a public inquiry on several grounds, including after the implementation of the Inquiries Act 2005. Since the late 1990s these grounds have included that the disaster was considered 'too long ago'. This is clearly arbitrary.

Secondly since devolution, the UK government has maintained that the decision whether to hold an inquiry into the Lockerbie bombing is a Scottish government responsibility. Yet given that the aircraft took off from Heathrow airport (where it is said that the bomb was loaded into the hold) and other national as well as international ramifications, in the families' view this should not be purely a Scottish government decision. Lockerbie would appear to 'qualify' for an inquiry under section 1 of the Act. However, as of early 2014 government resistance to the holding of an inquiry remains steadfast.

Investigations by the Health and Safety Executive and the police into a disaster are now carried out with the assumption that a crime, such as corporate manslaughter, may have been committed, until or unless it is clear that an unpreventable accident has taken place. This marks a sea change from the period in the late 1980s when the assumption was that an unfortunate accident had occurred which had nothing to do with the organisation's decisions. The significance of this change in attitude and in investigative practices is set out in the next chapter.

NOTES

1 Anne Eyre, 'More than PTSD: Proactive Responses among Disaster Survivors', in the *Australasian Journal of Disaster and Trauma Studies*, 2 (1998) http://www.massey.ac.nz/~trauma/issues/1998-2/eyre.htm.

2 Pam Dix, in Disaster Action Newsletter, Issue 3, Autumn 1995, p. 5.

3 Eyre (1998).

4 Pam Dix, 'Disastrous way to treat grief', in the *Guardian* (17 May 1995).

5 Pam Dix, 'A hard crusade', in the *Guardian* (25 July 1998).

6 Anne Eyre, in Disaster Action Newsletter, 2002 Issue, pp. 3–4.

7 INQUEST: Working for Truth, Justice and Accountability, http://www.inquest.org.uk/.

8 Anthony Clarke, *Public inquiry into the identification of victims following major transport accidents report of Lord Justice Clarke*, Cm. 5012, TSO (The Stationery Office, 2001) p. 7, paragraph 5.2.

CHAPTER 8

CORPORATE RESPONSIBILITY AND THE LAW

> The usual background to disaster is, as history has repeatedly shown, a compendium of error and misjudgement – not only by individuals, but groups, boards and companies. Though the act or omission of an individual may precipitate disaster, the real cause lies much deeper within the systems, outlook and personnel of an organisation.[1]

A significant part of Disaster Action's mission has been to help create a health and safety climate in which disasters are less likely to occur; our focus on corporate responsibility has underpinned this intention. The degree to which Maurice de Rohan personally, and Disaster Action as a whole, succeeded in influencing government thinking is reflected in the remarks made by the then Home Secretary John Reid when he introduced the second reading of the Corporate Manslaughter Bill in the House of Commons on 10 October 2006. To our great regret, this came too late for Maurice, who had died just a few days before.

CORPORATE MANSLAUGHTER AND CORPORATE HOMICIDE BILL

The Secretary of State for the Home Department (John Reid): I beg to move, that the Bill be now read a Second time.

The Government are committed to a properly balanced criminal justice system – a criminal justice system that protects the public inside and outside the home and in the workplace.

In opening the debate, may I first pay tribute to Maurice de Rohan, who died late last week? Maurice de Rohan lost his daughter, Alison, and son-in-law, Francis, in the 1987 Zeebrugge ferry disaster, which claimed the lives of 187 people. He brought together people affected by a series of tragedies in the late 1980s out of which sprang the charity Disaster Action, which has provided an important advocacy and advisory service, giving voice to the survivors and the bereaved of major disasters and contributed significantly to the debate on corporate manslaughter. Maurice remained chairman of Disaster Action until October 2005 and was a trustee until his death. It is fitting that we mark his passing on this occasion.

Tony Lloyd (Manchester, Central) (Lab): I would like to associate everyone with those remarks. One important fact about Maurice de Rohan that is worth recording is that despite his personal tragedy, he maintained his own sense of humanity in every action that he took. It is wholly fit and proper for us to take note of my right hon. Friend's tribute today.[2]

Getting to that point in 2006 had been a long, committed and hard road for Disaster Action.

THE ROYAL COMMISSION ON CRIMINAL JUSTICE

On 13 November 1991, just two weeks after its national launch, a delegation from Disaster Action presented a submission to the Royal Commission on Criminal Justice. The proposal called for radical changes in the criminal justice system concerning the treatment of possible corporate crimes of violence.

> We are particularly concerned that the criminal justice system should fully investigate and prosecute corporate criminal conduct after disasters. Our common experience is that the present system of justice is biased against treating corporate crimes of violence – including those which lead to large scale death and injury – as seriously as it treats traditional crimes of violence.[3]

The submission was concerned with two particular areas of law and practice that came within the Commission's remit:

... the conduct of police investigations and their supervision by senior police officers, and in particular the degree of control that is exercised by those officers over the conduct of the investigation and the gathering and preparation of evidence; the role of the prosecutor in supervising the gathering of evidence and deciding whether to proceed with a case.[4]

The submission revealed failures by the police to undertake immediate and thorough investigation into the conduct of the senior management of companies involved in the long list of disasters from Aberfan in 1966 to the *Marchioness* in 1989. It argued that the criminal justice system had failed to bring to account those companies and senior officers who might have recklessly or negligently caused death or serious injury. Disaster Action argued in detailed proposals that the system of prosecution and investigation should be totally overhauled.

Deputy Chairman Peter Spooner, who handed in the submission, said that 'Disasters will be prevented only when companies are aware that their conduct will immediately be thoroughly investigated and subject to criminal prosecution if there is sufficient evidence of negligence or recklessness.'[5]

FUNDING FOR THE CORPORATE RESPONSIBILITY PROJECT

In 1993, The Joseph Rowntree Charitable Trust[6] agreed to fund Disaster Action for a further two years, thus building on the work of the Herald Charitable Trust's (HCT) pioneering project arising from the Zeebrugge disaster. The funding supported a corporate responsibility project focusing on promoting higher standards of safety. The overall aim was to make a significant reduction in the rate of deaths and serious injuries from other than natural causes primarily through more responsible behaviour by corporate bodies.

This is an example of the sort of work within Disaster Action that complements that of our member groups, also being a platform from which they could promote their separate and specific concerns. The project was chaired by Barrie Berkley and managed by Donat Desmond, who had survived the January 1989 Kegworth air crash in which his wife Marja had died beside him. Commenting on this task at the beginning of the project, Donat said:

When you look at the series of disasters that have affected the lives of members of Disaster Action they aren't merely accidents and as such many were preventable. If safety had been taken seriously at the boardroom level and given the same priority as the financial management of a company we wouldn't have had them in the first place. Ignoring safety is the most destructive form of corporate irresponsibility and in many respects safety and a company's attitude to it is a litmus test of its attitude to corporate responsibility.[7]

From the beginning of the project views were sought from the legal profession and academics on the HFA's publication *Disasters: Where the Law Fails*, which was researched and written by David Bergman.[8] David was later also to research and write *The Case for Corporate Responsibility: Corporate Violence and the Criminal Justice System*, on behalf of Disaster Action,[9] following which he founded the Centre for Corporate Accountability, about which more below. This networking discussion provided the opportunity to broaden contacts with like-minded individuals and organisations and to learn from their experiences.

The project leaders also looked at the various influences on the safety performance of companies. Papers prepared by group participants reviewed the relevance of the BSI standard for quality of service, BS 5750, and also surveyed the systems for safety management available to organisations. The main conclusion from this early work was that there were perfectly adequate safety systems available for implementation within both large and small companies. However, the extent to which organisations saw safety as an integral part of their management criteria varied considerably.

HEALTH AND SAFETY REPORTING IN COMPANY ANNUAL REPORTS

In 1996, as part of Disaster Action's aim to promote greater responsibility for disaster prevention, members Charles Norrie and Barrie Berkley researched and wrote a report on the extent to which the top 100 UK companies described their approach to health and safety in their annual report to shareholders.[10] The Disaster Action report recommended that all companies should adopt this vehicle to demonstrate their commitment to a high standard of safety management consistent with the type of operation in which they are engaged.

As a well-recognised and readily available listing of the foremost British corporate concerns, it was decided to use the Financial Times London Stock Exchange index of the leading 100 companies (FTSE 100). Although this excluded some nationalised concerns and foreign-based companies, it was considered that this listing would provide a sufficient cross-section of types of company for the purposes of the review. The latest annual reports available at that time (1995) were used as the source material.

In the absence of a mandatory requirement it was understandable that widely different approaches were taken to the nature and extent of the information provided on health and safety. Thus while 53 of these 100 large and prominent companies chose not to make any mention of health and safety, some of the other 47 had multiple entries describing their policies, levels of responsibility and review procedures.

As might be expected, companies in certain business sectors were more likely to describe these activities than others. Transport, oil, chemical and engineering industries were generally well represented. Conversely, some companies that might have been expected to mention health and safety because of the type of operations in which they were involved chose not to do so. Companies engaged in finance, insurance and retailing were generally poorly represented.

Disaster Action's study then used the best examples of health and safety reporting to construct a set of guidelines for the type of health and safety information that would offer a corporation advantages if it were to be provided in annual reports. It was suggested the advantages could include:

• helping to demonstrate at a corporate level that the achievement of high standards of health and safety management performance has been recognised as a business objective

• showing that at the operating level the company is adopting a practical approach to health and safety issues

• acknowledging the right and need to know of shareholders, the workforce, regulators, insurers, the media and the wider public of a company's approach to this important area.

A further reason suggested for adopting the reporting guidelines was the growing evidence that the costs of poor health and safety performance had been grossly underestimated, as were the cumulative costs to society, not only in economic and societal terms but also in terms of the pain, grief and suffering of individuals and their families.

DISASTER ACTION'S SUBMISSION ON INVOLUNTARY MANSLAUGHTER

Since there were many bodies such as the Health and Safety Executive (HSE), RoSPA (Royal Society for the Prevention of Accidents) and the health and safety sections of professional societies already involved in promoting safety, we decided to take this work further by focusing on where we could make a unique contribution. An opportunity arose in 1994 when the Law Commission issued their consultation paper on Involuntary Manslaughter, containing proposals for improving the definition of the criteria by which corporate bodies would be judged for their safety performance. In view of his expertise in this field David Bergman was asked to assist Disaster Action in the preparation of our response.

In our submission, we stressed the fact that Disaster Action welcomed the more pragmatic and practical tests for satisfactory safety systems proposed, while highlighting three additional areas we considered essential to address if the law were to stand any chance of having a significant impact on corporate responsibility:

- deaths caused by organisations in the workplace or involving the general public had to be treated with the same seriousness as crimes perpetrated by individuals
- changes were urgently needed to make accident investigation and prosecution policies more effective
- penalties imposed on companies for manslaughter needed to be reviewed, with the emphasis not only on appropriate fines and terms of imprisonment but also on the need for rehabilitation of companies by demonstrating that their safety procedures had been satisfactorily improved.

The preparation of this response made it possible for Disaster Action's project leaders to exchange views on these legal issues with other interested bodies, such as the Health and Safety Executive, the TUC and the West Midlands Health and Safety Advice Centre (HASAC). Barrie Berkley was also invited by RoSPA to give a presentation on this subject at their health and safety congress in Birmingham.

A particular aspect of concern to Disaster Action's member groups was that at that time UK law relating to deaths caused by corporate activities was extremely difficult to apply and, as a consequence, there had been no case of a large corporation being successfully prosecuted either by the Crown Prosecution Service or by family groups for manslaughter. The collective experience across the organisation had made it evident that this situation, combined with the comparatively low fines exacted by the health and safety bodies on companies in cases of deaths or serious injury, was not providing sufficient incentive for guilty companies to put safety systems in place.

The words of bereaved mother Maureen Kavanagh about her experience of the law make it clear why change was so important on a personal level:

Following the death of our only son Peter in the 1997 Southall rail crash, our lives were changed forever. We had no other family, no support, assistance or information from any authorities despite our requests for help. We were trapped in a nightmare so terrible and had nowhere to turn.

British Transport Police were investigating the crash and train company procedures with a view to a criminal prosecution.

At this time a documentary TV company, Blakeway Productions, began filming a series of programmes on Southall and the investigation, embargoed until after any trial and inquiry. I was invited to be involved and in order finally to get some answers I agreed. The information revealed was both shocking and very enlightening. It made me determined to improve rail safety and 'Safe Trains Action Group' (STAG) was born. We received great support from the media in our campaign, which also supported train employees who feared for their jobs. We ensured that the first whistleblower phone line was put in place, with no comebacks on rail employees.

Eighteen months on, the criminal investigation and gathering of evidence was complete and the trial was ready to begin at the Old Bailey on 30 June 1999. This was to be the first time we had contact with other bereaved, as we had been forbidden to do so before then.

We were taken into a room where the Crown Prosecutor told us there would be no trial as the law was not right to do so – it would be a waste of time and money. He said that the driver (due to stand trial) would be 'slapped on the hand' and made to apologise to us. We were astounded and voiced our dismay but instead of answering our questions the Crown Prosecutor said we were not to keep the judge waiting…

The driver was called into the dock and the judge discharged him, saying that the law as it stood did not allow him to go any further and stating that the train operator (Great Western) would be fined for health and safety offences at a later date (the company was fined £1.5 million, at that time the largest ever such fine).

The families were represented by Richard Lissack QC, an expert in corporate manslaughter, who was the most fabulous person to deal with. He immediately said he would appeal the judge's decision. Meanwhile, the bereaved were directed to leave 'the back way' – I said we should speak to the press outside the court as we had certainly not received justice that day. The next day the papers were filled with the injustice of it all – and what, exactly, was wrong with the law? The resulting publicity helped with the rail safety march that STAG was organising with rail unions and the public in November 1999.

The appeal was heard at the Royal Courts of Justice with the draft judgement issued on 15 February 2000. The final paragraph stated that the judges did not think it appropriate to propel the law in the direction Mr Lissack was seeking, that it was a matter for parliament and not the courts. At this stage a draft Bill had been waiting for four years.

Appeal denied. At this point I knew the law must be changed. Although too late for my son, it was not too late for other disasters whose families would cry out for justice.

RAISING PUBLIC AWARENESS OF CORPORATE RESPONSIBILITY

Barrie Berkley was well aware of the importance of raising public awareness of the need for change:

> It is quite obvious that changes in the law and in the attitudes of corporate bodies towards safety are dependent on public attitudes and pressures. Priority for safety legislation, whichever political party is in power, will only be given if the government of the day considers that public demand is sufficiently strong.[11]

To this end, Disaster Action's work included contributing to television and radio programmes, articles and letters focusing on corporate responsibility and safety issues. One of the notions that we had to try to refute was the widely held and simplistic belief that survivors and relatives were seeking revenge. Nothing could be further from the truth. Accountability has nothing to do with scapegoating and everything to do with justice.

THE LAW COMMISSION'S DRAFT BILL ON INVOLUNTARY HOMICIDE, 1996

In March 1996 the Law Commission published a draft Bill on Involuntary Homicide, introducing a new offence of corporate killing. In relation to the three additional areas Disaster Action had highlighted, some positive changes had been incorporated into the Bill:

- The first requirement about treating corporate crimes as seriously as individual ones had essentially been met by the introduction of the new offence of corporate killing. This would arise 'where the body corporate's management failure is the cause or one of the causes of a person's death and that failure is conduct which falls far below what could be reasonably expected of a corporation. A management failure would arise if the way in which the corporation's activities were managed or organised failed to ensure the health and safety of persons employed in or affected by those activities'[12]

- The second point about making accident investigation more effective was not directly covered in the final report; however, Disaster Action felt that clarification of the law would help local authorities, the Crown Prosecution Service and family groups to obtain justice more effectively

- In relation to the third point regarding the review of penalties, Disaster Action was pleased to note that this concept was taken on board by the Law Commission: 'We now accept, and recommend, that the courts should have the power not only to impose a fine on a corporation but also to order it to take remedial steps. We regard this power indeed as an important feature of our recommendations.'[13]

With the above proposed changes, Disaster Action felt that the Law Commission's recommendations had gone most of the way towards meeting our legislative requirements. Having earlier considered drafting a private members Bill in this area, we decided instead to concentrate resources on getting the Law Commission's draft Bill before parliament.

A CHANGE IN GOVERNMENT AND ONGOING PARLIAMENTARY DELAY

The publication of the Bill was followed by a frustrating period of inaction. With a change of government in 1997, however, Disaster Action once again became hopeful of opportunities to pursue the issue, especially given that the Labour Party had shown some support while in opposition. Disaster Action's work has always been apolitical – seeking to influence process, procedure and the legislative framework necessitates working with politicians from all parties, opposition and government.

Efforts were made to establish links with activists in the field, articles were published and contact was made with TV and other media organisations so that Disaster Action would be ready to press for legislative action at the appropriate time. In 1997 Sophie Tarassenko, a lecturer in law as well as a key member of Disaster Action since its foundation, wrote the following article:

THE GENIUS OF OUR LAW

Laws exist primarily to serve the needs of the community to make all its members responsible for their actions. The very notion of Justice rests on holding those who fail to act responsibly accountable to the rest of us, whether they are reckless drivers, child abusers, or negligent dentists. So when dozens or hundreds of people are killed in horrific circumstances, it seems reasonable for most of us to have an expectation that the judicial system will endeavour to establish who is responsible and who should be held accountable.

The extraordinary thing is that this simply does not happen. And yet when relatives of those who are burnt or crushed to death, drowned or blown to pieces ask, in good faith: *Could a court of law please look at the question of responsibility and accountability?* they are perceived as hysterical or vengeful.

In every disaster associated with our organisation, each court in the land has in turn failed us and therefore the community. The criminal justice system, which is the forum most appropriate for society's rightful expectations to be fulfilled, will not prosecute a company for a death. Lesser health and safety offences, even where they cause horrific deaths, are not pursued, due either to lack of resources or lack of willingness (or if they are, the result is a fine smaller than the company's petty cash account).

When the criminal justice system fails in this way, the inquest and the pursuit of compensation acquire enormous importance; relatives begin to count on those courts of law as alternative arenas in which to examine questions of responsibility and accountability (this was recently demonstrated very clearly in the case of Stephen Lawrence). Sadly they hope in vain.

Inquests can become impossible as the jury is bound by the rules to find nobody responsible. Insurance companies' lawyers manipulate relatives into quiet capitulation after advising their client corporation that a quick admission of liability followed by months or years of ruthless haggling over pounds and pence will normally do the trick. The case either never gets to court at all, or if it does it is about amounts, not responsibility, and the victims are perceived as being greedy.

It feels not so much like being slapped in the face as being trod into a large dirty carpet.[14]

THE CASE FOR CORPORATE RESPONSIBILITY: CORPORATE VIOLENCE AND THE CRIMINAL JUSTICE SYSTEM

Disaster Action's Executive Committee decided that a book on corporate responsibility could help to galvanise activity, at a time when initial interest from government appeared to have waned. The book would serve to set out the reasons for the failures in the law as it stood, and to influence policy makers by providing proposals for a workable, appropriate law to cover the punishment, deterrence and rehabilitative aspects that were the bedrock of its purpose.

Given his commitment to legislative reform and knowledge as well as his long-term association with Disaster Action, we commissioned David Bergman to undertake the research and to write the book, which was published in June 2000. The launch was held at the Royal Society for the Arts, attended by individuals who had supported and played a part in the work. A significant contribution to the debate on this subject, the book continues to be used as reference for students and others seeking to understand the background to this still contentious subject.

CENTRE FOR CORPORATE ACCOUNTABILITY (CCA)

Arising out of his work on corporate responsibility and interest in workplace safety, in 1999 David Bergman set up the CCA as a not-for-profit human rights organisation. Given charitable status in 2004, the CCA was concerned with the promotion of worker and public safety. Its focus was on the role of state bodies in enforcing health and safety law, investigating work-related deaths and injuries, and subjecting them to proper and appropriate prosecution scrutiny. Until it closed in 2009, the CCA acted as an invaluable source of advocacy and advice to families affected by the devastating consequences of workplace negligence as well as being a strong campaigning voice in an often complacent environment.

THE CORPORATE MANSLAUGHTER AND CORPORATE HOMICIDE ACT 2007

In 2005 a disappointingly watered down version of the previous draft Bill was published by the government, and in June that year Disaster Action made written submissions commenting on these proposals. We were invited later in 2005 to give oral evidence to the House of Commons Work and Pensions Select Committee as a result. This was a rare and welcome opportunity for Sophie Tarassenko and Pam Dix to give voice to the concerns of more than 20 years to those responsible for creating the laws of the land. The Bill then went back through committee, with the final version published on 31 October 2006 – including some of the amendments Disaster Action had suggested.

In July 2007 the Bill was debated in parliament, progressing through the two Houses, although the House of Lords and the government were at odds over one single aspect of the bill: the House of Lords wanted the corporate manslaughter offence to apply to deaths in custody, while the government was against this, and the House of Commons would vote to defeat the entire Bill if it contained this provision. Other organisations such as INQUEST and the CCA were campaigning for deaths in custody to remain part of the Bill. If the matter could not be resolved by July, the Bill would fail. Disaster Action wrote to all MPs and several key individuals in the House of Lords in a plea for support:

> To contemplate the Bill being defeated now would be an appalling waste of the considerable effort of the past 17 years. The original, central purpose of this Bill was to ensure that other companies should not replicate the sloppy corporate behaviour that led to the 'unlawful killing' of so many people on the *Herald*. This is not about scapegoating, nor retribution, but about what is just. The law would act as an important deterrent, offering the protection denied to those killed on the *Herald* and in numerous disasters that have followed.
>
> ... We urge your support for this Bill, as the potential implications of losing it are incalculable. The devastating and life-long consequences for those who may be affected cannot be overstated.[15]

The Bill ping-ponged back and forth several times between the House of Commons and the House of Lords. The tension and sense of expectation inside Disaster Action were considerable. Would this be the point at which so many years of dogged research and campaigning would come to fruition, or would it all end in failure? At last, after much debate about amendments made by the House of Lords, a compromise was reached, whereby the Home Office's potential corporate responsibility for deaths in custody would be introduced at a later date. On 26 July 2007, the Bill was passed. On 6 April 2008, the Corporate Manslaughter and Corporate Homicide Act came into force.[16]

Reflecting on the impact and implications of the new Act from Disaster Action's perspective, Sophie Tarassenko wrote the following in response to an article about the issues raised by the new law for emergency planners, for the Emergency Planning Society magazine *Blueprint*. It sums up how, and why, new legislation was essential, and what has driven Disaster Action to be part of the movement for change in corporate attitudes and governance.

THE CASE FOR CORPORATE RESPONSIBILITY

David Watts's article [published in the same magazine] rightly aims to allay the fears of emergency planners who see the Corporate Manslaughter and Corporate Homicide Act 2007 as a threat to their job and even their liberty. He also explains that the purpose of the Act is to concentrate the mind of senior managers who run dangerous organisations, not to punish those who ensure the safety of their employees and customers. This short article will attempt to set out the reasons why this piece of legislation is not to be feared, but, on the contrary, to be welcomed by everyone.

Disaster Action was one of the organisations at the forefront of the campaign to promote this change in the law. Our membership consists exclusively of survivors and bereaved people from major disasters, including all modes of transport incidents, and, lately, a range of terrorist attacks in the UK and abroad. We share the experience of being traumatised by sudden death or serious injury, and we are united in the desire to prevent future disasters from ever happening again.

Maurice de Rohan, who first chaired Disaster Action, was himself a company director, whose young daughter and son-in-law, along with 191 others, drowned in March 1987 when the *Herald of Free Enterprise* capsized in 90 seconds because it had sailed with the bow doors open. Such waste of lives not yet lived, and the ensuing years of sorrow suffered by hundreds of family members and friends, could have been prevented by the use of a simple indicator light which had been suggested to P&O by their employees. These lights were, in fact, fitted within days of the tragedy. Maurice became a driving force behind the work of Disaster Action, and in particular the corporate responsibility project. He missed his daughter every day until he himself died last year.

My own involvement with Disaster Action stems from the horrific death of my brother at the age of 25 in the inferno that was King's Cross underground station on 18 November 1987. Part of my personal trauma was having to identify his body and then tell my parents the awful truth. The Fennell report which followed the fire identified a 'collective failure from the most senior management level downward over many years to minimise the outbreak of fire and, more importantly, to foresee and plan for an uncontrolled outbreak of fire at an underground station with a real potential for large scale loss of life'. Many simple recommendations made after previous, smaller fires had not been acted upon.

In the late 1980s members of Disaster Action all came to the inescapable conclusion that all the disasters in which they had been involved were preventable, but that the absence of accountability that was prevalent in English law led to a climate of complacency in certain large corporations. It was from that point that we began to campaign for the prosecution of companies that were indifferent to safety.

Within two weeks of our formation in 1991, on 13 November, a delegation from Disaster Action presented a submission to the Royal Commission on Criminal Justice, which sought radical changes in the way the criminal justice system treated crimes of corporate violence. We argued that for as long as the law failed to bring to account companies and their senior officers who might have recklessly caused death or serious injury, the safety of the public and their employees would be at risk. Peter Spooner, then Deputy Chairman of Disaster Action, said: 'Disasters will be prevented only when companies are aware that their conduct will immediately be thoroughly investigated and subject to criminal prosecution if there is sufficient evidence of negligence or recklessness.'

Over the past 17 years we have set up the Corporate Responsibility Project (funded by The Joseph Rowntree Charitable Trust), lobbied one government after another, contributed to radio and television programmes, written hundreds of letters and articles, made written and oral submissions to parliamentary committees – in the hope that one day the law would change, and the firm belief that when it did, lives would be saved.

We have often been asked if wishing for guilty companies to be prosecuted does not stem from a thirst for revenge. It does not. It comes from a conviction that individual and corporate behaviour can be changed through appropriate legislation. I am old enough to remember the days when wearing a seatbelt was not compulsory, just a good idea. When faced with the prospect of being fined for failure to do so, however, thousands of us changed the habit of a lifetime and started being safe even on short journeys.

We have also been told many times that a new offence of corporate manslaughter would add nothing to current Health and Safety legislation (for example the Health and Safety at Work Act 1974). We say that the threat of prosecution for health and safety offences has not been a sufficient deterrent for those corporate bodies that routinely place the lives of workers and the public at unreasonable risk, since the offences are not considered 'real crimes' and are unrelated to causing death. For some, they have been the acceptable price of doing business.

We are used to being referred to as a 'victims' group' with a gripe against disaster professionals and the media, but we are ordinary people, company directors, housewives, scientists, writers, lawyers. We are human beings who have sought to change the social conditions that brought about the premature and horrific ending of lives dear to us. We think every person who has a husband, wife, partner, son, daughter, brother or sister should welcome the passage of this Act. We believe its mere presence on the statute books has brought about changes in attitudes, and possibly saved lives already.[17]

In April 2013, Jonathan Grimes (partner and health and safety law expert), and Richard Fox (partner and head of employment at Kingsley Napley LLP) reported in People Management/the Chartered Institute of Personnel and Development that, as is common with new legislation, cases brought under the Act have been relatively slow in coming, but that they are beginning to gather pace.[18]

The first case, Cotswold Geotechnical Holding, involving a death in 2008, resulted in a conviction following trial in 2011. Since then two more companies, JMW Farms and Lion Steel, have been convicted. But there is evidence of an increase in cases – five companies have been charged since July 2012. Grimes and Fox stated that the Crown Prosecution Service was still reviewing a number of new cases and that inevitably more corporations would be charged in future.

The Act is testament to the power that can rest in ordinary people, when those people are committed to a justice system that truly represents their interests.

NOTES

1 Stuart Crainer, *Zeebrugge: Learning from Disaster: Lessons in Corporate Responsibility* (Herald Families Association/Herald Charitable Trust, London, 1993) p. 1.

2 *Hansard*, Volume 450, Part No 197, Column 191 (10 October 2006).

3 Disaster Action Newsletter, Issue 1, Spring 1992, p. 6.

4 Disaster Action Newsletter (1992).

5 Peter Spooner, in Disaster Action Newsletter, Issue 1, Spring 1992, p. 6.

6 The Joseph Rowntree Charitable Trust, http://www.jrct.org.uk/.

7 Donat Desmond, in Disaster Action Newsletter, Issue 2, Autumn 1993, p. 2.

8 David Bergman, *Disasters: Where the Law Fails* (Herald Families Association/Herald Charitable Trust, London, 1993).

9 Disaster Action, *The Case for Corporate Responsibility: Corporate Violence and the Criminal Justice System* (Disaster Action, 2000).

10 Disaster Action, *Corporate Responsibility: Health and Safety in Company Annual Reports* (Disaster Action, 1997).

11 Barrie Berkley, in Disaster Action Newsletter, Issue 3, Autumn 1995, p. 3.

12 Barrie Berkley, in Disaster Action Newsletter, Issue 4, Spring/Summer 1997, insert.

13 Disaster Action Newsletter (1997).

14 Sophie Tarassenko, in Disaster Action Newsletter, Issue 4, Spring/Summer 1997, p. 1.

15 Disaster Action letter, 9 March 2007.

16 Corporate Manslaughter and Corporate Homicide Act (Crown Copyright, 2007) http://www.legislation.gov.uk/ukpga/2007/19/contents.

17   Sophie Tarassenko, 'The Case for Corporate Responsibility', in *Blueprint* (Emergency Planning Society, November 2008).

18 Jonathan Grimes and Richard Fox, 'Corporate manslaughter cases increase', in *People Management* (The Chartered Institute of Personnel and Development (CIPD), 12 April 2013) http://www.cipd.co.uk/.

CHAPTER 9

NEW MILLENNIUM, NEW DIMENSIONS – RESPONDING TO FURTHER DISASTERS

The much anticipated disaster threat associated with the 'Millenium Bug' did not materialise at the turn of the century, but there would be no shortage of disasters as the new decade unfolded.

As new members joined the charity, they brought with them different experiences. While these were inevitably devastating, sometimes aspects of these experiences reflected the difference Disaster Action had been able to make. There were instances when individuals and families were referred directly and quickly to Disaster Action, giving them the opportunity to make contact early on with people who could offer valuable information, support and guidance. The impact this can have on those who find themselves involved in tragic events is evident in the words of Jelena Watkins in this chapter.

THE SEPTEMBER 11 ATTACKS, 2001

The first year of the new century was to bring the worst terrorist attack to date on the United States, with the deaths of nearly 3000 people of 60 nationalities.

Straight after the attacks, seen live by Disaster Action members on their television screens as by so many around the world, we wrote to the Right Honourable Tessa Jowell MP – charged by Prime Minister Tony Blair with responsibility for the welfare of affected UK nationals – drawing her attention to what we anticipated their needs might be. For the first time, a government minister had been appointed to oversee what was to be done to help those affected by a major tragedy. 'Recovery' from disaster finally meant placing people's needs at the forefront of an emergency response. The outcome was the setting up of the Humanitarian Assistance Unit in the Department for Culture, Media and Sport; disasters and entertainment might appear to be an uneasy mix, but it was Tessa Jowell's personal involvement as minister for this department that brought this about.

We felt an extraordinary sense of empathy and responsibility for those involved in the 9/11 attacks, and believed that it was incumbent on us to use our past experience to improve the treatment of those affected by the shocking events of that day. We became increasingly involved, taking telephone calls from a number of those in Britain who had been bereaved, offering practical and emotional support – a listening ear, based on empathy and prior experience. People found this helpful because of the unique insight of the Disaster Action members who took the calls. We are not counsellors, but non-judgemental, practical advice based on our personal experience remains at the core of what we do.

Five months after the attacks, with the assistance of the British Consulate in New York, the Foreign & Commonwealth Consular Directorate in London and the Metropolitan Police Service, Disaster Action hosted a private meeting at a hotel in London to enable the 9/11 families to meet each other for the first time. This was a meeting filled with emotion, most evident when each of those present briefly explained why they were there, who they had lost. This was a continuation of the central focus of our work with families in facilitating the coming together of support groups – a primary source of self-help for those affected by a disaster. Following their initial meeting, the September 11 families went on to form their own group, with the continued support and guidance of Disaster Action. At the time of writing in 2014, the group continues to mark the anniversaries of the tragedy at the memorial garden in Grosvenor Square in London and its members remain committed to offering each other mutual support.

One such member, Jelena Watkins, writes about her experience of Disaster Action and why she later decided to join and become an active member of the charity's Executive Committee:

I lost my brother Vladimir in the 9/11 attacks. Vladimir lived in Canada and this was his first ever trip to New York City. There are no words that could describe the horror that we as a family have been through, especially in the early days and weeks after the disaster. The fact that none of us was based in the US made our situation additionally difficult. The early months were spent in a complete haze: due to the scale of destruction the process of identification of victims was very slow and confusing. In those early weeks and months what I desperately needed was information, but it was almost impossible to get, even for those who were living in NY. I felt very isolated and out of the loop here in the UK, where I didn't know anyone else affected by September 11.

I was determined to set up a support group from the very early days. In my search for other people affected by 9/11 I was put in touch with DA, who were present at a national memorial service at Westminster Abbey. I got in touch with them primarily because of my desire to set up a group and wanting to see whether they could help me. But once I did get in touch with Sophie Tarassenko who lost her brother in the King's Cross fire, I was immediately struck by how similar our experiences were. I met with Sophie one evening after work, four months after 9/11, and I talked and talked and talked. Sophie listened for as long as it took, and just occasionally added a few points from her own experience. Hearing that others before me have had similar problems made me feel better, or least more normal. It was at that meeting with Sophie that I came to realise two things: people from very different disasters go through some very similar experiences, and some of the problems that people go through are preventable if learning from one disaster was used for future disasters. It was already at that point that I knew I would want to get more involved with DA at some point in the future.

Disaster Action indeed helped me and the other 9/11 families get together as a group by organising our first meeting some months after the disaster. In that first meeting there were nearly 100 of us bereaved people, and the feeling of shared pain was palpable. It was in that meeting that we decided to form an organised group, September 11 UK Families Support Group. I was one of the founding committee members. We are active to this day and for many of our 300 members we have been a lifeline.

Once my own group was well established and my own life took on some form of functioning, I wanted to get more involved with DA. My main reason was that some of the problems I was going through in dealing with those in official positions appeared to be generic and I felt an urge to address them so that no one goes through it again. It was in December 2004 and I was in contact with Pam from DA about commenting on FCO guidance for humanitarian assistance to British nationals affected by overseas disaster.

Some days later the Indian Ocean tsunami happened, claiming hundreds of thousand of lives, with many of the missing being British. I was deeply affected by this tragedy, and could particularly strongly identify with a situation when a loved one was missing, far away from home, and all the logistical difficulties that would add to the already unbearable trauma. I took an active part in DA's response to the tsunami, first in providing advice to the government on dealing with the victims, then later in the creation of the support network for survivors and the bereaved. I facilitated a monthly support group for the bereaved people based in London.

In the following year the 7 July bombings took place. Again, as someone personally affected by terrorism and as a London resident, I was deeply shaken by the event. As a DA member I took part in regular management meetings for the responders and contributed my experience.

It's been nine years since the start of my active involvement with DA and I continue to feel passionate about our work. What I have gained is a sense of satisfaction for being able to use my own tragic experience to make a difference to the lives of others.

THE BALI BOMBINGS, 2002

Just over a year after the September 11 attacks, British nationals were again caught up in a terrorist attack, this time at the Sari nightclub in the Indonesian holiday resort of Bali. Of the 202 people killed, 28 were British nationals. In January 2003 Disaster Action hosted a meeting to provide an opportunity for those bereaved and those who survived the bombing (some of whom were also bereaved) and their relatives to meet each other. As with the meeting for the September 11 families, it was a highly charged event, which was to prove the beginning of a new lifeline for those affected.

Maurice de Rohan, with his inimitable measured empathy welcomed families and explained that one of Disaster Action's aims was to offer support to those affected by disaster. A number of members spoke about how helpful it had been for them to be in touch with those who had experienced other disasters, while emphasising that they were not there to tell people what they ought to be doing or feeling.

Following this meeting the Bali families established their own support group and meetings, affiliating with Disaster Action for ongoing communication and support. The words of Bob and Sandra Empson, who some time later became Disaster Action Executive Committee members, vividly record the impact of the loss of a beloved family member through a disaster, as well as the difference that contact with Disaster Action can make.

We made contact with Disaster Action more or less two months to the day after the Bali terrorist bombings of 2002 robbed us of the life of our beloved only daughter, Lucy, aged 30. Lucy was on a 10-day holiday to Singapore and Bali with her dear friend, Emma. The girls had been in Bali for less than a day when terror struck. Emma also lost her young life.

As of 12 October 2002 our lives changed forever. In our delicate, grief-stricken state we were immediately manoeuvred through a maze of officialdom, some gentle, some stark reality. Sometimes we had to fight to be heard yet other times help and support came from unexpected sources. When we look back nearly seven years on, the main players that supported us in those early months were family, good friends, the brilliant Family Liaison Service and the humble, the dedicated and the necessary Disaster Action.

Our Family Liaison Officer pointed us in the direction of this remarkable organisation and it was on 10 December 2002 that we first became acquainted. With incredible listening skills Pam Dix heard us out. She responded with comfort and wisdom, borne out by the fact that she was not only one of the main contacts for DA but had also lost her brother in the Pan Am Lockerbie disaster. To hear soft, caring tones from someone who had experienced a similar tragedy was instantly cathartic and our rapport with this organisation was sealed. We asked so many questions as to our way forward and she provided us with the vital information we needed. When we look back to our diary entry on that day we cannot believe that all the advice she gave us at that time has turned out to be 100% correct. We have no hesitation therefore in saying that DA's advisory service for those victims of disasters is second to none. Pam also directed us to the DA website which we now know to be an invaluable source of help, support and constant referral.

Disaster Action, the Metropolitan Police Service and the British Red Cross were all instrumental in organising an initial meeting for victims' families and individuals affected by the Bali Bombings. It was structured to bring people together to give them access to information and

---

support, not just in the immediate aftermath of the disaster but also in the months and years ahead. The meeting took place in London in early January 2003 and was a much needed and uplifting experience, giving us a moment's pause in our suffering and confusion. Those present had the opportunity to listen to the expertise of others. The Chairman and founder of Disaster Action, Maurice de Rohan, was one such person. He told us that he formed DA as a result of losing his own daughter and son-in-law in the Zeebrugge disaster. His talk was inspiring, delivered with such warmth and strength that we treasure it to this day. So powerful was his speech that we entered the meeting fragile and alone and left it with a sense of friendship and belonging, the result of which a group was formed, namely the UK Bali Bombings Victims Group. Our group is now firmly established as belonging to the family sitting under the umbrella organisation that is Disaster Action.

To this day our hearts will forever belong to Disaster Action, being an impartial organisation that seeks only to help and support victims of disasters. They were there for us during our complex years of trauma, issues and bureaucracy and still are to this day. They have never let us down. In turn we will forever be there for them. We trust that to date we have been able to contribute in some small way to this wonderful organisation in return for all the care they have given us.

We dedicate these words to the memory of our dearly loved and exceptional daughter whom we still sorely miss every waking moment of our lives.[1]

AL KHOBAR, SAUDI ARABIA, TERRORIST ATTACKS, 2004

In May 2004, an attack on an oil installation and housing complex killed 22 people of ten different nationalities and injured many others. Penny Hamilton's husband Michael was one of those who died.

PENNY'S STORY

I have been a member of Disaster Action since 2006, when I was introduced to the organisation by Tessa Jowell. I believe that the work Disaster Action carries out is invaluable to all those who have suffered as a result of disasters and terrorist incidents both in this country and abroad. After the initial help provided by the emergency services, survivors and relatives are often left to cope with the physical and mental trauma on their own. Disaster Action provides ongoing legal, practical and emotional help at an extremely difficult time.

My personal involvement has been extremely positive. My husband was murdered by Saudi members of Al Qaeda on 29 May 2004. Although a number of people were killed that day, Michael was the only British victim. As a result there is no specific 'survivors' group. I have been lucky in that I have a strong and supportive family and have received professional and ongoing help from the Foreign Office and the anti-terrorist police. In particular the police family liaison officer assigned to me was compassionate, empathetic and a source of great strength both to me and my family at a time when we were all traumatised and confused by what had happened.

But Disaster Action has given me an opportunity to share my experience with people whose involvement in similar incidents has given them a unique insight and understanding into what others might be suffering. It has also given me an opportunity, in a small way, to contribute towards the ongoing help we give to individuals and organisations preparing for possible future disasters.

THE INDIAN OCEAN TSUNAMI, 2004

On Boxing Day 2004 the Indian Ocean Tsunami (sometimes referred to as the South East Asian Tsunami) swept across a number of countries, killing many thousands of people.

A phone call to Pam Dix from then Metropolitan Police Service (MPS) Chief Inspector Mick Free to ask whether we would advise on the police response could result in only one answer: 'Yes'. A journey to Yorkshire for a family holiday was interrupted, and the destination instead became Hendon Police Training College, where Charles Norrie and Pam Dix met Commander Cressida Dick, the police silver commander, part of whose responsibility was family liaison. At that early stage, although the appalling loss of life and impact on so many people was already evident, the level of involvement of UK nationals was still unclear.

Guidance from Disaster Action to the police and the Foreign & Commonwealth Office included dealing with coronial and mortuary arrangements, collection of forensic and other evidence, repatriation of survivors and bodies, communication with families and survivors, and death certification for those whose bodies were not recovered. We were in a position to highlight the issues that would be most important in terms of the impact on those affected. Pressure from Disaster Action helped to persuade the government to waive the seven-year rule, so that interim death certificates could be issued for those missing presumed dead. Otherwise families could have had to wait years to settle estates and organise their financial affairs, adding greatly to the already highly distressing circumstances.

Our advice continued through conversations and emails, which undoubtedly improved the quality of the police service considerably. Police officers (particularly family liaison officers) also made use of our existing resources – the website and leaflets – in their provision of information to families. Cressida Dick, appointed Assistant Commissioner at the MPS in 2009, reflected in September 2005 on the difference we had made: 'Disaster Action's impact was extraordinary, the advice proving to be entirely sound. I would regard what they did as a model of good practice, which had a very great real impact on the experience of those most affected.'

At the beginning of 2005, Disaster Action met with the British Red Cross and Foreign Office officials to discuss ways of meeting the ongoing needs of families and survivors in the UK. The result was the establishment of the Tsunami Support Network (TSN) by the British Red Cross, which coordinated the multi-agency response to the disaster. Sitting at the table for the first meeting of this service, Pam Dix reflected on the importance of the event, the first time efforts had been made to create such a coordinated service at the behest of central government for those directly affected by a disaster.

Disaster Action sat on the Steering Group for the TSN and continued to offer advice over the following two years or so, including on the arrangements for memorial services. We were to learn much about what works for families and survivors, and what doesn't work, at the very first meeting for those affected. They felt patronised by those who led the meeting, and so we rapidly had to revise the way in which it was organised. Eventually, an independent support group, Tsunami Support UK, was formed with start-up funding support from the Red Cross. This group has joined Disaster Action, which continues to be available to offer advice and support to the group as well as to individuals affected by the Tsunami.

One survivor, Sasha Pagella, who joined Disaster Action as an individual, offers his views on the organisation:

I first learnt about Disaster Action from the Red Cross when I phoned their Tsunami support helpline. On my return to the UK I felt extremely isolated and had a strong need to meet and share my experiences with other survivors, as I didn't know anyone else in the UK who'd survived the Tsunami. I'd been holidaying on my own in Penang, Malaysia and the only other survivors I knew were living in Australia and Asia.

In the few months after the disaster the British Red Cross hadn't yet had the opportunity to establish a physical support group where survivors and bereaved could meet and it was DA that was able to facilitate a quick exchange of contact details between consenting survivors.

On contacting DA for the first time I was struck by the fact that everyone involved had been directly affected by a disaster themselves and to my mind were uniquely placed to understand what I was going through. I can't begin to stress how important this was, and talking with them I soon realised that the mental turmoil I was experiencing was a natural and shared reaction to an extreme event and not unique to me. For me this first early association with DA marked the beginning of my long road to recovery.

A few months after the Tsunami I felt a strong need to channel my experience into something positive to benefit others. DA was able to provide me with practical advice, ideas concerning my wish to help as well as understanding and support. As a member of DA I was able to use my experiences to help train the police family liaison officers and social workers that deal with both bereaved and survivors. I was also able to provide constructive feedback through DA to other government agencies such as the Foreign Office and Department of Culture, Media and Sport's Humanitarian Assistance Unit.

Importantly, Disaster Action made me feel welcome and never sought more from me than I felt able to give. I feel an immense sense of gratitude towards Disaster Action and a bond that I will no doubt share with them for the rest of my life.

Edie Fassnidge explains why she too joined Disaster Action some years after the deaths of her mother and sister in the Tsunami, which she and her partner (now husband) Matt survived:

I joined Disaster Action with the aim of helping other people who experience disasters and to try and give something back following the support that I received. After the Tsunami I benefited from Disaster Action through the 'support for survivors and bereaved' leaflets which I accessed online and were really the only source of information I could find that was relevant to my personal experience of both surviving the Tsunami and also being bereaved through the death of my mother and sister. The information was practical and provided clear guidance on disaster victim identification. It was also comforting and enabled me to realise that the feelings that I was experiencing were quite normal in the aftermath of a disaster.

I found Disaster Action's presence at meetings of survivors and bereaved after the Tsunami to be informative, calm, non-judgemental and pragmatic – exactly what is required at such events. I was also impressed by their work in engaging with the police, government and other agencies to improve the experience for people who are affected by disasters.

THE LONDON BOMBINGS, 2005

On 7 July 2005, London witnessed the biggest terrorist attack seen in the UK since the Lockerbie bombing of 1988, when four bombs exploded on the public transport network during the morning rush hour. Fifty-two people were killed as well as four suicide bombers.

The coincidence of being present on Upper Woburn Place just 100 metres from where the bus bomb exploded that morning was not lost on Pam Dix. She was on her way to an event to discuss 'humanitarian assistance in emergencies', the phrase coined by those of us working on putting the needs of affected individuals at the heart of emergency planning and response.

Within two days, the Metropolitan Police Service called upon Disaster Action to help. Not normally frontline responders, we felt compelled to do as much as we could to assist those caught up in such a brutal experience. During the first week after the disaster various members became actively involved, spending time at the Family Assistance Centre and visiting the temporary mortuary to comment on the viewing facilities being set up for families who might wish to see the bodies of their loved ones.

One reason why we were more involved than usual was that Disaster Action had been part of the steering group, led by the MPS, which was working with the Department for Culture, Media and Sport Humanitarian Assistance Unit to create national guidance on the setting up of assistance centres for those affected by disaster.[2] This guidance was still in draft at the time of the bombings, and with Moya Wood-Heath of the British Red Cross (also on the steering group), we were therefore some of the few people who were equipped to put into practice for the first time the kind of assistance centre set up after the bombings. (The guidance was published in autumn 2005.)

With Mick Free of the MPS and Moya Wood-Heath, Disaster Action members Charles Norrie and Pam Dix were instrumental in convincing then Secretary of State Tessa Jowell of the need for an appropriate assistance centre to meet the practical and emotional needs of those affected by the bombings. Our overriding concern was for central government to take on board that a disaster with such national implications required an unprecedented response from our government. This we succeeded in doing.

Within a week and a half of the disaster, Disaster Action had helped create opportunities for those affected to meet each other informally at the Family Assistance Centre, with two members attending at one such meeting where people could get together in a private, secure and comfortable setting. The Centre provided a range of other facilities for visitors, including Disaster Action leaflets, which were heavily drawn on and used.

John Stoker, Chief Executive of the London Bombings Relief Charitable Fund, which was set up to manage and distribute money raised for the survivors and bereaved donated by people all round the UK as well as from the government, invited Disaster Action to present the perspective of those who had been recipients of previous disaster funds – or had been turned down as recipients. (The extensive experience of our members and further research was later to result in our 2010 report and guidance leaflet on the *Management & Distribution of Disaster Funds*.)[3]

It soon became apparent – as with other disasters – that the responses from the organisations involved were mixed, and many of those affected by the bombing received no information about the support on offer in general, or Disaster Action in particular. A number of individuals affected by the London – and later the Sharm El Sheikh bombings, and who subsequently came into contact with Disaster Action – revealed that they had not been told about the organisation at an early stage, even though they would have appreciated the opportunity for this contact. This was another reminder to members not to feel complacent, highlighting the ongoing need for Disaster Action to communicate its existence and role.

From the outset, Disaster Action offered real-time advice to the Centre management group that sat for a number of weeks at the Royal Horticultural Society Halls (the location for the Centre) and to the Next Steps programme that followed. Pam Dix sat on the advisory group for the pan-London NHS mental health response, which set up the first ever dedicated 'screen and treat' programme for those affected by a disaster. Inevitably the programme had difficulties and limitations, but it provided recognition of the potential trauma for those affected by a disaster, and steps towards how to assess and treat those who might be in urgent need of help.

We eventually learned that survivors in particular felt that the name of the Centre, with its emphasis on the word 'family', had excluded them. Such centres are now planned for by local authorities all over the country, as Humanitarian rather than Family Assistance Centres. This is a good example of the way in which the experience of those directly affected can – and should – be reflected in planning for future emergencies.

Part of the learning for Disaster Action was that in terms of capacity we are not in a position to offer a frontline service. Circumstances prevailed that made it possible for us to do so on that occasion – availability and proximity of members to London, relationships with key responders, knowledge of the draft plans – but such response is outside our normal remit and scope. The personal price paid by members for such levels of commitment should also not be underestimated in terms of its emotional demands.

THE SHARM EL SHEIKH BOMBINGS, 2005

Later that same month, a number of Britons found themselves caught up in a shocking suicide bombing attack in Sharm El Sheikh, Egypt, including Trevor Lakin whose son Jeremy was killed with his girlfriend Annalie Vickers. With the focus of government and the country so much on what had happened just a few weeks before in London, official support for those affected was not what it should have been. The families were to learn of Disaster Action far later than they should have done, indeed by which time they were considering setting up such an organisation themselves.

DISASTER ACTION AND THE DEVELOPMENT OF POLICE FAMILY LIAISON

As these examples show, police family liaison is now an integral part of the response to disasters, with family liaison officers (FLOs) deployed to bereaved families as an integral part of the identification and investigation procedures. Their role is to work with families to make sure that ante mortem data and material (to assist in the identification of the dead) are gathered quickly, compassionately and effectively. This is to ensure that identification and repatriation of people's loved ones takes place as quickly as possible, although for families the wait may well still feel too long. The value of this approach includes families having a single point of contact for accessing information and further support, and today FLOs are specially selected and trained for what is a complex and sensitive role.

This was not always the case. Family liaison in its current form did not exist for those bereaved in the disasters associated with Disaster Action's early days, a factor that in part contributed to the negative experiences of those exposed to earlier identification and investigatory methods and procedures. All too often those processes had been carried out without sufficient compassion, coordination or care.

Disaster Action has witnessed and been proud to help shape and support the development of this aspect of the police service over the last 20 years, working with a number of individuals and forces involved in disaster-related training and response. In this endeavour a key influence and friend of Disaster Action has been Duncan McGarry MBE, formerly National Police Family Liaison Advisor. As a serving police officer Duncan's role included the development of family liaison from 1998 until 2013; he advised on a number of mass fatality incidents including the Ladbroke Grove Rail crash, 11 September attacks, the Bali bombings, the Indian Ocean Tsunami and the 2005 London and Egyptian bombings. At the time of writing in 2014, Duncan is the Family Liaison Advisor to the Hillsborough Inquiry.

Of Disaster Action he says:

'I have worked closely with members of Disaster Action throughout my career and not only in areas related to disaster. Their insight and knowledge has been a tremendous resource to all police practitioners down the years. I personally feel that the current police family liaison system would not be as advanced as it is had we not been able to approach DA for advice and guidance.

Theirs is a unique insight into disaster incidents, in areas police officers can only be grateful never to have experienced. They have shared their own painful experiences in an educated and non-judgemental fashion for the benefit of survivors and responders alike. They have made a difference.'

NORTH SEA HELICOPTER CRASHES, 2009 AND 2013

In April 2009 a helicopter returning from a BP oil platform in the Miller oilfield off the Scottish coast crashed, killing all 16 people on board in the worst such crash in 23 years. As arrangements were being put in place for setting up the first Scottish Humanitarian Assistance Centre of its kind under Scotland's new national guidance, Disaster Action representatives were invited to attend the multi-agency planning and advisory meetings. Two of us spent a number of days in Aberdeen offering advice and support to those staffing and managing the assistance centre as well as to those working with families at such a difficult and sensitive time. As ever, we took our leaflets with us for passing on to responders, families and others, knowing that (as proved to be the case), it is often some weeks, months or years later that those affected might need or wish to be in touch with Disaster Action.

Aberdeen City Council Emergency Planning Officer Joy Stamp writes:

> I already knew of the work Disaster Action undertook from a previous emergency planning role in aviation and so they were invited to join the multi-agency team co-ordinating the setting up of a Humanitarian Assistance Centre in the city for the relatives, friends, colleagues and basically anyone directly or indirectly affected by the tragedy.
>
> Disaster Action's input was a great reassurance to us all as we strove to achieve the provision of a welcoming, calming and relaxing atmosphere for our visitors where they could access the support they needed and meet with relatives, colleagues and others affected by the disaster. Disaster Action did not leave us until the day after opening and it was further reassurance to know that, if needed, they were at the end of a telephone.

Four years later another fatal helicopter crash occurred in the North Sea and we were in contact once more with responders there. Again they passed on our details at their initial meetings and included Disaster Action on their Humanitarian Assistance Centre information leaflets.

Sadly, the end of 2013 witnessed another fatal helicopter crash in Scotland, this time in Glasgow; nine people died and a number were seriously injured when a police helicopter crashed through the roof of a city pub. It was a further reminder, if any were needed, of the impact and suffering caused to those involved in and affected by sudden, unexpected tragedy.

The examples we have given here illustrate our ongoing activities since 2000, particularly in the aftermath and further initial phases after disasters. But it would be a distortion of our work to suggest that this is our primary activity and focus. Thankfully disasters do not happen every day or week in the UK and yet there is always work to be done, keeping Disaster Action members busy, particularly at the office and within our informal and internal networks. This includes supporting each other and other individuals who may contact us for support at significant times such as anniversaries or when personal experiences and emotions are triggered through new disasters. Media interest and coverage can play a role here and so it is to a consideration of Disaster Action and the media that we now turn.

NOTES

1 Bob and Sandra Empson, in Disaster Action Newsletter, Spring 2010, p. 9.
2 HM Government, *Humanitarian Assistance in Emergencies: Non-statutory Guidance on Establishing Humanitarian Assistance Centres* (Crown Copyright, 2006) https://www.gov.uk/government/uploads/system/uploads/attachment_data/file/61221/hac_guidance.pdf.
3 Dr Anne Eyre, *Disaster Funds: Lessons & Guidance on the Management & Distribution of Disaster Funds* (Disaster Action, 2010).

CHAPTER 10

EXPERIENCES OF THE MASS MEDIA

The human interest angle has always made bereaved people and survivors attractive to the mass media. The continuing issues associated with disasters also ensure that victims' stories continue to be of interest. Since its earliest days, Disaster Action has received regular requests for interviews, analysis and comment and offered feedback on the personal angle, from outlets as diverse as the *Lancet*, the *BMJ*, *Police Review*, *Woman's Own*, the *Guardian* and the *Sunday Telegraph* as well as specialist magazines and journals.

In our experience, journalists often rely heavily on survivors and the bereaved for background information and context, sometimes giving the impression that they are looking for unpaid researchers or ways to flesh out their stories. There is often intense pressure on reporters from their editors to meet daily newspaper and programme deadlines, which can mean a loss of factual accuracy and a breach of the trust of those who may be the focus of the story.

By contrast, the commitment and skills of investigative journalists such as the late Paul Foot have been an invaluable support not only to individuals within Disaster Action but to the charity as a whole. Foot's assistance in persuading The Joseph Rowntree Charitable Trust to fund the Herald Families Association's work on corporate responsibility helped to lay the foundation for all that was to follow. He was mindful of the potential impact on individuals and families of stories that might be published about their experience or campaigns, and understood how important it was to develop mutually trusting relationships. On receiving a request for an article in the mid-1990s about why people traumatised by tragedy campaign for change after their experience, Foot's answer was to refer the editor to Pam Dix so we could write the story for ourselves.

The advent of 24-hour news has also meant increasing pressure to find stories to fill the time, leading to more speculative reporting, while the facts are being established. The rapid development of technology means that disasters can now be captured on video or mobile phones as they unfold, as in the 2005 London bombings. This potentially offers rapid news and updates and valuable insight into disaster experiences. But it also encourages the acquisition and dissemination of images that may be distasteful, exploitative and harmful to the feelings, rights and welfare of those affected by disasters.

As in our other work, Disaster Action members have sought to influence journalists' perceptions and treatment of those they seek to interview. This includes giving presentations to journalism and research students at colleges and universities, contributing to the work of the Dart Centre for Journalism and Trauma,[1] and the production of a leaflet with guidance on interviewing, which spells out what it is like to be on the receiving end. One of the most rewarding parts of this work is contributing to education for the next generation of journalists.

THE MEDIA: FRIEND OR FOE?

Media intrusion in those minutes, hours and days after disaster strikes has amplified the grief of many victims, their friends and relatives. But the media can help as well as hinder. In October 1993, Pam Dix wrote an article for the *Guardian* reviewing a new book, *The Media and Disasters – Pan Am 103* by Joan Deppa and others.[2] The article, which considers the role of the media based on Pam's personal experiences and reflections, echoes those of other members of Disaster Action. This article was the first one Pam wrote about her experiences of Lockerbie and the media, in an effort to reclaim control over what was said. An adapted version is presented below.

The death in a disaster of someone you love is a nightmare that happens to other people. But that nightmare came true for my family when, on December 21 1988, Pan Am 103 was destroyed over Lockerbie, taking with it my oldest brother Peter. We found out about his death not from any official source, but by asking a reporter friend to get into the Pan Am system at New York and confirm our suspicions. So my earliest experience of the disaster showed the potential of the media to get things done when all else fails. I did not watch the first TV coverage. I can still feel how I recoiled after working out what the graceful and arty photograph on the front of the *Independent* newspaper was – a body draped over a roof. How many wondered whether it was their relative?

It was impossible to see the face, and I accept the necessity of showing the full force of what the explosion of an aircraft at 31,000 feet really means. Yet, before Lockerbie, I had no sense of how deep the effect of every image and reference to the disaster is on someone personally affected. Even now, if I glance at a paper without concentrating, pictures turn into debris, words beginning with L become Lockerbie and those beginning with D become death and disaster.

We went to Lockerbie on Christmas Day, to see the site and come face to face with the reality of what had happened. To walk past a reporter speaking on a public telephone, filing a story about bodies falling out of the sky was a surreal experience.

The media had to be given proper access to the site but the relatives' need to know seemed to be secondary. After much cajoling, we managed a few moments silent contemplation in front of the nose cone, while the reality sank in. We owed this to the efforts of a social worker, who was told by an overwrought policeman: 'You are in deep shit – get these people out of here.'

The instinct of the police was to protect the relatives from media intrusion. But there is a price to be paid for lack of direct contact, as I would have disputed some press reports.

Peter's identification seemed to take forever, for reasons which took years to discover. One relative, frustrated in his efforts to get his wife identified, went to the press. Was it coincidence that her body was released next day? My family agonized over going to the press with our experiences in the first few weeks after the disaster, when virtually all our contact with the authorities had done little but fuel our anger. In the end we did so, and we have no regrets.

I have come to understand that the media can be friend or foe. I now realize in order to learn the truth and get things changed, it is essential to work with them. But one false move can leave a relative feeling exposed and exploited. One journalist I trusted for years after Lockerbie was using me for his own purposes, and the only way to prevent him from publishing his version was to get a solicitor.

News organizations should have a disaster plan. A disaster will put reporters and editors under intolerable pressure, and even the best-intentioned may make decisions they will regret.

The necessity for such a strategy is clear from one example from Lockerbie. Only a couple of hours after the disaster, when Pan Am had not released any passengers' names, a TV station in Syracuse showed a list obtained from the airline. The stations' reporters were devastated when they had to contend with distraught phone calls from those who called in for confirmation of the deaths.

So what role should the media have in a disaster? I still do not know where the line should be drawn. Should the photograph have been printed in the *Independent*? In the end we have to rely on the good judgement of journalists. But reporters and editors must understand the immediate and long-lasting effects of their behaviour on the bereaved and survivors.

As the years go by my task as a bereaved relation has been transformed from avoiding the media to badgering them when interest in 'my' disaster falls off. The effect of too little media interest in a disaster can be deeply frustrating to relatives.

People often ask me if it is hard when Lockerbie resurfaces in the news. Of course it is. Yet if effective preventative measures are to be put into place, there must be a full exploration of what has happened. However long it takes, those of us in the relatives' group, UK Families Flight 103, will continue to fight to gain that truth. We have no choice but to use whatever media resources we can, as my dealings with the authorities have taught me that for them political expediency may take precedence.

Five years after Lockerbie most people are unaware that it is still possible to place an unaccompanied bag into many airline baggage systems in the way that the bomb suitcase ended up on Flight 103. Only public opinion can change how governments create and enforce rules for the protection of passengers.

If all the information that individual journalists hold on Lockerbie could be pooled perhaps the jigsaw might fit. Ideally what we need is for the notion of scoop to be swallowed up by the notion that truth matters more. Such an approach may yet come about through the efforts of those journalists dedicated to uncovering the whole Lockerbie story.

The media response has had a very negative impact on those involved in a number of disasters. When the *Marchioness* riverboat sank on the river Thames in August 1989, 51 young people were drowned. They had been attending a party. Articles appeared in the press, one in the London *Evening*

Standard suggesting that the dead had been born with 'silver spoons in their mouths' and were at a drink and drug-fuelled party. A significant consequence was the detrimental influence on public sympathy for the dead, survivors and bereaved: the disaster trust fund, set up to raise money for those affected, raised approximately £89,000. This is in sharp contrast with figures of over 4 million pounds raised after the 1985 Bradford football stadium fire and the 1987 Zeebrugge ferry disaster.[3] Yet later, the focus of the media on the unfinished business of the *Marchioness*, when the Marchioness Action Group needed all the support it could get for a full inquest and inquiry, was instrumental in keeping the disaster in the news. This mixed experience of media interest and coverage has been one of the points of common ground and connection between members of Disaster Action and, more broadly, those affected by any collective private tragedy that becomes public commodity. This is despite the fact that the nature, technology and techniques of the mass media have changed so radically since the time of Aberfan, when television coverage of the rescue effort became one of the first live outside broadcasts.

There are also distinctions between local and national media coverage of disasters that touch particular communities. In our experience, local media may offer support and understanding to those directly affected and the broader community, as is illustrated by the experiences of those affected by the Hillsborough disaster.

Much has been said and written about the impact of inaccurate and negative media coverage by some news agencies in the immediate aftermath of the Hillsborough disaster in April 1989. In particular one tabloid newspaper, the *Sun*, under a front page headline 'The Truth', manufactured untrue stories alleging violent and offensive behaviour by Liverpool fans caught up in the disaster. The paper suggested that the dead and survivors were responsible for what had happened. Such myths continued to be perpetuated over the years and the victims blamed, adding to the traumatic injury of those affected.

In response to the *Sun*'s initial coverage, the regional newspaper the *Liverpool Echo*, in the days after the disaster, produced accurate accounts under headlines such as 'The Real Truth'. In subsequent years, the *Echo* continued to show a special understanding and appreciation of the disaster and its consequences. A successful and enduring campaign by a Hillsborough disaster support group led to the *Sun* newspaper being boycotted by the community in Liverpool.

The victims and survivors were eventually exonerated and the real causes of the disaster revealed through the work of the Hillsborough Independent Panel Report in 2012,[4] an event which itself received much media coverage. This came at a time when the culture and practices of the media both historically and in the present day were being exposed and scrutinised through broader reviews such as the Leveson Inquiry (see below).

The media coverage of the Hillsborough Panel Report brought the disaster, bereaved families and survivors back into the public eye, along with the outstanding issues around accountability, support and prevention. It brought new opportunities for the bereaved, survivors and support groups to air their views and experiences, usually reserved mainly for anniversaries when the interest of the media can be a mixed blessing. In 2014, Hillsborough has been in the news almost as much as in the immediate aftermath, with the new inquest, criminal investigations and the 25th anniversary.

Disaster Action issued a press release following publication of the Panel Report, calling for a parliamentary debate on the disaster investigation process. It stated:

> Organisations must not divert attention from corporate and individual failings in order to blame those unwittingly caught up in a disaster. *Every* disaster must be investigated with the objective of establishing the truth and bringing to justice those responsible, not in an endeavour to minimise responsibility and reputational damage. The conspiracy of silence around Hillsborough is to be abhorred, but sadly the lack of a rigorous, effective inquest and inquiry process after disasters has been all too common.
>
> Much has changed over the past 20 years due to the committed efforts of individuals and organisations such as Disaster Action. Yet the openness and transparency advocated in the House of Commons must be underpinned by an ongoing commitment to legal as well as moral accountability.
>
> Hillsborough would not have happened had known and preventable risks been acted upon. Yet 2012 has seen the abolition of numerous health and safety laws, with Prime Minister David Cameron vowing to 'kill off the health and safety culture for good.'[5]

Disaster Action Co-chair Iain Philpott, a survivor of the *Marchioness* disaster, which happened four months after Hillsborough, said:

> We have spent 20 years giving a voice to those on the receiving end of

disaster, but clearly successive governments have not really understood the message. It's time for an open parliamentary debate on the investigative process, so that concerns are heard and robust measures put in place to ensure that never again will it take 23 years for the truth to come forth. The investigative process has failed many disasters, not just Hillsborough – it's time to look in depth at why.

The relationship between those affected by the Hillsborough tragedy and the media is not unique, in so far as it illustrates the more general experience of many affected by disaster in feeling sometimes abused by and at other times able to use the media. As highlighted throughout our accounts in this book, the difference often comes down to the extent to which our engagement with journalists includes acknowledgement, compassion, honesty, accuracy, consent and control.

CONTRIBUTING TO THE WORK OF THE DART CENTRE FOR JOURNALISM AND TRAUMA

The Dart Centre for Journalism and Trauma is a global network of journalists, journalism educators and health professionals dedicated to improving media coverage of trauma, conflict and tragedy. The Centre also addresses the consequences of such coverage for those working in journalism.

In March 2005 Pam Dix contributed to Dart's work by giving a talk at a discussion session run by the Centre on a new guideline for the treatment of post traumatic stress disorder (PTSD). The National Institute for Health and Care Excellence (NICE) had just launched the guideline that day.[6] Pam was invited because of her role as a lay representative on the PTSD guideline development group and as someone who had experienced the trauma of disaster.

As well as introducing the guideline, the purpose of the meeting was to focus on the reporting of trauma, the best support for members of the public who become involved in traumatic events and how journalists may keep themselves well in relation to traumatic environments.

In her presentation Pam acknowledged that many of the journalists in the audience might have been through traumatic events themselves and would be able to understand it from a personal as well as professional point of view. She talked about the difference between the perceived and actual needs of people in situations similar to that in which she and her family found themselves after the Lockerbie tragedy. She also commented on how people picking up a newspaper after disasters may see references to 'counselling' for those affected, but that this term may mean different things to different people. The main purpose of her talk was to convey to the journalists, therapists and others in the audience what it felt and feels like to have been through traumatic events, and what people in this position may need, with reference to her own experience and the testimony of others.

In the subsequent discussion the then Dart chairman Mark Brayne (journalist and psychotherapist) posed questions to the audience about how the media portray trauma and how more intelligent reporting could be encouraged. The discussion highlighted the important role the media can play in informing the public about the effects of trauma and how to access help. Commenting on the negative experience of media attention, particularly in relation to their agendas, Pam said:

> I've been on the receiving end of some exceptionally difficult media experiences in which it was very clear to me that they didn't actually want me to tell my story but they were telling me what they wanted to hear. I have sat with many a journalist asking me questions [and] demanding I give the answer that is required, and I have learned how not to do that – but that's taken ten years.

GUIDANCE FOR THE MEDIA

In 2007, the personal views and experiences of members of Disaster Action led us to write a leaflet for those conducting interviews with survivors and bereaved people – *Interviews about Disaster Experience: Personal Reflections and Guidelines for Interviewers*. The purpose of the leaflet is to minimise the risk of interviewees feeling unprepared, exploited or abused by researchers and interviewers. It reminds readers that being interviewed can be either a positive or negative experience, or both.

The reflections of those who have been interviewees give an insight into what it is like to be in this position. The second part of the leaflet sets out guidelines for prospective interviewers – journalists, students and researchers – many of whom have approached the charity over the years in their quest for information and ideas.

We have lost count of the number of approaches from journalists looking for disaster survivors who fell in love with their rescuers, or female survivors in their 20s who could tell their invariably 'inspirational' story of overcoming adversity. Certainly there will always be examples of a fulfilling life to be led after trauma, but most of the time we find that the agenda for these stories has already been set by the editor, magazine or newspaper in question. They are interested in real-life experience only in so far as it fits into their preconceived notions.

During the course of an interview with a national tabloid on a visit by then Prime Minister Tony Blair to Libya, it was clear that the journalist was seeking inflammatory headlines. The reasoned view from a relative who wished to see appropriate diplomatic relations re-established between the UK and Libya did not make it into the article.

The often young and inexperienced researchers and journalists instructed to locate survivors and bereaved for a new radio or television documentary can find it hard to understand that people might wish to keep their experiences private rather than airing them publicly. In an era of reality TV, in which it has become fashionable to reveal all without considering the consequences, Disaster Action tries to keep a balance between protecting our members and providing opportunities for them to be involved in media projects if they choose to be.

John Mosey's 2011 programme in the BBC Radio 4 series 'A Life Less Ordinary', on his experiences of the media since the death of his daughter Helga in the Lockerbie bombing, provides a revealing insight into the way in which the lives of those affected by disaster can be affected by involvement with the media.[7] John speaks frankly not only about the way in which he sought to use the media to keep the unfinished business of Lockerbie in the public eye, but also of his sense that the story was becoming about him instead of about the disaster itself.

The *Sunday Telegraph* helped to publicise the 20th anniversary of the founding of Disaster Action by publishing an article about our work in October 2011.[8] A woman whose husband had died in an air disaster 30 years before was prompted to get in touch having read the article and has since become a member. Editor Ian MacGregor and chief reporter Robert Mendick have also given the Lockerbie families a voice, and the opportunity to continue to highlight the need for a public inquiry into all circumstances of the disaster.

The year 2011 was a busy one for Disaster Action and involvement with the media was on numerous occasions important for the charity. We made a submission to the Leveson Inquiry into the Culture, Practice and Ethics of the Press,[9] in which we wrote from the point of view of those on the receiving end of media attention. In the submission we sought to highlight the impact, both positive and negative, that media interest can have. The efforts of families and survivors to memorialise and integrate the events of the past into current experience can be rewarded through some media attention, though there can be a price to be paid in terms of individual privacy. The media can offer survivors and the bereaved a public voice to express thoughts and feelings that would otherwise be denied, as in the powerful 'Letter to ... Mum and Alice',[10] written by Edie Fassnidge for the seventh anniversary of the Tsunami and published in the *Guardian* 'Letters to…' series, a fitting end to this chapter:

I have thought about writing to you for years, but somehow it has never felt quite right. I am not exactly sure what has changed and why I have chosen this moment, almost seven years after you both died. Well, it would have been a big year for us. Alice, you would have turned 30 in May, and Mum, we'd have celebrated your 60th birthday in October.

I thought about you so much around your birthdays and felt I should do something to mark them, but was at a bit of a loss as to what to do, who to invite etc. … so I'm sorry about that. Please don't think that I've forgotten about you though. On 9 October, we had a lovely lunch with Karen, Andrew, Katharine and James, and raised a toast to you both.

As well as a big birthday year, at long last, and after a lot of hard work from a group of thoroughly committed individuals a tsunami memorial was unveiled at the Natural History Museum. It is really quite impressive, a huge piece of rock outside in a garden, and your names are right there in the middle, which I guess makes sense given that your name was Macgill. Matt and I met the Duchess of Cornwall, or Camilla Parker Bowles as you would have known her. We spoke about both of you and your many achievements.

So I imagine you would like to know a little about what has happened to me since I last saw you on Boxing Day 2004. Following some time in hospital in Thailand and the UK and a nasty head wound, Matt and I spent a few months of convalescence in Devon under the attentive, loving eye of Tessa. With the help of Uncle Pete we sold the house in Burley and bought a little cottage in north London. We are still there now and love it. It feels like a safe, calm place to be and we are surrounded by happy memories of you both – photos, paintings and musical instruments.

The best news is that after 10 happy years together, Matt and I got married in November 2009 in a little village in Devon. I know you were both with us on the day, as the sun came out at just the perfect moment as we left the church, so thank you for that.

Mum, I have followed your example and taken up triathlon, which I love, although I will never be as speedy a swimmer as you. Alice, we set up a charity in your name to support musicians … oh, and I have learned to be a little more relaxed about spending money and would even go so far as to say I'm (very) occasionally frivolous.

I once read that it takes seven years to 'recover' when someone close to you dies. I'm not sure what that means for me, having lost both of you, and I hope you don't mind me saying this but, seven years on, I can honestly say I am happy. Matt has looked after me through every step of the turbulent journey. I would not be the person I am today without him. I am also so fortunate to have the most incredible support network of friends and family and a loving family-in-law who make me feel so very loved.

Still, not a day goes by without me feeling at least a moment of sadness, and I am haunted by what happened that day. Matt and I were on a trip of a lifetime when you so kindly came out to visit us for a holiday in Thailand, and we were all together when the waves came and took both of you, but left Matt and me. I will never understand why.

You are, and will always be, part of me. You are my strength and source of optimism and resilience. You will always be in my heart and mind.

With love for ever, Your daughter, sister, boo, E x

NOTES

1 Dart Centre for Journalism and Trauma, http://dartcenter.org/.
2 Joan Deppa et al., *The Media and Disasters: Pan Am 103* (NYU Press, New York, 1994).
3 Dr Anne Eyre, *Disaster Funds: Lessons & Guidance on the Management & Distribution of Disaster Funds* (Disaster Action, London, 2010).
4 Hillsborough Independent Panel, *Hillsborough: The Report of the Hillsborough Independent Panel* (The Stationery Office, London, 2012) http://hillsborough.independent.gov.uk/.
5 Speech by David Cameron to small business audience, Maidenhead, Berkshire, 5 January 2012.
6 National Institute for Health and Care Excellence (NICE), 'Post-traumatic stress disorder: The management of PTSD in adults and children in primary and secondary care', Guideline number 26 (The Royal College of Psychiatrists and The British Psychological Society, 2005) http://www.nice.org.uk/nice-media/pdf/CG026fullguideline.pdf.
7 'A Life Less Ordinary' (BBC Radio 4, Episode One, 30 May 2011) http://www.bbc.co.uk/programmes/b011j303.
8 Nigel Farndale, 'From the Marchioness to Southall: when disaster strikes how do people survive the unimaginable?', in the *Sunday Telegraph* (22 October 2011) http://www.telegraph.co.uk/women/mother-tongue/8836170/From-the-Marchioness-to-Southall-when-disaster-strikes-how-do-people-survive-the-unimaginable.html.

9 Leveson Inquiry into the Culture, Practice and Ethics of the Press http://www.levesoninquiry.org.uk/.

10 Edie Fassnidge, 'A Letter to ... Mum and Alice, seven years after the tsunami', in the *Guardian* (24 December 2011).

CHAPTER 11

CONSOLIDATING DISASTER ACTION'S INFLUENCE AND CONTRIBUTION

Within ten years of its foundation, Disaster Action had become well established as an organisation and increasingly participated in consultations on planning for and responding to the needs of those directly affected by disaster. The involvement of our members in committees and specialist working parties continued to develop as the emergency services, emergency planning professionals and others sought to improve and develop procedures, guidance and legislative processes for disaster prevention, planning and response. As from the beginning, our purpose was to bring the voice of experience to the theory, to shed light on how every decision and action would affect those directly affected by disaster, and to highlight the gaps and inadequacies of the law.

Since the turn of the century Disaster Action has continued to offer advice rooted in our experience on a range of issues relating to the most difficult aspects of disaster – victim identification; viewing, recovery and release of bodies; police family liaison; the inquest, investigation and inquiry processes; communication channels; death certification; support networks and family and survivor support groups. As of 2014, we are still regularly consulted by the statutory and voluntary services on how people's practical and emotional needs can best be met in the aftermath of disaster. Disaster Action normally does not charge a fee for this service, in order to maintain our independence; our role has been described by retired assistant chief constable Graham Sunderland as that of 'critical friend'.

Some refer to Disaster Action as 'experts'; we are not. Although some of our members have gone on – often as a direct result of their disaster experience – to specialise in their own independent capacity in related fields such as counselling, psychotherapy and trauma management, within Disaster Action we regard ourselves simply as ordinary people who can offer the perspective of personal experience. We see our role as seeking to ensure that the needs of survivors and the bereaved are taken account of at strategic as well as operational levels.

It has become clear over the years that the influence of the organisation had spread far beyond its size, and that we are 'punching above our weight'. This is shown by the extent to which we continue to be invited to give presentations and participate in more and more national and international events and consultative processes.

DISASTER ACTION'S WEB PRESENCE

Set up in 2001, the Disaster Action website has attracted increasing numbers of visitors each year, reflecting public interest in our work and activities. There was an estimated doubling of visitors to the site over the period 1 October 2005 to 30 September 2006. In that year the number of real visitors (as opposed to automated services that trawl websites compiling an index of their contents) was estimated at around 25,000, with an average of 70 visitors per day. By comparison, in the three months after the website was first launched (in October 2001) the average number of visitors per day was five.

In the first five years of www.disasteraction.org.uk being set up, referrals to the site came predominantly from government, news and charity organisations. In those early days, the pages most frequently requested were those about the organisation rather than the advice it offered. By 2006 the advisory side of the site was becoming the main draw for visitors.

Since their relatively recent introduction, there has been a steady increase in readership of the Guidance for Responders leaflets as well as the leaflet providing guidance on setting up and running e-forum discussion groups. The 'When Disaster Strikes' series leaflets continue to be regularly requested by visitors to the website, in particular those leaflets in which individuals offer their own experiences of disasters.

Most visitors arrive via search engine services and are often either searching for Disaster Action itself, setting up an online forum or looking for survivor support information. Direct/referred visitors make up around 20 per cent of the total visitors to the site, with a significant number of referrals coming from Wikipedia. In general, the visitor numbers have remained fairly constant over the past three years, though there is a slow increase in those arriving via social media and using devices such as tablets and smart phones.

Over the years, the website has become the ideal place to hold all the resources that have become such a significant part of Disaster Action's contribution. One example of this is our guidance report *Disaster Funds*. This was a project we had wished to undertake since our foundation, as this aspect of the response to so many of our disasters had been beset by problems, maladministration and poor management. For years we struggled to attract the funding needed to carry out an independent piece of work on disaster funds, until in 2008 Frances McLeod of the Department for Culture Media and Sport (DCMS) enabled us to take the work forward with a grant from the DCMS.

This press release was issued with the launch of the report in November 2010:

DISASTER ACTION PUBLISHES NEW REPORT ON DISASTER FUNDS

Controversy surrounds many disaster funds, even decades after they were launched. Little guidance is available to those who take on the responsibility of managing and distributing funds in accordance with the wishes of the donors. *Disaster Funds* is a unique report that fills that gap. It is an essential resource for emergency planners, fund trustees, administrators and managers.

Minister for Tourism and Heritage John Penrose said: 'This report will be incredibly valuable in providing useful guidance for everyone involved in planning and responding to disasters. In these situations it's imperative that victims receive the right support promptly and I'm glad DCMS was able to fund this report, which will help all those involved in future disasters.'

Disaster Funds draws on the first-hand experience of beneficiaries, administrators, fund managers and trustees. Case studies include events such as the Cumbria floods (2009), the London bombings (2005), the South East Asian Tsunami (2004), the Ladbroke Grove rail crash (1999), the Zeebrugge ferry sinking (1987), the Bradford football stadium fire (1985) and Aberfan (1966).

Sophie Tarassenko, Co Chair of Disaster Action, said today: '*Disaster Funds* should make a substantial difference. The real beneficiaries will be those whose lives have yet to be affected by disaster.

Our thanks go to the DCMS humanitarian assistance unit for providing the funding for the report.'

Setting out lessons learned from numerous disasters, the report contains specific guidance that should help prevent negative experiences – often described as 'a second disaster' – by future beneficiaries of disaster funds. This guidance is also available as a separate leaflet for easy reference.

In the words of Margaret Lally of the British Red Cross Society: 'We have a responsibility to ensure that how we manage disaster funds is transparent and sensitive to the needs of individuals who have already had a traumatic experience. Any money distributed should help them rebuild their lives and be a light hope in a dark period. This report provides excellent learning for all of us involved in the management of disaster funds.'

Disaster Funds is referred to as a useful source within the 2012 Charity Commission's 'Disaster Appeals: guidance on starting, running and supporting charitable disaster appeals', a clear indication of the difference we have been able to make in this controversial area.

In 2013 we decided that the site was in need of modernisation and our web host Steve Bradley set about creating a new design, giving us the opportunity to create new pages and revise and add to the leaflets series. The new site was launched at the end of March 2014.

INTERNATIONAL ACTIVITIES: ACROSS EUROPE

Although the charity has remained small, its developing reach and influence is highlighted through our work within Europe and increasingly all over the world. Disaster Action's membership has always been open to those of any nationality affected by a disaster wherever it happens, provided that they normally live in the UK. While much of our work on consultations and training has focused within the UK, this focus has widened to include conferences and events in Europe.

In 2009, Disaster Action was invited to contribute to the Informed Prepared Together project, initiated by Moya Wood-Heath, who was spending much of her time working in the Red Cross European Union office. The project was co-financed by the European Commission and the Red Cross European Union Office. It was founded on the recognition that individual citizens and organisations have the capacity to work together to develop and improve resilience. In order to bring this recognition to life, the Informed Prepared Together project aims to encourage European Union Member States and European Economic Area Countries to acknowledge the added value of using every resource – from individual citizen and volunteer to voluntary and statutory organisations – to enhance community and national resilience in civil protection.

Disaster Action played a key role in the initial development of the project, including setting out the principles for the human aspects of disasters, which lie at the heart of the initiative and feature on the Informed Prepared Together website (see text box). The website continues to grow as a repository of toolkits and other resources, with resources available in French, German, Spanish, Polish and Turkish as well as English.[1]

INFORMED PREPARED TOGETHER: HUMAN ASPECTS IN CIVIL PROTECTION

The four key principles of the human aspects approach are being **Informed**, being **Prepared** and working **Together** to build **Resilience**.

Informed

Enabling citizens to access relevant information about potential risks and hazards and the consequences of emergencies and disasters, and to know how they can equip themselves to be prepared and to cope better during emergency situations

Educating and training responders to understand that meeting needs includes communicating with citizens and each other in a timely, appropriate, honest, open and transparent way

Enabling citizens to feel informed about decisions, to make informed choices, and to participate in recovery activities to mitigate the effects of emergencies and disasters.

Prepared

Engaging citizens as active participants in planning, preparedness, response and recovery activities

Assisting citizens, communities and organisations in the development of personal, family and organisational emergency plans, capacities, capabilities and skills

Giving volunteers and responders appropriate skills, knowledge and training in order for them to feel prepared to meet citizens' needs in emergencies and disasters.

Together

Integrating the needs of citizens within and across all phases of emergency planning, preparedness, response and recovery strategies

Including citizens, volunteers and communities as active partners in emergency planning, preparedness, response and recovery activities

Assisting organisations to work together co-operatively and in a coordinated way to meet medical, practical, emotional, social and cultural needs during and after emergencies and disasters.

FURTHER WORK THROUGH EUROPEAN AND INTERNATIONAL RED CROSS SOCIETIES

The end of 2012 brought an opportunity for Pam Dix to participate in an international workshop at the Brocher Foundation in Geneva, 'Naming the dead: social, ethical and legal issues of disaster victim identification by DNA', organised and run by Professor Jackie Leach Scully and colleagues from Newcastle University. This was a rare opportunity to focus on the issues that lie behind scientific approaches to identification.

As a result of contacts made at the seminar Pam was invited to speak at two international mass fatalities seminars for the International Committee of the Red Cross (ICRC) in Geneva. Meeting delegates from countries as diverse as Greece, Somalia, Pakistan, Libya, Brazil and Honduras who were learning to plan for and respond to emergencies in often highly challenging and under-resourced environments was enlightening. The differences in scale between the disasters faced by most of our members and those in ongoing conflict zones and areas prone to natural disaster might seem insurmountable; in fact the seminars served to emphasise the universality of the needs of individual survivors and the bereaved in mass fatality and casualty situations.

One area of common concern, the location and identification of the dead after conflict and disaster, was highlighted by a conference organised by the International Commission on Missing Persons (ICMP) at The Hague in 2013. The conference drew together scientists, anthropologists, government ministers and officials as well as the bereaved from all around the world. Pam Dix's input to the conference on behalf of Disaster Action clearly had an impact, as shown by a letter from Ambassador (retired) Thomas Miller, chair of ICMP:

On behalf of the International Commission on Missing Persons (ICMP), I would like to thank you for participating in our conference, *Missing*

Persons: An Agenda for the Future. Your presentation was excellent and contributed to the overall success of the event.

The conference received a large amount of media coverage and as such, we believe it contributed significantly to raising the global profile of the issue and the need for a coordinated international response.

This conference is just the beginning of a much broader discussion on the topic of missing persons and we look forward to continuing this inspiring and thought provoking dialogue with you on specific thematic topics through meetings that we will organize in the future.'[2]

The contacts developed by Disaster Action were further extended by participation in an ICRC/University of Milan conference in that city, also in 2013, with particular reference to issues around locating and identifying migrants who have died in their efforts to reach Europe from Africa and elsewhere. While the circumstances may again seem very different from those faced by the families of the dead from disasters we are familiar with, the principle of extending the same rights to migrants and their families is entirely relevant.

GLOBAL NETWORKS AND PROFILE

International awareness of our work has also been influenced by research and publications conducted by individual members in their independent and professional capacities. In 1998, for example, Anne Eyre, already a sociologist and by then a lecturer in disaster management, undertook a series of qualitative interviews with Disaster Action members. Her research article, entitled 'More Than PTSD: Proactive Responses among Disaster Survivors', was published in the *Australasian Journal of Disaster and Trauma Studies* in 1998.[3]

Anne has also given presentations on this study and related work at conferences focusing on trauma and disaster management in the United States, Canada and New Zealand. As well as highlighting the unique nature of our organisation – as it seems there are no other umbrella disaster-related groups in the world with a membership functioning in quite the same way as we do – this work has raised awareness of Disaster Action overseas and as a result we continue to have dialogue with policy makers, planners and responders abroad.

In June 2010, when 12 people were killed and a further 11 injured in a mass shooting in Cumbria, the news and impact of yet another community tragedy resonated with members of Disaster Action. Once the community Recovery Group was formed they contacted us for help and advice. It so happened that at that time we were in contact with colleagues in the

Australian Red Cross who were able to put us in touch with those from various agencies who had coordinated personal and community support services following the tragic shootings in Port Arthur, Tasmania in 1996. We were therefore able to consolidate and collate information and advice for Cumbria responders, combining our own collective experience with lessons and guidance from professionals across the world.

It is often said that communities come together after disaster; in this instance we were able to reflect on the positive impact of new technologies such as the internet and email in helping put people in touch with each other both for local and for global outreach and support, despite the geographical distances involved.

Our leaflets and resources are relevant, accessible and used by emergency planners, responders and those directly affected by disasters well beyond the UK. Sometimes we are contacted by individuals and organisations from other parts of the world seeking information and advice from our experience for their own research projects or information services. Examples include the Aviation Disaster Family Assistance Project in the US, which gives details of Disaster Action within the resources section of its website,[4] and a review of Disaster Action's leaflets which featured in the third edition of the Australian Red Cross's Disaster Digest (May 2012).

The Disaster Digest is a regular summary of articles, reports and other materials that are published that could assist the Red Cross locally in emergency situations. The reviewer, Kate Brady, National Recovery Coordinator for Australian Red Cross Emergency Services, affirmed the value of the leaflets as succinct and helpful reading for:

• 'People who want to know more about first hand reactions after emergencies but feel awkward asking
• Hand outs for training
• Additional information for volunteers
• To get people to start thinking about some of the emotional reactions to emergencies.'

During 2013–14 we worked with Japanese TV station NHK in their documentary exploration of corporate responsibility and how the bereaved from the 2005 Amagasaki rail crash in which over 100 people were killed can learn from the experience of Disaster Action.

The front cover of the pamphlet produced for Disaster Action's launch in October 1991.

The memorial garden for Aberfan, created in 1991 for the 25th anniversary, sits at the end of the arched headstones, which represent the children holding hands.

For ten years Herald Families Association meetings were held at St Mark's Church, St John's Wood in London. The plaque in the church was unveiled during the HFA's final service there in September 1997.

In loving memory
of the 193 people who died
in the Herald ferry disaster
off Zeebrugge Belgium
on 6th March
1987
Herald Families Association

The memorial plaque at King's Cross underground station on the left was organised by the King's Cross families soon after the disaster; the plaques on the right were added some years later, after the King's Cross Disaster Fund closed.

IN MEMORY OF
THE THIRTY ONE PEOPLE
WHO LOST THEIR LIVES
IN THE KING'S CROSS
UNDERGROUND FIRE OF
18TH NOVEMBER 1987

KINGS CROSS DISASTER FUND
IN MEMORY OF THE 31 PEOPLE
WHO DIED
IN THE TERRIBLE FIRE
AT KINGS CROSS
UNDERGROUND STATION
ON THE NIGHT OF
18th NOVEMBER 1987

BETTY AFUA AGYAPONG	MICHAEL HOLDEN
TERRENCE ALONZO BEST	RALPH HUMBERSTONE
MARK DAVID BRYANT	BERNADETT KEARNEY
ANDY BURDETT B.A.(HONS)	M.A.BOBBY KEEGAN
ELIZABETH N.BYERS	MOHAMMED SHOIAB KHAN
TREENA CHAPPELL	MARCO LIBERATI
DEAN T.COTTLE	PHILIP G.MARKS
SUSHEILA N.COTTLE	LAURENCE V.MORAN
FELIX DEARDEN	LAWRENCE S.NEWCOMBE S.R.N.
NEVILLE H.EVE	STEPHEN A.PARSONS
JANE A.FAIREY B.A.(HONS)	CHRISTOPHER WALLACE ROOME
NATALIE A.FALCO	RAI SINGH
JONATHAN R.GEORGE	JOHN F.JOSEPH ST.PRIX
KUTTALAM GOVINDARAJAN	IVAN TARASSENKO
GRAHAM D.HALL	STATION OFFICER
	COLIN J.TOWNSLEY G.M.

AN UNIDENTIFIED MAN
LATER IDENTIFIED AS ALEXANDER WILLIAMSON FALLON

One of the memorials to those killed in the bombing of Pan Am 103, Dryfesdale Cemetery, Lockerbie. The picture was taken on the 25th anniversary of the disaster.

The Hillsborough memorial at Anfield Stadium, Liverpool Football Club, photographed on 12 September 2012, the day the Hillsborough Independent Panel Report was released.

The plaque dedicated to the memory of all those who died in the sinking of the *Marchioness* on the river Thames on 20 August 1989, Southwark Cathedral, London.

A memorial garden, with one plaque to commemorate those who died and one to give thanks for the efforts of the emergency services and others, was opened on the sixth anniversary of the Southall rail crash, next to Southall railway station, London.

In loving memory
of all those killed in the
Southall rail crash
on September 19th 1997

May they rest in peace

Mr Peter Dobson Allen
Mr Clive Brain
Mr David Waring Eustace
Mr Peter Patrick Kavanagh
Mr Marcus Olander
Mr Anthony Richard Petch
Mr Gerard Martin Traynor

On Friday
September 19th, 1997
at approximately 1:15pm
a high speed Swansea to Paddington
train collided with a freight train at Southall
7 people were killed and 139 injured

This stone gives thanks to all the
emergency services, British Transport Police
and members of the Southall community
who courageously give comfort, support
and sympathy to the injured
and dignity to the dead.

May God Bless you all

Some of the 140 people who worked on the construction of the UT 772 memorial in Niger, including Tuaregs, Tubus and Haoussas from Niger, and Guillaume Denoix de Saint Marc, whose father was killed in the crash.

An aerial shot of the finished UT 772 memorial, which is visible on Google maps.

A memorial garden in Grosvenor Square, London, to all those who lost their lives in the attacks in the United States on September 11, 2001, which was officially opened in 2003, on the second anniversary of the tragedy.

The memorial to those killed in the Bali bombings, King Charles Street, London, unveiled by their Royal Highnesses Prince Charles, The Prince of Wales and Camilla, The Duchess of Cornwall on 12 October 2007. Many family members attended, as did ambassadors from every country whose citizens died in the attacks.

The memorial to those who died in the 2004 Indian Ocean Tsunami, at the Natural History Museum, London. Constructed from silver-white granite from the Tarn quarries, Toulouse, France, it was unveiled by their Royal Highnesses Prince Charles, The Prince of Wales and Camilla, The Duchess of Cornwall on 6 July 2011.

'Expressing the inexpressible'. Located in Hyde Park, the memorial to those killed in the 2005 London bombings is comprised of 52 solid cast stainless steel pillars (stelae), each representing one of the lives lost, grouped in four interlinked clusters reflecting the four locations of the bombings.

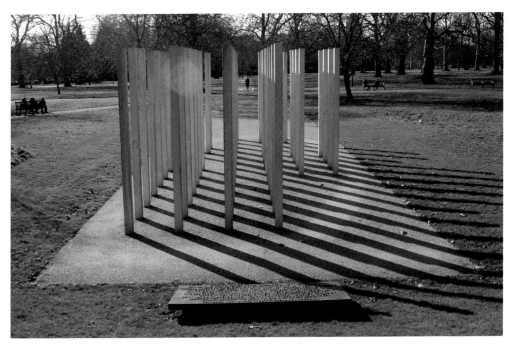

Commemorating the worst civilian disaster of World War 2, the Stairway to Heaven memorial, Bethnal Green, London. As well as the list of victims' names and ages, individual plaques are sited along the plinth, with testimonies from survivors, victims' relatives, rescuers and emergency services personnel.

The late investigative journalist and campaigner Paul Foot, in his office at *Private Eye*, London.

Founder of Disaster Action, Maurice de Rohan AO OBE and his wife Margaret, at the January 2006 Australia Day dinner, Australia House, London.

Anne Eyre, Vice Chair of Disaster Action, receiving the Winston Churchill travelling Fellowship Award in 2008, with the late Lady Mary Soames, Winston Churchill's daughter.

Disaster Action trustees, Iain Philpott, Moya Wood-Heath and Sophie Tarassenko, at the reception to mark the 20ᵗʰ anniversary of the founding of Disaster Action, Australian High Commission, October 2011.

Judy Cooper, Secretary/director of Disaster Action since 1991.

Disaster Action Executive Director Pam Dix with her husband John Francis.

Disaster Action members Rosemary Mayes and Julie Nicholson.

Disaster Action members Henry Luce and Marilyn Robinson.

Charles Norrie with Iain Philpott and Margaret Lockwood-Croft – all founder members of Disaster Action.

Home Office mass fatalities adviser Lucy Easthope with Disaster Action members Maureen Kavanagh and Mary Campion.

Disaster Action members Sandra and Bob Empson, with Phil Storr (centre) of the Department of Health.

Jeff Goodright, College of Policing, with Disaster Action members Penny Hamilton and Pam Dix.

Disaster Action members Edie Fassnidge and Nigel Pike.

Tessa Jowell MP, at the anniversary reception.

Alan Goodwin, Deputy Chief Constable, Derbyshire Constabulary, speaking at the anniversary reception.

William and Linda Beckett, founder members of Disaster Action.

Disaster Action members at the anniversary reception.

RECOGNITION FOR DISASTER ACTION: AWARDS AND COMMENDATIONS

SOCIETY GUARDIAN CHARITY AWARD, 2004

In 2004, Disaster Action won the Society Guardian Charity Award for excellence in our field. Of 756 charities that applied for the award Disaster Action was one of only five winners. The award had at that time been running for 15 years, giving small charities providing a unique service the opportunity to obtain some funding and recognition.

In our application we explained what winning would mean to us:

Our work is demanding and carried out at some personal cost. However, it is highly rewarding to perform what we believe to be an important public service that cannot be replicated by others. It gives us great personal satisfaction to know that we are in a position to make a positive difference to the social welfare of those affected by trauma.

We value our independence as an advocacy organisation. Winning would give DA public recognition for our unique work. It would enable us to extend what can be done by a small number of committed individuals whose time and resources are necessarily limited. It would ensure that DA reaches the wider police, emergency planning and corporate community at a time when responding to major incidents is unfortunately a key feature of twenty-first century life. Above all, we would reach the survivors and the bereaved of the future, at the most traumatic and vulnerable time of their lives.

In granting the award, the *Guardian*'s public services editor David Brindle commented that our application was 'topical, focused, clear and innovative'. The Award consisted of £5000 and a computer. Disaster Action used the funding to produce further leaflets in our 'When Disaster Strikes' and 'Guidance for Responders' series. These were on setting up family and survivor support groups, best practice for professionals in dealing with people after disaster and on dealing with longer-term issues.

NATIONWIDE AWARD 2005

A year later Pam Dix was recognised in the Nationwide Awards for Voluntary Endeavour in the adult group category. Peter Spooner of the Herald Families Association also received a Nationwide Award nomination for his work.

LETTERS OF COMMENDATION

Over the years Disaster Action's influence, and appreciation for its role, has been reflected in private letters of thanks and official letters of commendation. By way of example, in 2005, letters were received from the Consular Directorate of the Foreign & Commonwealth Office, the Home Office, the Metropolitan Police Service, the Association of Chief Police Officers (ACPO) and the British Red Cross.

The following letter from Deputy Chief Constable of Derbyshire Constabulary Alan Goodwin highlighted the sort of recognition and appreciation offered by such senior professionals in relation to Disaster Action's contribution:

At a time when the police service is dealing with the ongoing threat of terrorism and the tragic impact of the 7 July attacks in London, I felt it would be appropriate to write to express my appreciation for everything that Disaster Action has done, and continues to do, in support of policing across the country.

As Chair of ACPO's Emergency Procedures Committee, I have been extremely grateful for the contribution made by Disaster Action, not only in terms of the practical response to specific incidents and tragedies, but also the tremendous contribution made to the formulation of policy and procedures aimed at providing the best possible service to the bereaved and the survivors of such events.

The ACPO/Home Office/Cabinet Office document *Humanitarian Assistance in Emergencies* (scheduled for publication in the very near future) provides the responding community with excellent and detailed guidance on how best to provide that service and I am indebted to Disaster Action for their massive contribution made in producing such a significant document. The quality of deployment of family liaison officers in major disasters, the concept of Family Assistance Centres such as the one now established in Vincent Square in London, and the wealth of good practice now available to the responding agencies are all due in no small part to the invaluable input from Disaster Action colleagues.

I also wish to record my appreciation here for the time you and your colleagues invest in supporting the numerous conferences, seminars and other events organised by the ACPO EP Committee to raise awareness amongst police colleagues of disaster response issues. Although the police professionals can provide detailed training and

guidance on technical processes and procedures, it is vitally important that we retain the focus of ensuring that all these techniques are
aimed at achieving the ultimate goal of providing a service of the
highest quality possible to the bereaved and survivors of major incidents and disasters. The powerful and impactive inputs provided by
Disaster Action colleagues at our training events ensure that this focus
is very much at the centre of all that we do and all the policies and
procedures that we construct … I am indebted to Disaster Action for
all that you do.

A number of committed individuals from key organisations worked over a
period of years to draw Disaster Action into their work. Retired police chief
inspector Mick Free was one of the first to involve us in training for police
body recovery officers, listening to and encouraging our participation in
training from the mid-1990s and then more broadly in his role as Emergency
Procedures Coordinator for ACPO.

Disaster Action's impact on Mick Free's working life is clear:

I first came across Disaster Action in 1998 when I was responsible for
running a training course at the Metropolitan Police College, Hendon.
The purpose of this course was to teach police officers to recover the
dead from the scene of a disaster. My colleague at the time, Gary
Locker, invited Pamela Dix from DA to address our students. To his
great credit, Gary had the foresight to recognise that if officers were
going to perform this difficult and unenviable role, they should be
exposed to the experience of someone who had lost a loved one
in a disaster. He felt that it was crucial for officers to have a better
understanding of the needs and expectations of people like Pamela, if
they were going to perform this role with a real sense of purpose and
regard for the dignity of the deceased and their family and friends.

I can vividly remember the first time Pamela addressed our students
and the impact that her presentation had – not only on them, but also
the directing staff. It was a huge learning experience for me and one
from which there was no turning back. The most important aspect
from my perspective is that ultimately it is Pamela and people like her
that we are working for: if we fail to listen to what they expect and
need, how can we even begin to provide a meaningful response?

My work with Disaster Action continued after my retirement as
a serving police officer in 2009. Throughout the last fifteen years I

have found DA invaluable in informing my decisions in just about all aspects of my work: from training to operational response to drafting policy and guidance. On reflection, I strongly believe that the lessons from working with DA in the field of disaster management can be applied to other aspects of policing and public service. For me this is about a real commitment to engage, listen, respond and develop an enduring working relationship based on trust and confidence by both parties.

As referred to earlier in the book, Moya Wood-Heath, first of the Metropolitan Police Service, and then for many years emergency planning consultant to the British Red Cross, gave Disaster Action the opportunity to engage with and influence the work of the Red Cross, itself going through a period of immense change as it sought to professionalise its approach and contribution to emergency planning and response. Disaster Action has continued its productive relationship with the Red Cross, the police and many other agencies into 2014.

NOTES

1 Informed Prepared Together http://www.informedprepared.eu/.
2 Letter to Pam Dix, 14 November 2013.
3 Anne Eyre, 'More than PTSD: Proactive Responses among Disaster Survivors', in *The Australasian Journal of Disaster and Trauma Studies*, (Volume 1998-2) http://www.massey.ac.nz/~trauma/issues/1998-2/eyre.htm.
4 The Aviation Disaster Family Assistance Project http://www.connectingjourneys.org/resources.html.

CHAPTER 12

LOOKING BACK AND LOOKING FORWARD – SIGNIFICANT ANNIVERSARIES

In Chapter 6 we made reference to the interest of researchers in the medium and longer-term psychological impact of disasters on those directly affected. As the tenth and 20ᵗʰ anniversaries came and went, the question of how those involved had fared over time and memories of their experiences also became of interest to occasional journalists looking for an anniversary angle on a story. But there was value too in individuals writing and owning their own accounts, as the production of *Jupiter's Children* illustrates.

JUPITER'S CHILDREN: SURVIVORS' ACCOUNTS PUBLISHED

Ten years after her own involvement in the disaster, Disaster Action member Mary Campion, schoolteacher and survivor, compiled a collection of memories produced by herself and other survivors. The book, published by Liverpool University Press in 1998, tells the story of what happened to 16 girls, one boy and two adults when their educational cruise ship *Jupiter* sank within 40 minutes following a collision off the port of Piraeus, Greece on 21 October 1988.

Mary had helped to lead many previous school trips. After such journeys booklets had been produced containing itineraries, menus, comments and happy memories; these booklets were personal souvenirs. There would be no booklets on this occasion, but while dealing with the essential paper-work a few days after their return the head teacher said: 'Why not? Why not write about what happened?' Everyone in the group was encouraged to write their account. Very few children have written of surviving shipwreck, and counsellors reinforced the idea that writing would help the healing process. As compiler of the collection, Mary described how a series of first-person accounts, which were factual and very detailed, emerged.

It was as though the scenes we had witnessed were glued inside our brains. That instant recall, that non-stop video playing in our heads, was a symptom of post-traumatic stress disorder, a term we did not know at that time. I promised to produce a book, when one girl asked: 'It will be a *proper* book won't it? Not an A4 booklet?'

The accounts are a major part of the book – about the disaster and what followed on our return home. I craved information. How had the disaster occurred? Who helped us survive? I needed to make logical sense of an abnormal experience. This led to contacting so many useful people who are acknowledged in our book. Many must have doubted my sanity as they deciphered handwritten letters, with ten queries demanding a reply as soon as possible! But they did answer and extra chapters developed. For example, after hassling the Minister for Transport for a translated copy of the Greek Inquiry, I tackled the International Maritime Organisation (IMO) about the non-publication of the material.

I asked my ex-naval husband to read only one chapter. 'Gibberish!' he said. A blazing row developed and a night of utter fury as I re-wrote the whole chapter. In the spring of 1998 the Deputy Director of the IMO read the same chapter and diplomatically suggested 'a few alterations, perhaps?', and wrote them in. This on the very day he had to deal with a major environmental coastal disaster in his Spanish homeland.

All the areas investigated were unknown territory to me. Sorting through hundreds of pictures of shipwrecks in picture agencies, I felt faint on recognising three of our little girls.

Handwritten lists arrived from the Greek harbourmaster, detailing those who had risked their lives in tiny boats to save us from a sinking ship in a dark oily sea. In 2018, under the 30-year ban on the publication of Government documents, we may be able to read telegrams sent to Greece by our Government.

The local library was ransacked for information on survival at sea –
most of it was horribly detailed...

Some children have never really discussed with their families what
happened on the *Jupiter*. I hope the book will help those and other
families to understand more. The personal accounts are primary
sources about a disaster so that GPs, solicitors, counsellors and emergency planners who read this will hear the voices of real people. Forty
per cent of the profits are going to charity.

The promise of a book has been fulfilled. It is a proper book, a
record of an experience and it has been a privilege to compile it.[1]

Mary Campion's words concerning the promise of a book are echoed in
the pages of *Collective Conviction*. Our own writing and contributions to
others' publications testify to experiences that were to change the lives of so
many individuals, but also offer opportunities to transform those seeking to
understand and humanise the world of emergency planning and response.

As the 20th anniversaries of the disasters of the 1980s approached, interest
in each of them was again generated by the mass media. Investigations and
reports delved into and discussed the longer-term impacts and personal
welfare of those directly involved. Some also examined outcomes and developments relating to accident prevention, and health and safety cultures
within those organisations that had failed people so badly in the 1980s.

For members of Disaster Action, the approach of the anniversaries of
the disasters that had led to the creation of the charity was experienced as
a personal and organisational reminder of how much had changed, what
achievements had been brought about and what work still needed to be done
in relation to the founding aims and objectives.

FINALLY GETTING TO THE TRUTH OF THE SINKING
OF THE MV *DERBYSHIRE*

The following account draws on the reflections of Vivienne King of the
Derbyshire Families Association, a founder member of Disaster Action
following the death of her son Paul on the ship. Over the years, she kept
Disaster Action updated on developments in the search for the truth about
the fate of the MV *Derbyshire*, which sank in 1980. As in so many other
instances documented in these pages, without the commitment of Vivienne
King and others, the truth about what happened to the ship would not have
been established.

When on 11 June 1987 the Secretary of State for Transport directed that a formal investigation should be held into the shipping casualty of the motor vessel *Derbyshire* in September 1980, it seemed that almost seven years hard and often frustrating work by those intent on finding the cause of the tragedy was at an end. Yet despite the evidence of structural weakness gathered from her five sister ships, the court concluded that *Derbyshire* was probably overwhelmed by the forces of nature. The evidence available did not support any firmer conclusion.

In 1993, with the development of technology came the opportunity to gain further evidence by searching for the wreck. To finance such a venture was a daunting task far beyond the means of the families and the UK seafaring unions the National Union of Marine Aviation Shipping Transport (NUMAST) and the National Union of Seamen (NUS), which had already incurred heavy costs whilst representing the families at the formal inquiry. Following representations form the National Union of Rail, Maritime and Transport Workers (RMT) and in furtherance of their concern for the safety of seafarers of all nationalities, the International Transport Worker's Federation generously agreed to fund the expedition.

Oceaneering Technologies of the United States, specialists in deep sea water search and recovery using their remotely operated vessels, were awarded the contract. In May 1995 the Japanese-registered offshore support vessel *Shin Kai Maru* set out for the site earmarked in 1980 by upwelling oil and updated later by computer calculations.

During the search of the sea bed a huge debris field was located by the side scan sonar and later filming of this field showed the bow of the *Derbyshire* with the last five letters of her name clearly visible. With funding depleted, after placing a bronze memorial plaque on the forecastle of the ship, the *Shin Kai Maru* returned to port.

A report of the mission together with the film of the underwater evidence was sent to the Marine Accident Investigation Board (MAIB), with the recommendation that the UK government undertake a further expedition to gather more information from the wreckage field and to hold a new inquiry into the loss of the *Derbyshire.*

The story of the *Derbyshire* investigation was to take further dramatic turns in the search for the truth, which was finally established through the government reopening of the formal investigation in 2000, at the insistence of then Deputy Prime Minister John Prescott. The blame that had been laid at the door of the crew now fell on the design of the ship, which was unable to withstand the violent typhoon to which the vessel had been exposed. Contradicting the findings of an earlier inquiry, Mr Justice Coleman found that there had been no negligence on the part of captain or crew.

In 2004 the Derbyshire Families Association was awarded the Marine Society's Thomas Gray Silver Medal for campaigning for better safety regulations for bulk carriers.

September 2012 saw an exhibition at Merseyside Maritime Museum called 'MV *Derbyshire* – Search for the Truth', opened to the public. The display tells the story of the discovery of the wreck, the various inquiries that took place into the ship's disappearance and the families' efforts over so many years.

MANCHESTER AIR DISASTER:
'IT TAKES A LONG TIME TO RECOVER'

On 22 August 2010, a memorial service took place at Manchester Airport to mark the 25th anniversary of the disaster. The airport's chaplain, Kevin Ball, commented on how relatives and survivors still need to grieve and remember to enable them to live with the impact of the event:

> We've found that people want to be in the area where things have happened. People feel very close to their loved ones at the incident scene and so it's appropriate that we do welcome them … The whole day was very moving and tears were shed. It's something we will never forget and the services were very dignified and respectful in keeping with what the survivors and families wanted.[2]

At the time of earlier key anniversaries SCISAFE member Lindsay Davies had reflected on the continuing need for the campaign's messages. In 1995 she commented in a Disaster Action newsletter on the fact that outstanding safety procedures, recommended ten years earlier, had still not been implemented. The group remained dissatisfied that not enough had been achieved to improve air safety with regard to getting out of a plane and toxic fumes.

By 2005 some further changes had been made to improve passenger safety, an ongoing and lengthy process which the campaign group had continued to call for, but not without personal cost. In an interview at the time of the 20th anniversary, bereaved father William Beckett had said: 'In achieving what we did in the end we know that new aircraft will be safer to fly in the future. The big difference that occurred from our campaign was that all these organisations are far more accountable than they were.'

He added: 'In some ways the campaigning detracted from the recovery process. It takes a long time to recover, but there was comfort in others who were going through the same experience and that is very important.'

COMMEMORATING THE ZEEBRUGGE DISASTER, 6 MARCH 2007: 'EVERY YEAR IT IS A DIFFICULT TIME'

On 4 March 2007, survivors and bereaved families from the Zeebrugge disaster gathered at church services in Dover, Kent and in Zeebrugge, Belgium to remember those who died when the *Herald of Free Enterprise* capsized shortly after leaving Zeebrugge for the Kent port.

During the memorial service at St Mary's Church in Dover the vicar referred to the 'selfless work of the crew' and their suffering in the aftermath of the disaster, as survivors and employees of the company Townsend Thoresen, which was blamed for causing the disaster. The church has a commemorative stained glass window honouring those lost in the disaster and also an illuminated scroll showing the names of the 193 people who died.

On the anniversary itself a further service was held at the Dover centre of the British and International Sailors' Society, at which the names of all those who died were read out. A bereaved man, whose father had been the ship's senior chief engineer, spoke of the deep community impact in his village, which lost three of its members. He commented that every year is a difficult time and expressed disbelief regarding the 20th anniversary. The images of the *Herald* on its side still made his heart stop and he said there had not been a day he had not thought about his father over the last 20 years.

A source of sadness for all those affected by the loss of the *Herald* as well as Disaster Action members was that Maurice de Rohan had died five months before this anniversary.

KING'S CROSS REMEMBERED: 18 NOVEMBER 2007

In 2004, the identity of the last named victim of the underground fire was finally confirmed. Body 115 – named after its mortuary tag number – was confirmed as Alexander Fallon after extensive police investigations and forensic analysis. His family, who had suspected that he was the 31st victim for a number of years, received the final confirmation after he was identified.

The former mayor of Camden, Barbara Hughes, commented on the relief for all now that this unknown victim had finally been identified. She added that his name would be inscribed on the grave and on a memorial to the 31 victims – replacing an inscription that up until then read simply 'unknown man'. The Interpol Resolution passed at the General Assembly meeting of 1996 setting out that '... for legal, religious, cultural and other reasons, human beings have the right not to lose their identities after death...' was thus finally fulfilled in this instance.

In 2007, speaking about the impending anniversary, Sophie Tarassenko, who had headed the King's Cross Family Action Group after the disaster, commented that 20 years on, the grieving process was now less about the fire and more about her brother:

> For the first three months I cried every day. The next three months I cried every other day. The next couple of years I cried once a month and after 20 years I cry two or three times a year. But it doesn't mean I don't think about him because I do – it just becomes less excruciatingly painful.

A local Roman Catholic priest, who helped respond to the disaster and its impact, commented on the sense from the families that a dedicated Mass would be appropriate to mark the 20th anniversary rather than anything more elaborate: 'We wrote to all the families to ask if they wanted to do something for the anniversary, but the overwhelming feeling is that they want to leave it where it is because in a sense everything has been done.'[3]

THE ANNIVERSARY OF PIPER ALPHA: 'SEEMS LIKE ONLY YESTERDAY'

Speaking on the 20th anniversary of the Piper Alpha oil platform disaster, bereaved family members talked of memories of the day being just as traumatic as it if was yesterday. One floral tribute left at the memorial garden said: 'Thinking of you on this sad day and every day as long as I live.' Ann Gillanders, whose husband Ian was one of the 30 men whose bodies have never been found, had this to say:

> Ian's remains were never found, which has made it hard to let go and say goodbye properly, but this year we have decided to put up a headstone. Ian was a very loving family man and I can still hear the sound of his laughter. Some days the tragedy seems like it happened centuries ago but on others it seems like only yesterday. I think the trauma of the whole thing just does not go away.

Leading the 20th anniversary memorial service, the Reverend Andrew Jolly, chaplain to the UK oil and gas industry (who died of cancer in 2010), said:

> There must always be names with faces, stories of sacrifice and of love, devotion and faith, so that what has gone on before does not become just

another statistic. If we as a community, or as an oil and gas industry, or as a city, or as a country allow that to happen, we should hang our heads in shame.[4]

In 2007, the Health and Safety Executive released a report on nearly 100 offshore installations and their equipment. Based on a three-year inspection, it stated that some key issues identified at the time of Piper Alpha had yet to be properly addressed, adding that in more than 50 per cent of platforms, the overall condition of the plant was poor. Critics wondered whether all the lessons from the deaths of 167 men on Piper Alpha had really been learned.

Commenting on the responses made to the report in May 2008, Chris Allen, the health, safety, social and environment director of Oil and Gas UK, the industry body, said:

> While Piper Alpha touched the lives of every person in the industry at the time, there is now a new generation starting their offshore careers who will not know about the lessons learned, and Oil and Gas UK, the industry body, is keen to ensure the corporate memory is not lost.... It is important that we remember what happened on July 6, 1988 and that we do not forget the lessons learned from this tragedy, making sure that the next generation of offshore workers does not have to learn the hard way.[5]

For the 25th anniversary of Piper Alpha, in addition to the memorial service and other events an online teaching resource was created about the disaster, so that new generations will understand its continuing significance. Unveiling the Piper Alpha learning community, where teachers can share ideas and discuss approaches to using the disaster in lessons, First Minister Alex Salmond said Scotland had an 'obligation' to ensure there was never a repeat of the devastating fire which took the lives of 167 people.

THE CLAPHAM RAIL CRASH:
FROM ISOLATION TO 'MY FAMILY GROUP'

Disaster Action Executive Committee member Marilyn Robinson reflects on her experience of surviving the Clapham rail crash and the impact it has had on her life.

As a survivor, the memories of the Clapham train crash of 12 December 1988 live on both physically and mentally, although these days more in the background, with occasional sharp reminders through personal physical pain and returning memories when other disasters occur.

No survivor group offered support then as most of the victims and survivors were scattered along the South West Trains line from Bournemouth to Waterloo, travelling alone, either intermittently or daily.

The memorial erected later at the site, just outside Clapham station, had been a regular yearly anniversary meeting point, with a tenth year 'specific' memorial service in 1998, this being the only time each year it was possible to meet others (albeit mostly bereaved and responders).

For the 20th anniversary the majority contacted by Bournemouth City Council felt the tenth had been a watershed for collective rather than personal memories.

Unlike other family groups, Disaster Action became for me the focal meeting point, although initially it was isolating being a survivor in the midst of mostly bereaved. The work we have collectively progressed has enabled the ever-present question of why I lived whilst others sadly did not, to form a positive outcome.

The very fact of making sure others did not suffer more than was necessary through using our personal insights and experience positively, benefiting future disaster survivors and bereaved, has meant that there need never be nowhere to turn for empathetic comfort, non-judgemental support and advice for both those involved or affected and responders alike.

On the odd day when physical pain or sadness encroach how good to be able to say there was a positive outcome from those initial desperate isolating days, thanks to my family group, Disaster Action.

The year 2009 brought further anniversaries – Kegworth, Hillsborough and the *Marchioness* – the last of the 20th anniversaries of the 1980s disasters that were the catalyst for Disaster Action's foundation.

TOWARDS OPENNESS AND HONESTY:
AFTER THE *MARCHIONESS* DISASTER

The inquest into the sinking of the *Marchioness* in 1989 was originally opened within a few days of the disaster and then adjourned. It was resumed in April 1990 and adjourned again. Nearly two years later, the coroner admitted that the hands of 25 of the deceased had been removed but no explanation was given as to why. The coroner refused to resume the inquest at this stage.

Eventually, after continued campaigning by the relatives and survivors, a new inquest was granted in April 1995 – six years after the sinking. The jury brought in a verdict of unlawful killing, but 15 months later the Crown Prosecution Service ruled that there was insufficient evidence to take further action.

The Marchioness Action Group only heard a full account of the events on the river Thames at the second inquest in 1995, when a police statement was read out in full. Given that this was six years after the disaster, relatives and survivors were angry that they had been denied an opportunity to hear such information sooner and instead had had to fight to learn about the events that night and what went wrong.

The evidence at the second inquest was not new – it had simply not been heard at the previous inquest. On the basis of this and dissatisfaction with inquest procedures following other disasters, members of Disaster Action continued to raise questions about the politics of inquests and the role, training and authority of coroners. The eventual success of this work can be found in the much-needed coroners' reforms of 2009 and later (see Chapter 7).

Margaret Lockwood-Croft reported on the reopening of the inquest again in March 1995, which lasted for four weeks:

> Evidence that had always been available was released for the first time, causing shock and bewilderment for the bereaved relatives and survivors, and dismay for our legal representatives. Limitation of damage against government, industry and insurers is the name of the game; after all, the 'dead are dead' and in time if obstacles such as deception and extended delays prevail long enough the bereaved and survivors will retreat.
>
> After a protracted legal fight over 4 years to obtain an inquest, far from allaying our fears, it presented more questions than answers. The inquest system showed it was impotent to deal with a major disaster.[6]

In 1999, Barbara Davis, whose son survived the sinking of the *Marchioness*, commented similarly on the continuing quest for information by families: 'The public perception continues to be that many questions surrounding the sinking of the *Marchioness* remain unanswered. We continue to push for a full public inquiry into the events of that night, together with the need for improved river safety.'[7]

As discussed in Chapter 1, ten years after the disaster a public inquiry was finally ordered. The outcome of Lord Justice Clarke's *Inquiry Report into the*

Identification of Victims Following a Major Transportation Accident caused landmark changes in the way in which individuals are now treated following disasters, in particular with regard to an open and honest approach now being recognised as right in principle with relatives being given information in a timely manner.

LEGACY OF LOCKERBIE: 'THEIR SPIRIT LIVES ON'

The 25th anniversary of the Lockerbie disaster in December 2013 was marked by services across the globe. The largest of these commemorations were a service arranged by members of UK Families Flight 103 at Westminster Abbey and memorial events in Lockerbie and the United States. Addresses from Jim Swire and John Mosey, both of whom lost daughters on Pan Am 103, at the Abbey service called not for revenge but for a just resolution, echoing the principle of appropriate accountability that has been so important to Disaster Action as an umbrella association.

By contrast, the theme of the memorial service at Dryfesdale Parish Church in Lockerbie, 'Looking Forward', highlighted the tensions between the desire of the town to move on and the need of the families for that just resolution. The decision not to read the names of the dead at this service left some relatives feeling very disappointed, given that without the 270 deaths there would have been no reason to gather there at all.

Every year Lockerbie Academy sends two students to study at Syracuse University, 35 of whose students died in the bombing, on scholarships. The close bond that has developed between the town's people and the university is significant, yet it also serves to underline a sense that the disaster 'belongs' to Lockerbie and to the United States rather than necessarily to those of all 21 nationalities who were lost.

The impact of a disaster on the next generation can be seen in the experience of Alana and Liam Francis, who travelled for the first time as adults to Lockerbie with their parents John Francis and Pam Dix for that 25th anniversary. Indeed, some of Alana's work as an artist investigates the personal and political consequences of being affected by an act of terrorism from the perspective of the second generation. She has worked over a number of years to understand the event that shaped her life and the lives of so many others. Alana's artwork is one example of the different and enduring ways meaning has been given to our disaster experiences, alongside other physical representations such as memorials and literature.

'LOOKING FORWARD?'

Disaster Action members are mindful of the sentiment of the themes reflected in commemorative services, and the question often posed by those outside our experiences as to whether we have yet got 'closure' and 'moved on'.

For all affected by these tragic events, significant anniversaries are in part about reconciling and assimilating the past into their everyday lives. For some, the passage of time means that the tenth, 20th and 25th anniversaries can represent an opportunity to look forward; for others, personal loss and the fact that fundamental questions about these events remain unanswered and unaddressed mean that notions such as 'moving on' or 'letting go' are simplistic and unhelpful.

The challenge for those organising and conducting commemorative events after collective tragedy is to ensure that moving on does not mean moving away from the connection with the tragedy. Commemorations need to be inclusive in order to avoid individual survivors or bereaved, or the wider community, feeling that their loss and experience are somehow lesser, or not recognised; the whole point of commemoration is to feel validated.

Disaster Action member Jelena Watkins has spoken of the 'legitimate mourners' who in some way become the face of a tragedy: 'In every disaster there is a group of people who fit some kind of simplified myth and they then become the legitimate mourners. The rest are ignored. It is very hurtful.'

REMEMBERING THE INDIVIDUAL IN COLLECTIVE MEMORIALS

When thoughtfully considered, the way in which permanent memorials and memorial services are designed and conducted can embrace the sense of remembering the unique character and loss of individuals within the collective experience of disaster. A good example of this is the consultation, development and final production of the enduring memorial to those killed in the 2005 London bombings, as described by Disaster Action member Julie Nicholson:

> The character of the memorial was informed by the singular and collective loss, inviting contemplation, journeying and touch as visitors meander through. Each pillar bears an inscription of date, time and place. Names are inscribed collectively on a plaque, set into the grass bank at the eastern end of the memorial. Each pillar is made unique in texture through the casting process while appearing identical from a distance.

The pillars of the memorial reflect and absorb light; they also cast long shadows, echoing the lives as well as the loss of the 52 killed.

An enduring theme championed by Disaster Action has been enabling a participatory approach, a core principle that has been adopted in guidance and recommendations focusing on the care and treatment of those affected by disaster. An example of our influence in this regard is on the Scottish Government steering group, which in November 2013 produced guidance on 'Responding to the Psychosocial and Mental Health Needs of People Affected by Emergencies'. The guidance included this statement on anniversaries: 'Memorial services, acts of remembrance and cultural rituals marking the anniversaries of the emergency should be *planned in conjunction with the people who have been affected.* They may want to do this independently or as a group. Some people may require additional support at this time.'[8] (Our italics.)

REMEMBERING FOR THE FUTURE

In researching and writing this book, we found ourselves having discussions about the meaning of our disasters now, their lasting consequences and legacy and how we may and should remember and mark them in the future. We have reflected on the fact that in some ways the passing of time has extended ownership and interpretation of 'our' disasters, with new generations, historians, and other commentators all having a say about what they mean or how they should be remembered and represented. This can be a mixed experience for us.

We appreciate that living with the reminders of a disaster in the place where it happened must be difficult. This issue is not new and is familiar to small towns and villages associated with terrible loss of life – Ypres, Passchendaele and others across the world. Had it not been for the events that marked them most people would never have heard of these places, as is true of villages and towns such as Aberfan, Lockerbie and Dunblane. Yet in Disaster Action's view it is possible – and necessary – to reconcile and assimilate the legacy of the past without rejecting it.

Disasters and conflicts are remembered and commemorated throughout the UK and indeed across the world. In April 2012, commemorative services and acts of remembrance were held across the world for the 100th anniversary of the sinking of the *Titanic*; these included events to remember single individuals who had died. In Cobh, Ireland, the last port of call for the ship, the commemorations lasted a full year. Survivors and bereaved from the 1943 Bethnal Green underground disaster held their 70th anniversary commemorations in March 2013 (and, indeed, their 71st in 2014). They continue to remember the dead, acknowledge the experience of survivors, recognise their loss, and assimilate this into their ongoing lives with the active involvement of those new to the community.

The continuing impact of disasters on the lives of those left behind is eloquently summed up by Sophie Tarassenko:

> When things go wrong it is irreversible ... my brother's been dead for 25 years ... the potential loss of such precious human lives has to be in people's minds when they are making decisions about safety ... the overwhelming emotion is still sadness that he never got to live life as he should.

That this sadness has proved to be, in the end, not disempowering but part of the motivating force behind Disaster Action's work is the extraordinary legacy that those who died can never be aware of. What remains difficult to accept is that it takes so many such deaths and serious injuries before systems, regulation, guidance and the law are changed so that others will be safer for the future.

NOTES

1 Mary Campion, in Disaster Action Newsletter, Spring/Summer 1999, Issue 5, pp. 3–4.
2 BBC News online, 22 August 2010, http://www.bbc.co.uk/news/uk-11050362.
3 BBC News online, 17 November 2007.
4 BBC News online, 6 July 2008, http://news.bbc.co.uk/1/hi/scotland/north_east/7490142.stm.
5 Chris Allen, in The Herald, (20 May 2008), http://www.heraldscotland.com/oil-industry-cannot-rule-out-another-piper-alpha-disaster-1.881511.
6 Margaret Lockwood-Croft, in Disaster Action Newsletter, Autumn 1995, Issue 3, p. 4.
7 Barbara Davis, in Disaster Action Newsletter, Spring/Summer 1999, Issue 5, p. 4.
8 Preparing Scotland: 'Responding to the Psychological and Mental Health Needs of People Affected by Emergencies: Supplement to Care for People Affected by Emergencies' (The Scottish Government, 2013).

CHAPTER 13

DISASTER ACTION'S LEGACY – AND THE FUTURE

Throughout his time as Chairman of Disaster Action, at the start of every annual general meeting Maurice de Rohan would pose two questions: has Disaster Action met its objectives? Should the organisation continue to exist or is it time to call a halt?

These were difficult questions for those so emotionally attached to the organisation to consider, particularly since many attending the meetings had been part of Disaster Action since its origins. Yet the question should continue to be asked, as all organisations need to be clear about their mission and purpose. The expectation of completing the work a charity was set up to fulfil may seem contrary to expectations of charities, most of which do not have an end point in mind. There is a precedent, however, in the Zito Trust, founded by Jayne Zito in 1992 after the fatal stabbing of her husband on the London Underground by a schizophrenic. The Trust had the aim of shedding light on and changing the inadequate mental health system that had let both her husband and his killer down. Having achieved as much as she felt the organisation could, Zito closed the charity some years ago.

In Maurice de Rohan and Peter Spooner's guiding hands, the Herald Families Association had asked itself the same questions, eventually choosing to close as a formal association in September 1997, as outlined earlier in the book. With Disaster Action, the continuing occurrence of disasters, their human impact and the issues arising each time from their management clearly indicated the need for the organisation to continue its unique and important work. At the time of writing in 2014, there has not been an incident resulting in many casualties or major loss of life in the UK since 2005.

Disaster Action's focus has, rightly, evolved over the lifetime of the charity, in recent years being as much on addressing the human aspects of disasters as on their prevention. New members have joined, bringing their different experiences and issues, which have affected the shape and direction of the organisation. In many ways their contributions have reinforced and reminded members of the universal and consistent needs of those affected by disasters. At the same time, their expectations and concerns reflect the dynamic nature of emergency management, the changing environments in which disasters occur and the need for a proper response, whatever the context.

FUNDING SUPPORT

In order to sustain our work the need for core funding for Disaster Action has remained paramount. Though many of the organisation's activities are carried out on a volunteer basis, its viability does depend on having a firm financial footing. As the grant from The Joseph Rowntree Charitable Trust came to an end, new sources had to be explored. Whilst we received excellent guidance from one funding adviser, unlike some organisations that employ professional fundraisers Disaster Action has taken a low-key approach to our funding needs, in keeping with our volunteer ethos. Members have generated some income for the charity through donations from Livery Companies with which they are associated and other sources. In March 2009, Disaster Action secured a grant from the Esmée Fairbairn Foundation for core funding over a three-year period. Unusually, the Foundation then agreed to fund the charity for a further two years, and this comes to an end in 2014.

Most recently, an application to the Golden Bottle and Bulldog Trusts was successful. A measure of Disaster Action's success lies in the fact that of 276 applications only three were successful – also an indication of how difficult it is for small charities to generate sufficient funds. Any future sources of funding for Disaster Action must enable the charity to maintain its independence from government or vested interest.

PUBLIC RECOGNITION

Unlike most charities striving for public interest in order to generate financial support and recognition, Disaster Action has chosen to remain under the radar, an organisation that is known about largely only where is there is sudden and extreme need. Some of our work has also necessarily been on a confidential basis, for example for police forces dealing with sensitive investigations and seeking guidance on appropriate family liaison strategies. Occasionally such consultation has generated some welcome income. In order to retain our trusted position as an adviser, however, this work often remains confidential to the client and Disaster Action; our satisfaction therefore has to lie in the difference we have made rather than in public recognition, and this inevitably reduces the potential for financial support from the wider public.

LEGISLATION AND GUIDANCE

Since 2008, when the Corporate Manslaughter and Corporate Homicide Act 2007 was implemented, the Crown Prosecution Service has investigated a significant number of cases, and that number is growing fast every year. Although there have only been five successful convictions at the time of writing, there are a further 100 or so cases listed for potential investigation. Another positive development is that coroners are referring more cases to the CPS. This means that deaths are being investigated properly, and that corporations, their shareholders and their insurers are having to pay proper attention to safety.

Most of the Coroners and Justice Act 2009 was implemented in July 2013, when the new Chief Coroner, Peter Thornton, said:

> I welcome the coroner reforms which come into force today. They will benefit bereaved families across England and Wales who will be the focus of a more efficient, effective and modern coroner service.
>
> Inquests will be heard earlier, usually within six months. Families will receive information earlier and will have greater access to documents and evidence. Bodies will be released earlier for burial or cremation. Fewer inquests will be needed as a result of early investigation. And there will be a special emphasis upon coroners reporting to prevent future deaths.[1]

We very much hope that this will mean consistent standards in England and Wales for those who come into contact with the coroners' service, a service that has, in our shared experience, been unacceptably patchy.

The 2013 House of Lords Select Committee on the Inquiries Act 2005 was set up to review the current system of statutory and non-statutory inquiries, and the committee's report on its review was published on 11 March 2014.[2] We welcome the careful attention the committee has paid to evidence submitted by Disaster Action and others on the importance of learning lessons from previous inquiries, and the implementation of recommendations made by such inquiries; the failure to do so is a shortcoming identified in relation to inquiries such as that into the 1987 King's Cross fire, as detailed in Chapter 7 of this book.

It is worth recording some observations from the report summary:

> Inquiries into matters of major public concern are now an integral feature of the governance of this country. They establish disputed facts, determine accountability, restore public confidence, and make recommendations for preventing recurrence of events and taking forward public policy...
>
> There is no consistency in ministerial decisions on setting up inquiries...
>
> We suggest that failures of regulatory and investigatory bodies should at the very least be grounds for considering setting up an inquiry.[3]

The committee report notes that broadly similar inquiries have resulted in an unacceptably wide variation in inquiry costs and refers to ministerial inconsistency in deciding whether to hold an inquiry, as well as making significant recommendations on:

- stronger control of government ministers
- capturing and learning lessons from inquiries
- government being held to account by parliament following publication of an inquiry report.

We also welcome the recommendation that victims and victims' families should be given the opportunity to make representations about the terms of reference of the inquiry, and that victims or the bereaved should meet the chair and counsel to the inquiry as early as possible.

It remains to be seen how the government will respond to the report, and whether these important recommendations are implemented – another monitoring task for Disaster Action and others.

DISASTER VICTIM IDENTIFICATION

In contrast to the traditional methods from our founding members' early experience of the identification of the dead in disasters, DNA analysis is now routinely used after multiple fatality disasters. It may be the only technique available in the case of severely damaged remains.

As of the tenth anniversary of the 9/11 attacks, 1124 of the 2753 people killed remained unidentified, yet efforts continue on the part of the Chief

Medical Examiner's office in New York, and 30 names have been added to the list of the identified since 2006.[4]

This is an illustration of the power of forensic science to deliver certainty. Those waiting for news that may come at any time remain in a different kind of limbo from families in earlier disasters, where identifications will never be carried out because of the circumstances and decisions taken at the time, including the cremation of unidentified remains.

More traditional identification methods include identifying individual physical characteristics, such as birthmarks, tattoos, or implants, fingerprint analysis and odontology, as well as clothing or jewellery. Visual identification by a friend or relative is, however, rarely used nowadays.

DNA identification testing, however, requires time and access to specialised services. The certainty provided by the new technology means that coroners may be tempted to use it, rather than other methods, in any mass fatality situation, and thus delay the identification even of those whose bodies are intact. Such an approach causes relatives, who often know that the missing person is likely to have been involved in the disaster, unnecessary painful days of waiting for definitive news.

In addition, the increasing use of scientific methods of identification has meant that relatives now have little, if any, involvement in the 'processing' of the deceased after the disaster. Very rarely is a confirmation of the identity of the person by the relatives required. Often the body is released, after lengthy delays, from the custody of the coroner, simply ready for burial or cremation. Psychologically, this is too late for many relatives to spend time with the deceased, and to feel part of their 'final journey'.

Disaster Action continues to advocate for coroners to inform relatives as quickly as possible of the death of their loved one, and to invite relatives to make a visual confirmation or viewing. This is a fundamental right routinely offered to families after individual acts of murder, manslaughter, or accident: to have a choice as to whether or not to see the body of their loved one.

Disaster Action spent many years lobbying to ensure that the design of major incident temporary mortuaries should, wherever possible, incorporate facilities for families to view their dead, such as were created in London after the 2005 bombings. Having reached a point at which this was accepted, there appears to be a shift towards not incorporating such facilities, partly on the basis of cost, yet worryingly also because of a lack of understanding of families' needs. This is a retrograde step and a classic example of the need to continue to learn from and apply lessons from past disasters into future planning.

THE FUTURE FOR HUMANITARIAN ASSISTANCE

A key area of interest for Disaster Action has been identifying and addressing the needs of survivors and the bereaved, known after 9/11 as 'family assistance' and at present in the UK as 'humanitarian assistance'.

The Humanitarian Assistance Unit (HAU) in the Department for Culture, Media and Sport was set up largely because of then minister of state Tessa Jowell MP's background in social work and her personal interest in the welfare of individuals following disasters. The creation of the Unit was driven by the 9/11 attacks in the United States; 65 UK nationals were killed in the tragedy and (encouraged by Disaster Action) central government had to take responsibility for the practical and emotional welfare of the many bereaved family members resident in the UK.

Led by civil servant Frances McLeod, the HAU went on to work in the interests of those affected by the disasters that followed 9/11 – Bali, the Tsunami, the London bombings, Sharm el Sheikh and the 2008 Mumbai attacks – as well as commissioning some important research on the needs of survivors and bereaved.

In 2010 the HAU was disbanded, leaving future responsibility for humanitarian assistance in limbo, although in March 2014 the DCMS was still listed on GOV.UK, the UK government website, as the lead government department for this vital area of emergency planning and response. Since 2012, government departments including the Cabinet Office and the Department for Communities and Local Government seem to have struggled to understand what is meant by humanitarian assistance. As of spring 2014, a decision on which department would take on responsibility for this area (and how it might be described, in order to ensure buy-in from local authorities) had still not been made public. While Disaster Action's input into the discussions has been welcomed, the apparent lack of urgency in getting to grips with such a gap in responsibility is disturbing. A government that introduced the idea of 'Big Society', devolving responsibility for local affairs to local communities, appears to have overlooked the importance of central guidance.

Government priorities revolve around current concerns, with the economic situation at the top of the agenda since the 2010 general election. As noted, given that in the UK there has not been a disaster involving large-scale loss of life since the London bombings of 2005, disaster management has fallen down that agenda. Yet the winter of 2013–14 brought with it consistently bad weather, resulting in coastal and inland flooding incidents all over the country, sorely testing both local council provision and preparedness. The impact on many rural and some urban communities has been considerable, and meeting the continuing and future challenges in terms of infrastructure and community resilience necessarily preoccupied government ministers at this time.

During the crisis it was clear that an overarching driving force was missing; while disaster response must have a local and regional focus, the lack of clear lines of responsibility within central government for the human aspects added to a sense that there was little strategic decision making and control over events.

Integrating an appropriate mental health response for survivors and the bereaved into humanitarian assistance after a multiple fatality disaster is essential. Yet there are no plans to replicate the National Health Service 'screen and treat' programme* in the event of a future national incident. If such a dedicated service is not set up, it is unclear how the potential mental health needs of those affected by future disasters will be identified and met.

CORPORATE MEMORY AND ENDURING PRINCIPLES: ACCOUNTABILITY, SUPPORT, PREVENTION

The Hillsborough tragedy demonstrates that lessons can, and must be, learnt after disasters, especially when the cost in human life has been high. The systemic failures that led to that disaster, the lack of accountability compounded by the very organisations that should have protected football fans in their efforts to cover up what happened, the unsatisfactory inquest, the failure fully and appropriately to inquire into the circumstances, and the media coverage, are a sad indictment of the national response. At the time of writing 25 years on, the results of the fresh inquest and criminal investigations are as yet unknown, but one valuable lesson should already be clear to the authorities: those who have been wronged will not stop in their efforts to achieve truth and justice, despite the many obstacles put in their way. Complacent statements such as 'Society has changed, it could not happen again' are not good enough: work must be done to *ensure* that this is the case – and remains so for the future.

Institutional memory is short. Our system of government, whereby ministers and civil servants are primarily generalists rather than specialists in any field, often prevents lessons being learnt. This increases the likelihood of a confused response and a potential failure to properly address the needs of those directly affected by the next disaster. Ministers change portfolios.

---

* Created after the 2005 London bombings to diagnose and treat those suffering from trauma-related conditions such as post traumatic stress disorder – see Chapter 6.

Civil servants who wish to improve their career prospects are expected to move from one role to another – a classic dilemma within the Foreign & Commonwealth Office, for example. This results in departments constantly 'reinventing the wheel' and we in Disaster Action have found that we are continually briefing those new to their roles in emergency planning.

The references in the previous chapter to the importance of corporate memory in preventing future disasters similar to Piper Alpha echo and reinforce the enduring principles that have underpinned Disaster Action from its beginning until now. Our core messages and aspirations are just as relevant for future generations as they were for us at the outset: corporate accountability, supporting people, and disaster prevention. Our personal experiences and collective conviction continue to inspire our work with individuals, institutions and organisations, promoting candour, care and compassion, not just as duties but as fundamental qualities of the kind of world we all want to live in.

The work that has been done over more than 25 years to change mind-sets, approaches and procedures cannot be set in stone. A new generation needs to take on the mantle of ensuring that the rights and needs of those affected by disaster remain at the core of responding to and planning for emergencies.

Key personnel in the statutory and voluntary services, practitioners, academics, civil servants and government ministers retire or move on, taking their individual and organisational experience of disaster with them. The corporate memory, shared experience and focused approach of Disaster Action are unique. This book has sought to encapsulate that memory so that it can be accessed by survivors, the bereaved, government and others for years to come.

NOTES

1 Peter Thornton QC, 25 July 2013, http://www.judiciary.gov.uk/media/media-releases/2013/ChiefCoronerImplementationOfRelevantPartsOfCoroners AndJusticeAct2009.

2 House of Lords Select Committee on the Inquiries Act 2005, Report of Session 2013–14, *The Inquiries Act 2005: Post Legislative Scrutiny* (The Stationery Office, 2014).

3 House of Lords Select Committee on the Inquiries Act 2005 (2014, p. 7).

4 Neil Tweedie, Telegraph Media, 11 September 2011, http://www.telegraph.co.uk/news/worldnews/september-11-attacks/8752980/911-Identifying-victims-10-years-on.html.

APPENDIX 1

DISASTER ACTION MEMBERSHIP, 2014

As of 2014, Disaster Action's members have been affected by the following 28 disasters:

Polish Air Force Tu-154, Russia (air crash, 2010)
Mumbai, India (terrorist attacks, 2008)
Dahab, Egypt (terrorist attack, 2006)
Nimrod, Afghanistan (air crash, 2006)
Sharm El Sheikh, Egypt, bombings (terrorist attack, 2005)
London bombings (terrorist attack, 2005)
Al Khobar, Saudi Arabia (terrorist attack, 2004)
Tsunami (Indian Ocean Tsunami, 2004)
Bali bombings (terrorist attack, 2002)
11th September (terrorist attacks in the US, 2001)
Ladbroke Grove (rail crash, 1999)
Southall (rail crash, 1997)
Dunblane (school shootings, 1996)
Hillsborough (football stadium crush, 1989)
Marchioness (riverboat sinking, 1989)
UT 772 – Niger, Africa (aircraft bombing, 1989)
Piper Alpha (oil platform fire, 1988)
Clapham (rail crash, 1988)
Jupiter, Greece (cruise ship sinking, 1988)
Lockerbie (aircraft bombing, 1988)

Zeebrugge (*Herald of Free Enterprise* sinking, 1987)
Enniskillen bombing (terrorist attack, 1987)
King's Cross (underground fire, 1987)
Manchester (air crash, 1985)
Saudia 163, Saudi Arabia (air crash, 1980)
MV *Derbyshire* (cargo vessel sinking, 1980)
Aberfan (coal tip slide on school, 1966)
Bethnal Green (underground crush, 1943)

APPENDIX 2

DISASTER ACTION TIMELINE – KEY EVENTS AND ACTIVITIES

This is a selection of Disaster Action's most significant achievements since the charity's foundation.

30 October 1991: Disaster Action launched, Regent's College, London
1991: submission on corporate crime to Royal Commission on Criminal Justice; The Joseph Rowntree Charitable Trust funds corporate responsibility project
1992: presentations to numerous health and safety and legal seminars and conferences; advises families affected by Kathmandu PK 268 air crash
1992–2009: first presentation on Management of Disasters and Civil Emergencies course, Bramshill police staff training college, then regular contributors during existence of the course
1993: first 'When Disaster Strikes' leaflets for bereaved people and survivors
1994: submission to Law Commission consultation on Involuntary Manslaughter
1995: published *Health and Safety Reporting in FTSE 100 Company Annual Reports*
1996–2014: member of London Resilience Forum voluntary sector sub committee; first presentation on Fundamentals of Accident Investigation course, Cranfield University, then regular contributors to course
1997: contributed to Home Office working party on inquiries and inquests

1998: contributed to Emergency Planning Society conference 'Responding to Disaster: the Human Aspects'

2000: published *The Case for Corporate Responsibility: Corporate Violence and the Criminal Justice System*; submission to Lord Justice Clarke's Public Inquiry into the identification of Victims Following Major Transport Accidents

2001: Disaster Action website launched

2002: hosted meeting for those bereaved in 11th September 2001 attacks

2002–06: sat on national steering group for *Humanitarian Assistance in Emergencies Guidance*

2003: facilitated formation of UK Bali Bombing Victims Group

2003–08: awarded core funding grants by The Joseph Rowntree Charitable Trust

2004: advised on Civil Contingencies Act; awarded Society Guardian Charity Award for excellence; assisted in formation of Ufton Nervet rail crash survivor network

2004–06: advisers to Metropolitan Police Service Silver Commander for the Tsunami and to British Red Cross Tsunami Support Network

2004–11: consultee on Home Office mass fatality planning and development of (inter) national procedures on Disaster Victim Identification

2005: member of NICE Post Traumatic Stress Disorder Guideline Development Group

2005–06: continued representations on draft Corporate Manslaughter Bill

2005–07: advisers to 7 July London bombings emergency responders (statutory and voluntary agencies)

2006–10: contributed to British Red Cross European Union projects on supporting individuals in disasters

2006–13: participated in consultations on Draft Charter for the Bereaved in Contact with the Coroners' Service, and Coroners and Justice Act 2009

2007: Corporate Manslaughter and Corporate Homicide Act passed; Disaster Action singled out for praise by Home Secretary in parliament; participant in FCO/Wilton Park international conference on 'Trans-border Consequence Management: Responding to Major CBRN Acts'; participant in OSCE – European Union security organisation – 'High Level Meeting on Victims of Terrorism', Vienna

2008: consulted on revised Association of Chief Police Officers (ACPO) *Guidance on Emergency Procedures*; presentation at Interpol Disaster Victim Identification Standing Committee Meeting, Lyon

2009: contributed to European Union Red Cross 'Informed Prepared Together' project; advised on Incident Support Centre, North Sea helicopter crash

2009–11: member of Cabinet Office Community Resilience Steering Group; consultee on ACPO *Guidance on Disaster Victim Identification*
2009–14: regular presentations on Multi-agency Gold Incident Command courses (police, local authority, fire and ambulance services, and military)
2009–14: awarded core funding grants by the Esmée Fairbairn Foundation
2010: contributes to Home Office consultation on counter terrorism; publishes report: *Disaster Funds: Lessons & Guidance on the Management & Distribution of Disaster Funds*
October 2011: 20th anniversary reception at Australian High Commission, London
2011–14: awarded Ministry of Justice peer support programme grant and capabilities building support
2012: reviewer for World Health Organization guidelines development group creating 'Guidelines for the Management of Conditions Specifically Related to Stress' (http://apps.who.int/iris/bitst ream/10665/85119/1/9789241505406_eng.pdf); consultee on Charity Commission Guidance on 'starting, running and supporting charitable disaster appeals'
(https://www.charitycommission.gov.uk/media/94175/CC40text.pdf); submission to Leveson Inquiry: Culture, Practice and Ethics of the Press
2012–13: consultee on Scottish Government guidance 'Preparing Scotland: Responding to the Psychosocial and Mental Health Needs of People Affected by Emergencies' (http://www.scotland.gov.uk/ Resource/0043/00439275.pdf)
2013: submission to Cabinet Office on future for Humanitarian Assistance; submission to House of Lords select committee on review of Inquiries Act 2005; presentation to Interpol Disaster Victim Identification Standing Committee meeting, Lyon; presentation to International Commission on Missing Persons conference, 'Missing Persons: An Agenda for the Future', The Hague; presentation to International Committee of the Red Cross/ University of Milan 'First Conference on Management and Identification of Unidentified Decedents with an Emphasis on Dead Migrants', Milan; consultee on London Churches Group Major Incident Plan; presentation to Preparing Scotland conference to launch guidance on 'Psychosocial and Mental Health Needs of People Affected by Emergencies'
2013–14: awarded core funding grants by the Golden Bottle/Bulldog Trusts
2014: provided guidance to police and the coroner's legal team on preparations for the Hillsborough inquests, and contributed to information workshops organised by INQUEST for Hillsborough families; updated and revised all leaflets and resources on re-launched website.

APPENDIX 3

'WHEN DISASTER STRIKES' AND 'GUIDANCE FOR RESPONDERS' LEAFLET SERIES

WHEN DISASTER STRIKES

This series of leaflets has been written for survivors and bereaved by Disaster Action members, with a view to helping them through the often difficult processes and procedures that follow a disaster. The starting point for each leaflet was to fill the gaps in information and support of the late 1980s. The series has been added to over the years, when it became clear that our knowledge and experience on subjects such as the return of personal property would be of help to others, and when new members brought their influence and experience to bear.

As published on the Disaster Action website, each leaflet has an introductory paragraph describing Disaster Action; these have been removed to avoid repetition in the book, as have sections such as 'Support Groups and Caring Organisations' and 'Useful Contacts'.

The leaflets were accurate at the time of writing early in 2014. The text is subject to change given developments in legislation and guidance and will also continue to evolve through the experience gained from new members and future disasters. We endeavour to keep the leaflets as published on the website as up-to-date as possible; these are free to download and distribute, as are those in the 'Guidance for Responders' series.

OVERSEAS DISASTERS CHECKLIST: THE IMMEDIATE AFTERMATH

Members of Disaster Action (DA), who have all been directly affected by disasters, have written this checklist for those whose friends and family may be missing in a disaster overseas. Every disaster is unique, but our aim is to suggest what you could do in the immediate aftermath. You may not feel able to do all this yourself. If not, try to get someone close to the family to do so.

Advice on what you need to do before leaving the UK is available from the Foreign & Commonwealth Office (FCO) website. Help may also be available from an airline, tour operator or if the missing person(s) was travelling on business from their company. General information on the disaster is likely to be available through Internet news services. See also DA leaflet *A Disaster Overseas*. The British Red Cross provides a tracing and messaging service to help people find missing relatives abroad, through www.redcross.org.uk/trace.

When you believe someone may be missing overseas
Try to:
- Establish their last known location
- Call their mobile phone
- Visit any social networking sites they may be members of
- Contact their hotel
- Call the mobile phones of friends who may be with them

- Contact friends and family in the UK to check if they have heard from them.

If you still cannot locate them:

In the event of a crisis the FCO may issue an emergency number, advertised through the media. Otherwise, you can contact them on 0207 0081500. Alternatively, any airline/tour operator involved may set up an emergency number. Try to have the following information ready before you call:

- Details of their travel itinerary (flights, hotel and tour operator) if relevant
- Full names, address and date of birth for those missing
- Photocopy of their passport if possible
- Name of their travel insurance company if known

- Keep trying the emergency telephone number – it is likely to be very busy. When you do get through, the operator is unlikely to have specific information about the person you are calling about at that time. They will record the details you give to assist in the process of identifying those who are likely to be involved in the incident
- See FCO information leaflet *Missing Persons Abroad*, at https:// www.gov.uk/government/uploads/system/uploads/attach-ment_data/file/193666/Missing_Persons_web_13.pdf   for information on what consular staff can and cannot do to help
- NB: If your missing relative or friend is found, let the FCO or police know. This will help those who are still missing and their families.

Credit and bank cards

If you know what credit and bank cards they hold:

- Contact the card companies to see if they can confirm recent use and the location. Explain your circumstances, but remember that Data Protection rules restrict what can be disclosed. They can advise you of the procedures to follow.

Preparing to Travel to the Disaster Site

You may wish to travel to the site; if so, seek advice on issues such as whether it is safe to do so and the conditions you may encounter before making your decision. If you do decide to go, see the checklist below:

- It is best **not to travel alone** – take someone with you if possible

- Check that your **passport is valid and its expiry date** – some countries require six months validity for entry
- Check if a **visa** is required
- **Book travel** through the missing person'(s) travel company (if relevant)
- Tell the FCO if you are happy for your **name and contact details to be given to other families**
- Obtain the **British Embassy/High Commission/Consulate contact details** for where you are going from the FCO website
- Check **FCO Travel Advice** for the country you are travelling to (see www.fco.gov.uk). You can subscribe to their advice alert; follow FCOTravel on Facebook and Twitter. For real time travel advice updates follow the nearest British Embassy, High Commission or Consulate on Twitter and Facebook
- Check **weather at destination** and pack accordingly for 4/5 days
- Arrange **travel insurance** for yourself and anyone accompanying you
- Agree with family and friends one person to be the **single point of contact** in UK
- Get the **most recent photograph** of the missing person(s) and make multiple copies (height and body size should be clear – no sunglasses)
- Prepare a list of any **special identifying features** (scars, tattoos, piercings, birthmarks)
- Obtain their **dental records/X-rays** if possible
- Photocopy of **their passport**
- Photocopy/details of **their travel documents**
- Copy of **their insurance details**
- Ask their insurers **what will be paid for** (e.g. flights, hotel, meals, hotel phone, taxis)
- **Charge your mobile.** Pack the **charger** and **power converter** (remember it costs *you* to receive calls overseas – much cheaper to text. Travel insurers may be less likely to pay mobile than hotel phone bills). Cheap phone cards are available in some countries
- Get **foreign currency** for destination
- Tell your **credit card company** where you are going and check your card has capacity.

When you arrive at your destination

- Contact the British Embassy, High Commission or Consulate for latest information and to inform them of your location and plans
- Call your UK contact with your hotel phone number and room number
- Agree set times for daily contact (bear in mind time differences) and keep in regular contact with family and friends so they are aware of your whereabouts
- Get in touch with relevant local tour operator if appropriate
- Keep receipts for everything (for insurance reimbursement)
- Drink lots of water in hot countries and try to eat healthily for energy.

A DISASTER OVERSEAS

Although each disaster is unique, our aim is to enable you to understand what may happen in the days, weeks and months after the disaster, to give you the opportunity to maintain some control over events. As well as the emotional trauma, you may be faced with language, geographical, administrative and political difficulties.

This leaflet is divided into two parts. See Part One if you are reading this soon after the disaster has happened (the Disaster Action leaflet *Overseas Disasters Checklist: the Immediate Aftermath* may also be helpful at this time) and Part Two if you are reading it later.

Part One: Your Disaster has just Happened

After an overseas disaster, it can be hard to get information about what has happened. Details of the disaster and involvement of your family member or friend may not be clear. At this stage, try to make contact with: other relatives and friends; any company that may be involved (such as an airline, coach firm, holiday company, school or their employer); the Foreign and Commonwealth Office (FCO); and news organisations.

Keep a record of telephone calls you make, recording names, contact numbers and any relevant email addresses.

Family and friends

If family and friends are in the country where the disaster took place, they may be in a better position to find out what is happening. Try to share information with them, and share responsibilities if you can for making contact with the organisations involved. This can reduce the immediate stress and demands on your time. It is a good idea for only one person to contact each organisation.

Organisations

When you contact an organisation, explain who you are and why you are getting in touch. Following many, if not all, disasters an emergency telephone number will be issued through the media, which you should contact. You may need to be persistent as such phone lines can become very overloaded. If it is suspected that the disaster is the result of a crime, the police in the UK may assign you a family liaison officer (FLO) who will try to get information on your behalf.

The Foreign & Commonwealth Office (FCO)

If you are based in the UK, contact the FCO Consular Directorate. Explain who you are, who the person you are concerned about is, your relationship to them, what the disaster is and why you think they may be involved. The FCO can provide consular assistance in relation to British nationals who die or suffer injury abroad and to their families.

The FCO may not have special knowledge of the disaster, and you may be the first to alert them to a UK involvement, although they may well become the route by which you will be best informed about developments in the future.

Normally, the consular section of the British Embassy or High Commission of the country in which the disaster occurs will liaise with those who are responding to it. Information will be passed from the consular official on the spot to the Consular Directorate in London, who will ask the local police force to inform the family.

What you are told by the police should be authoritative. However, you may get information through a number of different routes. You may be informed of developments by a consular official in London, or by one abroad. Sometimes there will be direct contact with those in charge of responding to the disaster.

If you live in the country where the disaster has happened, contact the Embassy or High Commission before the local police if you can and it is legal to contact a third party before calling the police.

News organisations

Overseas disasters involving few UK citizens are rarely reported here as fully as they are in the local media. Discovering what is reported locally is now much easier, thanks to the internet. News agencies such as Reuters may also have more information than is used in media and newspaper reports here. On the internet you can search for national and local newspapers in the affected country. Some foreign newspapers may have an English edition. If not, you may be able to use a web-based translation tool to translate relevant articles. Such information, however, will only be of general use in understanding the disaster and will not usually contain details of your personal connection with it.

Dealing with the media

Information about what happened may become available through social media very quickly after the disaster or even while it is still happening, although this will depend on where the disaster has taken place and the circumstances. However, bear in mind that what you learn from all media sources may not give you the amount – or accuracy – of information that you would like to have.

You may be approached by the media, looking for photographs or interviews. The media may also try to speak to children and young people in your family. Think carefully about whether this is appropriate and the possible consequences of such exposure through the 24-hour news media.

It is your choice whether or not to talk to them, but remember that your aim (finding out what has happened to your relative or friend) will not be the same as theirs. Remember too that you cannot change your mind later about what you have said.

You may be unable to stop them taking photographs, but don't be afraid to tell them to leave you alone. If the media is bothering you or your family, tell the police or the FCO officials you are dealing with – their press office will be able to help.

Part Two: The Aftermath

What you have experienced may have a considerable effect upon you now and/or in the future. Although you may not have been physically injured or survived the disaster yourself, coming to terms with what happened may be difficult. Each person's experience of and feelings about a disaster are unique; some people may have problems because of it and others may not.

Legal advice

Getting appropriate legal help will be important. You are likely to need more specialised advice than your family solicitor can give you. In addition to a specialist lawyer in the UK, you may also need a lawyer local to the disaster. The Law Society or the Association of Personal Injury Lawyers can give you lists of lawyers with experience in this area.

It is important to bear in mind that if the death has occurred abroad and the body is returned to England or Wales, the coroner in whose district the body now lies is legally in charge of the body, until he or she releases it. If the deceased was cremated abroad before being returned, the coroner no longer has any duties or powers to deal with the matter in any way.

Going to the disaster site

Arrangements may be made for you to go either to the disaster site or some appropriate location to coincide with acts of remembrance or other such events. It is your choice whether to go. The advantages of going are that you may learn more about the disaster and benefit from sharing with others their and your experience. The disadvantages are that the trip may be emotionally demanding, will take you away from your existing sources of news and information and may be frustrating.

If you are offered a trip by one of the agencies involved in the disaster, even if you think there may be a future legal claim against them, your position should not affected by accepting their hospitality.

Identification

All those involved in a disaster will need to be identified, a process referred to as disaster victim identification or DVI. In some circumstances the UK police will assist in this process. This may be especially complicated when the disaster has happened abroad, in a country whose customs may be unfamiliar. The process may also take some time. The coroner in the UK will have to be satisfied as to the identification of each person, to prevent any problems arising at the time of repatriation to this country.

A police family liaison officer (FLO) may contact you for:
- A physical description of your relative, or friend, including any distinctive features, such as scars or tattoos
- Clear, recent photographs of them
- Name and address of their doctor and dentist (if they were living in the UK)
- Details of items they may have been wearing or had with them – driving licence, wallet, handbag, jewellery, keys
- Items that may contain fingerprints or DNA.

This information will probably be required whatever the circumstances of the disaster. The police may also need to take fingerprint or other samples from their house, if the person was resident in the UK. Your FLO should keep you informed about how the identification is being carried out. Even if you have no contact with the police, it can be a good idea to collect this information, in case it is asked for.

Registering the death

You may be faced with difficult decisions concerning the body and registering the death. The FCO may be able to help you decide what needs to be done and what is feasible. The process will be more complicated and take longer than a similar death in the UK. The local authorities will normally register a death in their territory and issue a local death certificate. Local death certificates are usually accepted by UK institutions if accompanied by a certified translation. In addition to the local death registration you can register the death at the Embassy or High Commission. There is no legal requirement to register the death at the High Commission or Embassy, although you may find this useful as you will be issued with a UK-style certificate, in English, and the General Registrar's Office in the UK keeps a record. The Embassy will need to see the original local death certificate when you apply for a consular death registration. A consular death registration may be applied for at any time. There will be fees to pay for consular registrations.

Non-identification

You need to prepare for the possibility, however distressing it may seem, that no body will be found. It may take weeks, months or even longer, before a decision is taken that an identification is not possible.

Personal property

After a disaster items of personal property may have become separated from their owners and later found at or near the site. If they have been recovered, you may have to wait some time for your relative's or friend's possessions to be returned to the next of kin – this may be particularly difficult in an overseas disaster. It is also possible that the items may have been destroyed in the disaster. You can ask your FLO, if you have one, about what will happen to the items. You may also find the DA leaflet *The Return of Personal Property* helpful in understanding how property is dealt with.

Contacting others who are involved

One of the ways in which people caught up in a disaster can best help themselves is by contacting others affected by the same disaster. Sharing your feelings and information with others who have had similar experiences can help at a time when you may feel alone. There may also be an advantage in belonging to a group when you need to approach the authorities, government departments, or lawyers.

Disaster Action can put families in touch with each other, if they make contact with us. We can also put you in touch with other Disaster Action members with relevant experience.

Groups may be set up to assist those who are local to the disaster, and they may welcome contact from you. Your FCO contact or FLO should know of any such groups, or find out about them on your behalf.

How might you be affected?

You may have a number of different reactions, such as loss of appetite or sleepless nights. You might find it difficult to concentrate. You might have anxiety attacks. You may find it hard to relate to family or friends who have not shared your experience. And you may keep re-living the disaster or have vivid flashbacks. It is important to understand that these reactions are not abnormal in themselves. If such reactions and feelings persist or disturb you, then you may find it beneficial to seek help. There's nothing wrong with knowing that you need help and trying to find it. Whether you feel you need help or not, take care in driving or doing other things that are potentially dangerous.

Where to find help

You can go to your doctor (who can refer you to a counsellor) to talk about how you feel, but if he or she has had no training in disasters, they may be unsure how best to help you. There are a few clinics, mostly in London, which specialise in helping those affected by disasters. Ask your doctor what is available locally, or speak to Disaster Action.

Some people will not want or feel the need to talk to anyone outside family and friends, although for others it may be essential. There is nothing wrong with knowing that you need help and trying to find it. If you contact a group but don't find it helpful, don't give up. It may be that whoever you spoke to was not the right person for you. It is never too early or too late to get help – the hard thing is to recognise, or admit, that you need it.

A telephone helpline may be set up by the local authority to offer guidance to those who need help. You should be able to get the number from your police contact or social services.†

---

† In order to avoid duplication of text, sections entitled 'dealing with the media', 'personal property', 'contacting others', 'how you might be affected' and 'where to find help' that appeared in the published versions of a number of the leaflets have been deleted from those that follow in this Appendix.

A SURVIVOR IN THE AFTERMATH

If you have been physically injured in a disaster, please read *A Physically Injured Survivor in the Aftermath*.

You may be reading this leaflet in a Survivor Reception Centre, in which case you should find Part One helpful. If not, please look at Part Two. (At a later stage the police and other agencies involved may set up a Humanitarian Assistance Centre, which could include virtual support through a dedicated website. This will be the focal point for information and assistance for families, survivors and others directly affected by the disaster.)

Part One: Survivor Reception Centre

A Survivor Reception Centre (SRC) may be set up by the police as soon as a disaster happens. Depending on the circumstances of the disaster there might be more than one SRC.

You can ask the police to call a member of your family, or call yourself, to let them know that you are at the SRC. Ask them to let other members of the family and your friends know that you are all right.

What happens at the SRC?

Survivors who were not physically injured may be interviewed here by the police to identify those involved and to find out what they saw and heard. A police officer will ask you for your personal details and ask you questions about what happened. The officer will fill in a form with the information and pass it to the Casualty Bureau (CB). The CB is where the police gather all the information coming from the disaster site (and from outside sources) about who may be involved. If you don't feel able to talk about the disaster right away, tell the police officer that you would rather be interviewed later, or at your home (if this is what you want). If you would prefer to have a member of your family or a friend with you while you are being interviewed, let the police know.

The police will also help you with any immediate needs you have as a result of the disaster. If, for example, you are temporarily homeless, they can assist you in finding emergency accommodation through social services. Depending on the circumstances, you may have the assistance of a police family liaison officer (FLO) or social worker.

What happened to those you were with?

This can be a deeply anxious time, especially if you got separated from relatives or friends who were with you when the disaster happened. It would help the police if you gave personal details about anyone you were with at the disaster scene. A police officer will fill in a form with this information, which will be passed on to the CB.

If the police have any news about those you were with, they will let you know, but feel free to ask about what is happening.

Part Two: The Aftermath

You may have left the scene of the disaster without having given your details to anyone and were understandably focusing on getting home. In the days and weeks following the disaster, what you have seen and heard may have an effect on you now and in the future. Although you may not have been physically injured, coming to terms with a disaster can be difficult. Each person's experience of and feelings about a disaster are unique; some people may have problems because of it and others may not.

Contact with the authorities

Following a disaster the police may contact you to interview you in order to identify those involved and to discover what happened. If you would prefer to have a member of your family or a friend with you while you are being interviewed, let the police know.

Other organisations may be able to help you with practical and emotional needs, including the local authority, social services or voluntary organisations. Details may be publicised locally or nationally. The local authority may set up a telephone helpline to offer guidance to those who need help. You should be able to get the number from your police contact or social services.

Survivor elation and survivor guilt

Survivors can experience elation or guilt. Both feelings are perfectly normal. Survivor elation is a reaction to the realisation that you have overcome an event where the outcome could have been much worse. Some people find that it can be a powerful aid to recovery. Survivor guilt comes at least partly from feeling you could have done more to protect those around you and that you survived when others did not.

If you feel you need help in dealing with such feelings, you can access further information and support through your GP and any dedicated services that may have been set up in the aftermath of the disaster. Some survivors find talking to others who have been similarly affected very helpful.

A PHYSICALLY INJURED SURVIVOR IN THE AFTERMATH

The information in this leaflet offers the experience of others that may be useful to you, your family and friends. While it cannot cover every eventuality, given the wide range of possible injury from cuts and bruises to life changing, the leaflet is relevant for those affected by a disaster in the UK and for those returning from overseas. At the end of the leaflet there are some explanations of the centres that may have been set up by the local authority and/or the police following the disaster, which you may not have been aware of or able to visit because of your injuries.

Part One: The Immediate Aftermath

If many people have been killed or injured in a disaster, the early aftermath is likely to be chaotic and getting information about who has been injured, which hospital you may have been taken to, and what has happened, may have been very difficult for your friends and family. Your workplace may well be used as a point of contact and your colleagues may find themselves inundated with requests from people seeking information.

Being in hospital

You and your family may have the assistance of a police family liaison officer (FLO) and/or social worker, depending on the circumstances.

Having been through a totally unexpected and traumatic event you may be trying to work out what happened to you and what the sequence of events was. You may also be trying to understand who – if anyone – was responsible for the disaster and why they did what they did. If you wish to do so, you can talk about this with your family and friends and the police.

The medication you may be on could affect your usual personality. You may also find that you experience nightmares and flashbacks – these are not unusual and should pass in time. When you feel well enough, you may find it useful to talk to other survivors; they will undoubtedly find it helpful to talk to you. Survivors from other disasters have found that talking about what happened with others can be beneficial.

Encourage family and friends to bring some of your clothes and personal possessions in to hospital so that you can return to being 'you' as quickly as possible. You will need to learn what hospital routines are and what everyone does.

The scene of the disaster

If the disaster happened in the UK, the police will have taken photographs of the debris after the disaster and you can ask about seeing these if you wish to do so. They may keep the debris for some time while the legal processes are ongoing, and you may also be able to visit this once you are physically able to do so. Others from past disasters have found it helpful to do this, as well as visiting the site, though the most important thing is for you to be able to make these choices for yourself.

Survivor elation and survivor guilt‡

Funerals and memorial services

If you are in hospital for some time, you may not have been able to attend events held to commemorate those who died. You may even have had to miss funerals for those you were with. It may be helpful to ask family and friends to make a note of who was there and what happened to tell you later.

You could also ask for the funeral to be videoed so that you can see it in your own time (remember to ask permission if you want someone to record the event). It has become increasingly common for audio and video recordings to be made of personal events such as these and many people find it helpful even when they have been able to attend and participate.

What happened to those you were with?

In the early stages after the disaster, if you are conscious and aware of what happened, this may be a deeply anxious time, especially if you got separated from relatives or friends who were with you when the disaster happened. The police may ask you for personal details about anyone you were with at the disaster scene. A police officer will fill in a form with this information, which will be passed on to the Casualty Bureau (CB). The CB is where the police gather all the information coming from the disaster site (and from outside sources) about who may be involved.

If the police have any news about those you were with, they will let you know, but you should feel free to ask about what is happening.

Part Two: The Longer Term

During and following your physical recovery, what you have seen and heard may have an effect upon you. In the future, this may be shown

---

‡ Please see A Survivor in the Aftermath for text relevant to this sub heading as it appeared in the published leaflet.

through feelings of anger and sadness, which are an entirely normal reaction to an abnormal (traumatic) event. Coming to terms with a disaster can be difficult even when the physical recovery is complete. In addition, you may have life-changing injuries to contend with. Each person's experience of and feelings about a disaster are unique; some people may experience emotional problems because of it and others may not.

An important milestone is when you can finally go home from hospital. There may be a mixture of excitement and apprehension about this event. You may find that this is a difficult period for you, something your family and friends may not understand. This is not uncommon. It may help to talk to people, whether family, health professionals or people who have gone through a similar experience.

This section of the leaflet is not a guide to everything that may have to be taken into account, but is intended to cover a range of the issues that may be relevant depending on your circumstances.

Assistance from your GP and local health service
Your ongoing needs should have been assessed by the hospital prior to your discharge. If you require continuing care, this will normally be through your local GP. Because of the nature of your injuries you may also continue to attend hospital services as an outpatient. Your GP will receive a letter from the hospital on your discharge concerning your condition.

Dealing with your employer
You may have to give up the job you were doing before the disaster happened, or you may find that your priorities have changed and you wish to do something completely different. The best option will be for you to make your own decisions about your future in consultation with others who can help.

Benefits and back to work schemes
The Department for Work and Pensions is responsible for a range of benefits and services for people of working age, providing financial help and support. On the DWP website you can access information on these services and what help may be available for you.

Driving
You may no longer be able to drive, depending on your condition once you get home, or will need to use a specially adapted vehicle. Information on any condition that you have to notify them about is

available from the DVLA (Driver and Vehicle Licensing Agency) website.

Legal/insurance claims
It is likely to be helpful for you to have the services of a solicitor who is experienced in dealing with issues arising from disasters. Please see Disaster Action leaflet *Legal Representation after a Disaster* for more information on this subject and some useful contacts.

Disaster trust funds
Depending on the circumstances of the disaster and whether it happens in the UK or overseas, a disaster trust fund may be set up by the relevant local authority or the British Red Cross. You may be eligible to make a claim on this fund, contact details for which will be publicised through the media.

Adaptations to your home
If you need improvements and adaptations to your home to help you continue to live independently there, you can ask the social services department of your local council to do an assessment of your home. Information on what may be available and how to access this and other help can be found on the Gov.Uk website.

Criminal Injuries Compensation Scheme
This provides for victims of crime to receive some compensation for their injuries, or in the case of the bereaved the death of their loved one. The scheme is supposed to be simple enough to use without the help of a solicitor, but it might still be advisable to seek advice and help in making and progressing your application.

If you were ordinarily resident in the UK and you were injured outside the UK in a terrorist attack, you may be able to claim under the Victims of Overseas Terrorism Compensation Scheme.

How might you be affected psychologically?
You may have a number of different reactions, such as loss of appetite or sleepless nights. You might find it difficult to concentrate. You might have anxiety attacks. You may find it hard to relate to family or friends who have not shared your experience. And you may keep re-living the disaster or have vivid flashbacks. If you have been recovering from serious physical injuries, these reactions may still occur while you are in hospital or when you are discharged. They may happen whether or not someone has been physically injured.

It is important to understand that these reactions are not abnormal in themselves. If such reactions and feeling persist or disturb you, then you may find it beneficial to seek help. There's nothing wrong with knowing that you need help and trying to find that help.

Local Authority and Police Reception Centres

You may find it helpful to have some information on some of the activities the police and local authorities may have carried out following the disaster.

Casualty Bureau

The Casualty Bureau is the centre where the police gather all the information regarding missing persons, casualties and survivors. It will also assess information coming from the disaster site, hospitals and other sources about who may be involved. It will seek to establish the number and identity of those involved in the incident. However, depending on the circumstances it is not likely to be able to provide information on an individual's involvement for some time. In serious cases the police will also normally speak to the family concerned in person. The purpose of this may be to take more details from the family and friends or provide sensitive information.

Family and Friends Reception Centre

A Family and Friends Reception Centre for those concerned about anyone who may have been caught up in the disaster is likely to be set up by the police and local authority. This will provide a place where people can attend to discuss their concerns with the authorities. It should be noted that it is not likely to have a telephone facility. Relevant information from here is also passed on to the CB to assist in identifying who is involved.

Survivor Reception Centre

The police and local authority may set up an SRC as soon as practicable after a disaster; depending on the nature of the disaster, there may be more than one Survivor Reception Centre. Survivors who are assessed as not physically injured may be interviewed here by the police to identify those involved and to find out what they saw and heard. This will help the police find out what happened.

Humanitarian Assistance Centre

After some disasters, the local authority, police and other agencies involved in the aftermath may set up a Humanitarian Assistance Centre. This will be the focal point for information and assistance for families, survivors and others directly affected by the disaster and could include virtual support through a dedicated website.

THE IMMEDIATE AFTERMATH FOR FAMILY AND FRIENDS

You may be reading this in a Family and Friends Reception Centre, in which case start with Part One. If not, please look at Part Two.

Part One: Casualty Bureau and Family and Friends Reception Centre

Soon after a disaster occurs, the police set up a Casualty Bureau (CB). This is where the police gather all the information coming from the disaster site and from outside sources about who may be involved. An emergency telephone number will be given out through the media as soon as possible after the disaster. The priority for the police is to find and identify those who may be missing.

A Family and Friends Reception Centre (FFRC) for those concerned about anyone who may have been caught up in the disaster is likely to be set up. Information from here is passed on to the CB. The local authority, police and other agencies involved may set up a Humanitarian Assistance Centre (HAC) at a slightly later stage, which could include virtual support through a dedicated website. This will be the focal point for information and assistance for families and others directly affected by the disaster.

There may be a lot of people around you – the police, social workers, volunteers. Make sure you know who you are talking to and check their identification. If you give information that may help identify your relative or friend, don't assume it will be passed on to the police. Always speak to the police directly.

As it becomes necessary, each family will be given a police family liaison officer (FLO), who will be responsible for co-ordinating information about your relative or friend and giving you news either in person or on the telephone.

Whether you go to the FFRC or stay at home is your choice, but there should always be someone that your family's named police officer can get in touch with; make sure that your police contact knows who that person is. Also ensure that you know who is replacing your police officer when they go off duty. If you go home, ask the police to telephone you at regular intervals even if they have no further news.

Identification

All those involved in a disaster will need to be identified.

What the police may need from you to assist in identifying your relative or friend:

- Physical description, including any distinctive features such as scars or tattoos
- Clear, recent photographs of them
- Name and address of their doctor and dentist
- Details of items they may have been wearing or had with them – driving licence, wallet, handbag, jewellery, keys
- Items that may contain fingerprints or DNA.

You can ask your FLO what identification methods are being used and to keep you informed with progress about the identification.

Can you check the hospitals?

If people have been injured in the disaster they will be taken to prearranged hospitals. It is your choice to go there if that is where you would most like to be. Bear in mind that treating the injured is the medical staff's priority and hospitals might only give out information when the police say they can.

What Happens Now?

Finding out what has happened to your relative or friend may happen quickly or it may take days, weeks or even longer. Throughout that time, your FLO will be your contact. The police will contact you as soon as they have any relevant information, but if some time has passed and you have not heard from them, telephone them again.

Don't feel you have to wait for news alone. Being with family and friends can be a great help at a time of such intense anxiety. The strain is great, however, and everyone will respond to it differently so don't be surprised if there is friction between you. It may also be helpful to talk to others who are waiting for news of their relatives and friends. Accept offers of practical help to deal with the necessities of life. Let someone else drive you wherever you need to go.

Part Two: When you Know what has Happened to your Relative or Friend

You may find out that they have escaped the disaster unhurt. This is good news, although it can be difficult to come to terms with what has happened, even if someone has not been physically injured. If they have been injured the police will tell you, either by telephone or in person if you are at home. If necessary, ask police advice about travel arrangements to visit them.

Your relative or friend may have been killed in the disaster. The first instinct of the police and others may be to protect you, and in so doing they may try to make decisions for you. This is okay if it feels right, but you can choose whether or not to take decisions yourself.

Access to the disaster site

While the emergency services are recovering those who have died, you are very unlikely to have access to the disaster site. The police may also suggest that you do not visit the site until it has been cleared of debris and in any case you will not be able to do so until it is safe. If it is physically possible, you can go to the site if this is what you want. It can help in making the disaster real to you although some people will prefer not to go. You should do whatever feels best for you.

Post mortem and release

When someone dies in a disaster, the coroner (or procurator fiscal in Scotland) will require a medical examination of the body. A post mortem is likely to be carried out (though sometimes the coroner will decide not to have this done) by a pathologist to find out how the person died. Relatives and friends will have no choice in this and it may delay the release of the body.

If it can be arranged, a medical representative for the family may be present at the post mortem. If the police suspect that the disaster was the result of a crime, the body may not be released to the family for some time. If the coroner is holding the body, you are entitled to ask for an explanation. The body will only be released to the family when the coroner is satisfied about the identification and the police have finished their first investigations.

Seeing the body and photographs of the dead

The body is in the care of the coroner until it is released to the family. You can see the body and/or photographs provided the next of kin agrees. It may be suggested to you not to see the body, however, if the person was very badly injured. What may seem morbid or unacceptable to those not directly affected can be quite a natural thing to do. You are entitled to know the circumstances of the death if you wish. It is your choice. However, you may want to make this choice with your family, the police, and/or a counsellor.

It is reasonable to ask about the photographs that will have been taken of your relative or friend, and to find out where they will be kept and for how long. If you do not wish to see them now you might be able to do so at a later stage. Everyone will have different reasons why they do or do not want to see such photographs. Think about it carefully. And get as much information as you can from those who can help you make the decision. If you do decide to see them, now or in the future, it may help to do so with a professional counsellor.

Non-identification

You need to prepare for the possibility, however distressing it may seem, that the body will not be found and an identification cannot take place. Depending on the circumstances, it may take weeks, months or even longer before the police and the coroner can be certain that an identification is not possible.

BEYOND THE FIRST ANNIVERSARY

Our aim is to enable you to understand the possible longer-term effects including ongoing legal processes and other issues that people face after disaster.

The Role of Family Liaison Officers (FLOs)

You may have had support from police family liaison officers and other authorities after the disaster. Their contact may have declined in the months after the disaster, though they may well stay in touch with you through the course of any investigations, events such as anniversaries and other disaster-related procedures. FLOs may be a useful referral point for other sources of information and advice.

Financial Issues

Many of the legal procedures set in motion after a disaster can seem lengthy, bureaucratic and impersonal. Claims for compensation, applications to disaster funds and other financial systems can be complicated and difficult to understand, especially when experienced for the first time. We have sometimes found that talking with others who have experienced the same or other disasters and are facing similar procedures can be helpful. Lawyers may be able to help. Although Disaster Action is unable to provide legal advice, we will be familiar with the issues and can make suggestions about what you can do.

Other Ongoing Legal Procedures

The legal and political aftermath of disasters is such that there may be separate investigations by different agencies and these can take a long time. These can include a public inquiry, inquest, Health and Safety Executive investigation, and civil and criminal cases. Where a disaster affects people from more than one country, investigative procedures can be further complicated by differing international systems and involve agencies such as embassies, consular departments and the Foreign & Commonwealth Office.

The police and other authorities should keep you informed and up-to-date with ongoing developments and procedures. Again, we have found that talking with others who have experienced the same disaster or similar disasters may be able to help. Members of Disaster Action have experience of both UK and international disasters and their legal aftermath.

Continuing Media Interest

In the build-up to the first and subsequent anniversaries, the media are likely to take an interest in those directly affected by a disaster. You can prepare for this by deciding whether or not you might wish to participate in interviews or other media-driven activities. If you have an FLO, they may be able to help by filtering requests. Some people have found it useful to have their own family spokesperson or produce their own short statements/photographs for the media. This will help give you more control over what goes out.

Some individuals and family/survivor support groups have found that the media can be allies in highlighting ongoing concerns and issues associated with the disaster. It is possible to produce press releases from time to time and it can be useful to keep contacts and build up working relationships with responsible journalists and reporters. At the same time, do bear in mind that you may not have control over the final content, interpretation and context of any communication.

On the Question of 'Closure'

It is often assumed by others that with the passage of time those who have survived and/or been bereaved by disaster should 'recover' in neat phases, return to 'normal' and be able to put 'closure' on their experience. Such assumptions and comments often feel inappropriate and unhelpful to those with first-hand experience of disaster, reflecting the views and expectations of others rather than how it really feels.

Family and Survivor Support Groups

Many people affected by previous disasters have talked about finding a different or 'new' normality and have found that in the longer term relatively few people can understand or share their experience. Some get greater understanding and support through family or survivor support groups. Even if being part of a group is not for you, long-lasting friendships can develop between people who have gone through a similar experience of disaster; such friendships can offer mutual support based on a special understanding.

Support Groups and Caring Organisations

Some people find that as well as self-help groups, longer-term coun-selling or therapy may help. It is not abnormal or unusual to have flashbacks or need specialist support from time to time over several years. Although the direct experience of disaster is universally trau-matic, the normal emotional and physical reactions usually diminish over time. (This is not to minimise the life-long impact of the death of a family member or close friend in a disaster, but to suggest that there may be ways to help you deal with the loss.) If these reactions persist or even intensify, it may be appropriate to refer to specialist help.

INQUESTS AFTER A DISASTER

Role of the inquest and public inquiry

The inquest is a judicial inquiry into deaths that have taken place. An inquest must be held where a death was violent or unnatural. A coroner seeks to establish the following information:
- who the deceased were
- when they died
- where they died
- by what means and in what circumstances they came by their death

In addition the coroner may make recommendations as to how such deaths may be avoided in future.

The role of a public inquiry into a disaster is 'to restore public confi-dence by carrying out "a full, fair and fearless investigation into the relevant events"'. It should also identify lessons to be learned. The decision as to whether or when to hold a public inquiry into a disaster is made by the relevant government department or Secretary of State.

The inquest will very likely be subordinated to the public inquiry (in order to avoid two hearings of the same evidence). If it is so subor-dinated, the inquest opens formally for identification and release of bodies for burial, then adjourns, resuming (if at all) only after the completion of the public inquiry.

The inquest cannot make or suggest any finding of civil liability, or any finding of criminal liability against any named person or company responsible for the deaths.

Immediately after the death

It is highly likely that the coroner for the area in which the bodies are found will handle all deaths that occur in England or Wales as a result of a disaster. The coroner therefore has legal custody of the body of the deceased until he or she releases it for burial or cremation.

If the disaster occurs overseas and the body is repatriated to England or Wales, the coroner local to where the body arrives takes charge. For example, if the arrival point is Heathrow airport the appointed coroner will be one of the London coroners. If a cremation has taken place overseas, however, and only the ashes of the deceased are brought back to England or Wales, the coroner has no jurisdiction and this means that there will not be an inquest.

As the coroner has legal custody of the deceased, s/he makes all the important decisions about identification, post-mortems and seeing the deceased. This can be a frustrating experience for relatives, who feel that the person who has died is still their loved one, and yet they cannot see them, hold their hand, say goodbye, or take them home if the coroner has decided that is to be the case.

The bereaved should expect the coroner, usually through his officer, to communicate with them in an open, honest and sensitive manner about the standard procedures that are going to be followed, and if there are to be any delays.

Although in the past many coroners have refused to let relatives see the body of the deceased before it is released for burial or cremation, there is now a greater awareness that this may be undesirable, as well as, potentially, an infringement of the human rights of the bereaved. Relatives who wish to see the body should make this very clear to the coroner.

Even if the body of the deceased is very badly damaged, relatives should be given an informed opportunity to see it, or part of it, if they wish to do so, as soon as possible after death. For advice on this please see When Disaster Strikes, *The Immediate Aftermath for Family and Friends*. See also the Government's Guide to Coroner Services.

Post-mortems

In cases of sudden death a forensic pathologist, who then produces a post-mortem report, usually carries out an examination of the body for the coroner. This contains a description of what was done by the pathologist to establish the cause of death, including the details of any laboratory tests.

The consent of the next of kin is not required for a post-mortem examination to take place, but the next of kin are entitled to have their own doctor present at the examination. They can also ask to have a second post-mortem examination carried out by their own pathologist but are expected to pay for this.

The next of kin must be informed, if they wish to be, of any organs removed from the body. Some relatives may prefer to wait for their return, in order for the whole body to be buried or cremated at once.

Opening and adjourning the inquest

Once the coroner has taken the steps required to identify the deceased and establish a cause of death, s/he is in a position to release the body for burial or cremation. This should, in straightforward cases, be done within a few days of the death, but where there are multiple fatalities, or where DNA testing is required for identification, it may take much longer.

The coroner then prepares to open the first part of the inquest and the next of kin should be advised as to where and when this is to take place. It is not necessary for anyone to attend, but many relatives wish to, because it is feels very much like being involved in the process. Their lawyer, if they have one, may also attend. The procedure, however, only takes a few minutes. The purpose is to enable the coroner to formally record the deceased's identity and to relinquish custody of the body. At this short hearing, the coroner issues an interim death certificate for the purposes of burial or cremation. The inquest is then adjourned, to be re-opened (if at all) very much later, in some cases not just months but even years later, depending on judicial investigations and whether there is a public inquiry or there are any criminal prosecutions.

Communicating with the coroner

When the coroner's investigations are complete, s/he sets a date for the inquest to resume. Only those whose details the coroner has at that time are notified, so it is important to get in touch with the coroner or coroner's officer if you wish to be kept informed. Any 'properly interested person' (see below for the list) can expect to be allowed to ask questions and be represented at the full inquest hearing.

Complex family situations, however, can mean that the next of kin may not pass on information to other family members, in which case any other interested family member should be in touch with the coroner's officer directly. The inquest itself is open to the public so anyone may attend, although only properly interested persons may ask questions during the hearing.

Before the inquest resumes you should receive information from the coroner in the form of a booklet, as well as details of where and when the inquest will take place. Some coroners provide a lot of information, some very little. It is important to form a good relationship with the coroner or the coroner's officer so that you are able to ask questions in advance of the inquest. Coroners vary greatly in their willingness to communicate directly with relatives. The Guide to Coroner Services, however, places much emphasis on the coroner making information readily available to relatives, and should be invoked where the coroner is not keeping to it.

Many, though not all, relatives especially want to know details of how the person died, whether they would have known they were dying, and whether they suffered physical pain. There are many different ways to die in a single incident and the coroner should not assume that relatives do not wish to know exactly what happened to each individual. This information should, of course, be given out sensitively and confidentially.

If such information is made available before the inquest begins, some of the most difficult aspects of the inquest can be avoided. Bereaved relatives will otherwise be in a position whereby the inquest is their first and only opportunity to find out exactly what happened to their loved one, and this can be made even more difficult by the public nature of the inquest.

Relatives who wish to have a copy of the post-mortem and special examination reports before the inquest opens should also communicate this to the coroner's officer. Normally the coroner's office would expect only to have to produce one copy, however, to the next of kin.

The coroner should also be able to provide a list of witnesses and a list of the statements that will be used during the inquest. Whether the relatives, or their lawyers, see the full statements well in advance will depend on the circumstances. The coroner has no legal duty to disclose the full statements.

In the past, relatives have also asked the coroner for information about:

- how long the inquest is likely to last
- whether there will be a private place to meet other relatives or their lawyers during the inquest
- how the inquest will proceed – whether the coroner will take each of the deceased in turn, and, if so, when. This is because

relatives are not always able to take long periods of time off work, or do not live locally, or wish to be present only when the death of their relative is being examined

- whether they will be able to see any documents or photographs before the inquest
- whether other parties will be legally represented. It can be distressing for a relative to arrive at the inquest and realise that every other party has at least one lawyer, yet there is no one representing the bereaved. Please see When Disaster Strikes *Legal Representation after a Disaster* for more information on this.

Attending the inquest

Multiple fatality inquests are held in large buildings so that there is sufficient room for the coroner, jury, lawyers for all the interested persons, and members of the press. Relatives should be prepared for a public, crowded room, but may wish to enquire ahead of the start date whether there will be private places for them to meet, discuss matters with their lawyers – if they are represented – and ask questions of the coroner or his officer.

If information has not been forthcoming before the inquest then this will be the relatives' chance to find out exactly what happened to their loved one. In that case, every effort should be made prior to the inquest to establish whether the coroner will make that information available to the bereaved during the inquest itself (including access to photos and post-mortem reports if that is their wish), preferably outside of the main court room and in private.

When the hearing begins, the coroner, having sworn in the jury, explains that the purpose of the inquest is to establish who each victim was, where and when they died, and how they came by their death. S/he also states that the inquest will not establish any criminal or civil liability or blame any named person or organisation for the death.

At some multiple fatality inquests individual time slots have then been allocated by the coroner to each deceased person, so that relatives can choose to attend only at that time rather than having to sit through details about the deaths of others, if they do not wish to.

The coroner's role, for the main part of the inquest, is to call witnesses and take them in turn through their witness statements. The coroner's duty is to ask all the questions that interested persons would wish to be asked of witnesses. Where – in the relatives' view – the coroner is not asking the questions which are of interest to them (as has happened in the past), it is possible for any properly interested person or their legal representative to question the witness themselves after the coroner has finished.

At some inquests, the coroner may also allow relatives to make victim impact statements, which aim to give the bereaved the opportunity to describe to the court and the public the effect that the death has had on them and their family and friends. Victim impact statements do not always form part of the inquest, but if the opportunity arises the statement should be written in advance. Some or all of the statement may be reported in the media.

The right to question witnesses ('interested persons')

This right, under the Coroners and Justice Act 2009, is given to:

(a) a spouse, civil partner, partner, parent, child, brother, sister, grandparent, grandchild, child of a brother or sister, stepfather, stepmother, half-brother or half-sister
(b) a personal representative of the deceased
(c) a medical examiner exercising functions in relation to the death of the deceased
(d) a beneficiary under a policy of insurance issued on the life of the deceased
(e) the insurer who issued such a policy of insurance
(f) a person who may by any act or omission have caused or contributed to the death of the deceased, or whose employee or agent may have done so
(g) a representative of a trade union of which the deceased was a member at the time of death (in certain cases)
(h) a person appointed by, or representative of, an enforcing authority
(i) a chief constable (in certain cases)
(j) a Provost Marshal (in certain cases)
(k) the Independent Police Complaints Commission (in certain cases)
(l) a person appointed by a Government department to attend an inquest into the death or to assist in, or provide evidence for the purposes of, an investigation into the death under this Part
(m) any other person who the senior coroner thinks has a sufficient interest.

This is something that should be considered well ahead of the inquest, along with legal representation.

Legal representation at the inquest

It is very difficult to feel confident enough to stand up in front of a full courtroom to ask the coroner or a witness a question, especially as the coroner can, under the coroners' rules, reject the question as not relevant to the purpose of the inquest or as breaching the immunity of the witness from self-incrimination. Some coroners have been known to do this less than sensitively. It may therefore be desirable to obtain the help of a specialist legal representative.

Generally, there only needs to be one legal representative, or a team of lawyers, acting for all the bereaved in a mass inquest. Where there is a parallel public inquiry, then the same legal representative(s) could, and should, be retained. Having one representative for all the relatives may not be appropriate in the case of a bereaved person whose deceased family member was, for example, the driver of a train that crashed after the driver was possibly careless in passing a red signal for example. In that case, separate representation must be obtained.

Dealing with the media

Major disaster inquests attract the attention of the media and bereaved relatives are always approached for comments. If you choose to speak to journalists it should be borne in mind that what is said in interviews is heavily edited, sometimes to fit a particular agenda. Some relatives have found it useful in the past to attend the inquest with pre-written statements that can be handed out to the media.

If you choose not to speak to the media you can say so firmly and ask to be left alone. Alternatively, you might wish to enquire about whether you can enter the inquest through a side entrance, for example, without having to pass through the assembled media.

The conclusion

Once all witnesses have been questioned and all the other evidence has been given, the coroner will commonly direct the jury to return a particular conclusion, which must in no way reflect the civil liability of anyone or the criminal liability of any named person. Where there is no jury, the coroner gives his or her own conclusion.

There are many possible conclusions for all types of circumstances (for example neglect or suicide) but in the case of a mass fatality disaster the likely conclusions are:
- accidental death
- unlawful killing (by 'gross negligence' which has been proved beyond reasonable doubt; this conclusion is very rare)
- open conclusion (where the cause of death cannot be established)

- narrative conclusion (a series of specific factual findings which describe how and why the death occurred: this is becoming more common even in cases where the death is not at the hands of state agencies such as the police or prison service).

For many relatives, a conclusion of 'accidental death' appears to exonerate all parties from any responsibility for the deaths, whereas a conclusion of 'unlawful killing' seems to hold that someone was criminally responsible. The conclusion – almost always 'accidental death' (unless a criminal act has taken place, for example, a terrorist incident) – can therefore cause considerable upset and anger.

Challenging a Coroner's decision

Appeal to Chief Coroner

Under the Coroners and Justice Act 2009 section 40, any 'interested person' may in due course be able to appeal most decisions of the coroner, including a decision that they are not an interested person. This provision will replace the former section 13 applications (see below) when and if the Act comes into force fully. It is not known at the time of writing exactly when this will be.

Judicial review

There are many grounds for applying for judicial review. This is concerned with the fairness of the procedure and whether the coroner has properly exercised his/her powers. Some of the grounds upheld in the past have included:

- insufficiency of inquiry
- rejection of relevant evidence
- refusal to allow representatives to make submissions
- pressure on jury to return a particular conclusion.

The application must be made promptly and in any case within three months of the end of the inquest.

Section 13 applications

Section 13 of the Coroners Act 1988 provided that an application can be made to the High Court on the grounds that the coroner either has refused to hold an inquest which ought to be held or, where an inquest has been held, because of irregularity of proceedings or insufficiency of inquiry, or the discovery of new facts or evidence, another inquest should be held. The High Court may order an inquest or another inquest to be held into the deaths. The application can be made at any time, but must be made 'without unnecessary delay'.

Complaints

The Judicial Conduct Investigation Office is responsible for coroners, although the local authority employs them. A complaint to the JCIO may result in the removal of a coroner from his/her office for inability to discharge his/her duty, misbehaviour or neglect of duty.

Scotland and Northern Ireland

In Scotland, where the death is reported to the 'procurator fiscal' (rather than 'coroner') the body is in his or her custody until released. The Lord Advocate then makes a decision whether to hold a 'Fatal Accident Inquiry' (rather than an 'inquest'). Fatal Accident Inquiries are far less common than inquests, but in a multiple fatality disaster it would almost always be 'in the public interest' to hold one. If the death occurs outside Scotland, there is no such inquiry, unless the deceased died on active service abroad.

In Northern Ireland, where the law was updated in 2006, an inquest is held where the coroner deems it necessary to do so. Most of the provisions otherwise are identical to those for England and Wales. There is, however, no provision for an inquest to be held where the death occurred outside Northern Ireland.

LEGAL REPRESENTATION AFTER A DISASTER

The purpose of this leaflet is to take you through what you need to consider in terms of legal advice and representation if you have been affected by a disaster. Our aim is to inform you about the legal process, and what your choices might be in the immediate aftermath and in the longer term. Legal language can be difficult to understand and may at times seem insensitive, but in order to properly explain the various processes, we have used some legal terminology in this leaflet.

Disaster Action cannot give you legal advice, nor recommend any particular firm of solicitors, but can offer our members' experience to assist you in this process.

Please note: the contents of this leaflet apply to England and Wales. Scotland and Northern Ireland operate under a separate (though similar) legal system.

It is important to bear in mind that if the death has occurred abroad and the body is returned to England or Wales, the coroner in whose district the body now lies is legally in charge of the body, until he or she releases it. If the deceased was cremated abroad before being returned, the coroner no longer has any duties or powers to deal with the matter in any way.

Part One: Introduction to the Legal Process

Whether you are a bereaved relative or friend, or a survivor, you are likely to find yourself involved in the legal process at some stage after a disaster. There are a number of very different aspects to this process.

The coroner and the inquest

The role of the coroner

After a person dies, if the death is sudden, the body of that person will be carefully recovered by a team of specialist police officers, and placed in the legal custody of the local coroner. The coroner organises the identification process, the release of the body to the next of kin, and the inquest. A designated police family liaison officer normally liaises between the bereaved and the coroner, but there is nothing to stop you contacting the coroner or his/her officer directly if you wish.

Sometimes the identification of those who have died, and the subsequent release of their body take longer than expected. Although all decisions of a coroner can be judicially reviewed, this process takes time and instructing a solicitor at this point will usually not be useful. You are, however, as a potential bereaved relative, entitled to seek explanations for delays directly from the coroner or his/her officer.

Once you are confirmed as a bereaved relative, you have the right to ask to view the body before it is released to the funeral director. You may also want to know what your legal rights are in terms of objecting to, or requiring, a post-mortem examination.

The inquest

The inquest usually takes place in two parts: a first court hearing which normally takes only a few minutes, which legally enables the coroner to release the body to the next of kin. Once this has taken place, the body of the deceased person is normally released to the chosen funeral director. The inquest is then adjourned, normally for several months, until such date as the coroner has gathered all the information he or she needs to establish the cause of death. It would be unusual for the next of kin to be represented by a lawyer for the first part of the inquest.

You may, however, find that you wish to have representation for the main part of the inquest. You should be informed about when and where the inquest will take place and how long it will last, well in advance by the coroner so you have time to decide what you wish to do. As an 'interested person', you have the right to attend the court hearing and ask witnesses questions yourself. In order to be reasonably prepared, you need to know in advance who the witnesses will be and what they are going to say. It may be that you wish to explore instructing a solicitor for this purpose, but it is crucial to have a solicitor who is experienced in this area. Before instructing a solicitor it would be sensible to contact an organisation such as INQUEST.

Public inquiry

Decision to hold a public inquiry

The aim of a public inquiry is to look into the causes of the disaster, to establish whether any lessons can be learnt and to make recommendations as to what actions may be taken to prevent such a disaster from happening again. It is up to the Secretary of State to decide whether to hold such an inquiry or not. If he or she opts not to have a public inquiry, this decision may be judicially reviewed. This legal process must be set in motion very soon after the decision is announced, and in any case within three months of the decision. It is a very difficult area in which to succeed, and the only type of solicitors usually interested in taking on such cases are 'human rights' law firms. If you feel strongly about a public inquiry, you might wish to make an exploratory phone call to such a firm. However, the costs of judicial review can be prohibitive, and the wrongness of the decision difficult – if not impossible – to prove. Seeking an appointment with the Secretary of State concerned, as a group of relatives or survivors, may be more effective.

Representation at the inquiry

If it is decided that a public inquiry should be held into the disaster, the inquest will be adjourned again, and will very likely never resume, while the inquiry looks into all the facts of how the disaster occurred.

It is common for lawyers to be funded by the government to take part in the public inquiry to represent survivors and the relatives of those who have died. They will often be chosen from the 'lead firm' or 'steering committee' (see below) representing the injured and the bereaved in proceedings for compensation.

It should be possible for relatives and survivors to obtain information in advance from these lawyers about the 'terms of reference' of the inquiry and the process. Once the inquiry begins, the lawyers representing the survivors and bereaved should be able to answer their questions and voice their concerns about any issue arising from the proceedings. There should be opportunities to meet them face-to-face.

Compensation claims

Making a claim

Survivors with physical and/or psychological injuries and bereaved relatives or partners may have a claim for compensation against a defendant company who could be liable for the injuries and deaths. Many bereaved relatives have found in the past that they are reluctant to 'make money from the death', and have mixed feelings about compensation. This is understandable, but it can also be said that the compensation claim from the bereaved is sometimes the only way that the defendant organisation can be seen to be held responsible. This is because in some cases there will not be any criminal, health and safety or any other proceedings against those responsible.

Choosing a solicitor

Some people choose to use their local solicitor, whom they know and trust, to pursue the claim on their behalf. If that is your choice, you must make sure that all the information your solicitor receives from the lead firm or steering committee is forwarded to you promptly.

If you do not have a solicitor in mind, then you should contact the Law Society who will advise you of specialists in the field of personal injury litigation. Your solicitor does not have to be local to you. You would normally only have to see him or her in person once or twice. You should ask the Law Society at the same time whether there is a lead firm or steering group set up for your disaster, as it may be more practical for you to use one of their lawyers rather than instructing a separate firm. Normally a steering group of lawyers is organised where there is to be a public inquiry or a group (or class) action.

Litigation

The compensation process is long and difficult. The levels of compensation are low, and the defendant lawyers will generally try to keep the amounts paid out to an absolute minimum. The defendants will sometimes accept liability for the injuries and deaths, so there will almost never be a civil court case. Most defendant companies have no wish to have the matter scrutinised in public, with all the attendant publicity.

It will then be for your solicitor, who must act according to your instructions, to negotiate a settlement on your behalf. There have been instances where a bereaved person or survivor has been put under enormous pressure to accept a settlement, without which the other claimants cannot recover their own compensation. It is a good idea for survivors or the bereaved to have contact with each other, at this point, away from the lawyers, in order to exchange information about this kind of issue. It may be that each survivor or bereaved relative thinks that they are the only person holding up the process. The defendant's lawyers can also bring pressure to bear by making a 'payment into court', or making an offer to settle which, if not accepted by you, could lead to you being awarded a lower sum by the court, and you then failing to recover some or all of your legal costs and even being ordered to contribute to the defendant's legal costs if the court were to find you have acted unreasonably in rejecting the offer. These tactics can be distressing but are within the rights of the defendant.

Group (or class) actions

How group actions work

If a number of people have been party to the same incident, they can bring a group action for compensation. Large personal injury firms tend to take these on, rather than the smaller firms, because the system for such cases is complex. Each claimant still has an individual solicitor, but all solicitors are answerable to a 'lead solicitor' who is responsible for making the decisions on the direction the case should take. You may find that this happens automatically in your case. You should find out from the beginning whether this is the way solicitors are conducting the compensation process, so that you can choose whether to be part of the group action or not and that you are aware of the rules if you do.

Advantages and disadvantages

There are advantages and disadvantages to this way of pursuing a compensation claim: the advantages are that you do not have to take on all the financial risks and burdens associated with litigation yourself, and that all the issues about whether the defendant is responsible are resolved together. The amount of compensation payable to each claimant remains an individual calculation, however.

The main disadvantage is that all members of the group have to wait until the group action has been brought to an end before they receive their compensation. It is not unusual that pressure is brought to bear on any member of the group who is not prepared to agree to a settlement, for whatever reason. If you prefer to take individual instead of group action, you can – but if there is already a group action in your disaster, you can only proceed if the court agrees you are able to fund your case.

Criminal Injuries Compensation Scheme

This provides for victims of violent crime to receive some compensation for their injuries, physical or psychological, or, in the case of the bereaved, the death of their loved one. The scheme is supposed to be simple enough to use without the help of a solicitor, but in many cases it might be advisable to seek advice regardless. The success of the claim will often depend on the quality of the medical evidence provided, and a good personal injury solicitor will know how to obtain an appropriately drafted medical report. In the case of a high profile terrorism case for example, such advice may be offered to the survivors and bereaved free of charge.

Due to the fact that this scheme is publicly-funded and open to all victims of violent crime, the levels of compensation for serious injuries and death tend to be lower than the sums awarded by the courts in civil litigation, and are based on a rigid tariff system. The maximum that can be awarded in regard to any individual claim is currently £500,000 and claims must normally be started within two years of the incident that caused injury or death.

Criminal prosecution

As a victim of crime you are not a party to criminal proceedings, only a potential 'witness'. You are therefore not entitled to legal representation. You are entitled to receive information about the process from Victim Support, however.

Legal proceedings overseas

There are likely to be additional complexities in the event of an overseas disaster such as unfamiliar language, culture and faith. It will be important to obtain the services of a firm of solicitors familiar with overseas disasters affecting UK nationals, who will work with legal representatives and authorities abroad. However, it is worth trying to find out at an early stage whether there are any organisations working with people in your position in the country concerned.

Group actions such as those outlined above may also apply in the case of an overseas disaster. Members of Disaster Action may have had experience similar to yours and may be willing to assist you as an individual, without sharing any confidential information about you with others in DA. Do bear in mind that such assistance does not constitute legal advice, but may help you through the process.

Depending on where the disaster happened, it may be very difficult to obtain compensation from those responsible. Criminal injuries compensation is now available from the UK scheme to those affected by an overseas terrorist incident.

The Law Society website has lists of lawyers specialising in personal injury and other types of litigation in most countries of the world.

Part Two: Instructing a Solicitor

When to instruct

In most disasters, the injured who have been identified by the authorities, and the next of kin of those who have died, are contacted shortly after the initial adjournment of the inquest, often by the defendant company. It may be at this stage that a solicitor is instructed. If not, you may instruct a solicitor at any point, and you may also change solicitors if you are not happy with the service provided by the firm you have instructed.

Whom to instruct

Generally, it is probably better to instruct a solicitor who specialises in personal injury litigation and, if there is a steering group, a member of that group. There are specialist law firms in London and other large cities that are well known for their participation in past disasters. Some of them specialise in claimant litigation, but many also work for insurance companies on behalf of their corporate clients. Lists of personal injury solicitors are available from the Law Society.

Personal injury lawyers also generally take on representation at the inquest, although other types of firms specialise in high profile inquests too. The Law Society does not recommend particular firms, however, so you have to make your decision based on reputation or word of mouth. Most firms have their own websites, and they will generally advertise the fact that they have been involved in high profile disasters in the past.

How much will it cost?

Whether legal aid is available, or whether you can instruct a solicitor on a 'no win no fee' basis, depends on the type of legal action in which you are involved. Free legal advice is also available, particularly if you are willing to form a group, from Lawworks for Community Groups.

The inquest

For the inquest, the following applies: generally legal aid (means tested) is available for advice in preparation for the inquest, but not for representation at the inquest hearing, unless it is an 'exceptional case' (which includes the necessity of representation in the wider public interest). If the person who died had a dependant aged under 18, funding for legal representation may also be available to that minor.

In some cases where there is going to be a claim for compensation, and some of the evidence at the inquest is relevant to that, the costs of representation or other attendance by your lawyers at the inquest can be included in the civil compensation claim. This is not unusual in a high profile disaster case. Finally, the organisation INQUEST (see below) can also sometimes help in finding lawyers who are prepared to work for nothing ('pro bono').

The compensation claim

Public funding is no longer available for claimants seeking compensation for injury or death, unless caused by medical negligence. Most solicitors, however, offer free initial advice sessions in which other methods of funding can be explored. A solicitor who is a personal injury specialist will be best qualified to suggest the most appropriate method of funding the claim.

You may have help paying for your solicitor through your trade union if you are an employee injured at work or if you are claiming as a relative of the deceased, who was an employee and died at work or in a situation connected with his or her work. Some household and motor insurance policies contain legal expenses insurance for bringing personal injury claims, and some credit card purchases can also have legal expenses insurance included in the transaction.

Most personal injury actions are now paid for on a 'no win no fee' basis. This is a complicated system based on a simple idea: if you win your case, the losing party will pay your legal costs. If you lose your case, you do not have to pay your legal costs. To protect you from having to pay the winner's costs if you lose, you are normally required to pay a one-off 'after-the-event insurance' premium (you usually get this back if you win). This is the one payment you may have to make at the beginning, although many insurers do not actually seek immediate payment of this premium.

A group action is funded in the same ways, including private funding, legal aid, individual conditional fee agreements and legal expenses insurance.

What to expect

Once instructed, your solicitor must explain the processes to you, and answer any questions you have about your case in good time. You are entitled to see most of the papers and reports pertaining to your case.

Your lawyer must also always follow your instructions on any decision to be made about the conduct of your case, provided the instruction you give is one which your solicitor can lawfully and ethically carry out. Relatives and survivors in past disasters have found it very useful to make contact with each other to discuss common aspects of their cases, however, including what information is being given out to individuals by their lawyers.

Lawyers are on the whole sympathetic to their clients, but it is their role to view your claim in terms of its financial aspects rather than the human cost to you of having been involved in the disaster. Unfortunately this 'human' cost is not something that has monetary value in our legal system, and it is our experience that the most painful aspects of injury or bereavement are not recognised by the law.

SETTING UP FAMILY AND SURVIVOR SUPPORT GROUPS

The aim of this leaflet is to help those setting up their own support groups after a disaster by sharing the lessons from our common experiences.

What is a disaster family and/or survivor support group?
A family and/or survivor support group is a group of people affected by the same disaster who support each other by sharing information, giving each other emotional and practical support and/or by focusing on issues important to them. The group can include bereaved family members, survivors and their families and others affected by the disaster. Depending on the circumstances of the disaster and the needs of the members, any group that emerges may be large or small, or divided into smaller sub-groups.

Why do you need a group?
People affected by a disaster often feel that the lasting effects of what has happened to them can only be fully understood by those who share experience of the same event.

Following any disaster, whatever its cause, there are likely to be practical problems to overcome. Any inquest and/or criminal inquiry process can be easier to cope with if you have the support and understanding of others affected. The process of seeking help from government services, voluntary agencies, the legal profession or insurance companies can also seem fraught with difficulty. Support groups, in which you can offer each other advice and suggestions about how to deal with specific issues, can be very helpful. A group can also be a forum for sharing information about matters of importance to everyone.

How do groups help?

The extracts below are personal views based on the experiences of individuals who have been affected by different disasters.

'You do have a common grief, therefore you feel no need to explain your pain or suffering, it is almost like having a shorthand in conversation and feelings.'

'As a group, we were heard by the government on issues such as memorial services. If we didn't have a group, decisions would have been made for us.'

'For some who grieve, to be involved in something positive, to have an agenda to follow (for example a memorial, or an intention never to let this happen again) helps, especially I think for men.'

'People bereaved by a horrific disaster – or afflicted by the shock of having survived one – are consumed by a mixture of grief and anger. These emotions are inescapable but quickly become destructive. The only remedy is to channel them into a constructive activity such as a support group.'

The Practicalities

First steps

If you are interested in setting up a family and/or survivor support group but don't know how to get in touch with others affected by the disaster, the responding police service(s) may be able to help. Central government guidance for emergency planners and others responding to the needs of people affected by disasters includes some information on assistance for families and survivors.

Depending on the nature of the disaster and where it happened, the Foreign & Commonwealth Office, and/or the police or relevant local authority may also be able to help. They cannot release contact details of people affected, for reasons of confidentiality. However, they should be able to contact everyone on their list with your request. Or they may help set up an initial meeting for survivors and bereaved families who may wish to attend, as has been done after some other disasters.

What next?

The initial meeting will be an opportunity for you to meet people affected by the same disaster and to find out whether they may want to be part of a group. Getting together for the first time may be a stressful and emotional occasion, but for many people the benefits of contact with others experiencing similar emotions and challenges will be worth it.

Our experience shows that the most harmonious groups are those that establish a clear purpose and aims. These may be very clear from the outset for some groups and for others it may take longer for these to emerge from discussion at meetings and informal get-togethers. Such aims may be to offer each other mutual emotional and practical support, to provide representation with external agencies, to share common experience and information, to campaign on issues specific to the disaster or to organise memorials. It may be helpful to set out a clear statement of aims and objectives for the group. (With the passage of time there is no reason why the focus cannot be changed, if that is what the group wishes.)

How should the group be structured?

There are a number of different options for the structure of family and survivor groups in terms of membership, legal status and manage-ment. Some groups have set up an unincorporated association, while others have decided to be as informal as possible. A few have chosen to apply for charitable status. You may find that legal advice on these options is helpful, particularly in circumstances where the group is given external funding. The important thing is for the status of the group to fit its nature and purpose. If you do seek legal advice, you can find contact numbers for solicitors who specialise in the charity field through the Law Society.

Whatever the nature of the group, committee members will need to be chosen and decisions taken about who will carry out key roles such as arranging meetings, taking notes and looking after the accounts. It may take some time for individuals to feel that they can take on these tasks and there should be no pressure to do so before people are ready. Some groups have found it helpful to rotate these roles so that people do not have a constant time-consuming commitment.

Group meetings (frequent or occasional, depending on the needs and wishes of the group) can then be organised by the committee. The group may choose to distribute a newsletter, occasionally or regu-larly and/or to set up a website. Some groups have found it helpful to set up smaller, regional subgroups where people can get to know each other better and focus on the issues they have most in common. Good communication channels between members are important and telephone-based meetings or email forums may make this possible if members live far apart or do not wish to attend all meetings.

Whatever option you choose for how the group is set up, advice and support is available from those who have done this before, and from other organisations.

Setting up and running an e-forum discussion group

Given that those affected by a disaster often live all round the UK and overseas, increasingly the opportunity (even necessity) to be in contact using online methods is important. Disaster Action's second leaflet on groups gives guidance and information on options on this area. See *Setting up and Running an E-forum Discussion Group*.

How will the group be funded?

Once the aims and objectives of the group are agreed, the group will be in a position to look for funding to cover its expenses. Funding may or may not be available through any disaster trust fund set up in the aftermath, or from other sources such as charitable trust funds, voluntary agencies or government departments.

How long should the group last?

In our experience all groups are different and differing views may emerge on how long individuals wish to remain part of a group. Some groups continue for many years, while others disband after they fulfil a specific purpose. A group should not be judged as a 'success' or a 'failure' because of how long it lasts. Many of us have made friends within our own groups and these friendships have lasted well beyond the formal life of the group.

What can the Pitfalls be and how can they be Avoided?

Differences within the group

Individuals will respond to a disaster in different ways and have both common and unique needs. While the group will need to have a core set of agreed aims, there are still likely to be different priorities for individuals at different times. Recognising and accepting these differences, rather than seeing them as a problem, may help the group evolve over time and focus when appropriate on the need for a common group response to key issues and concerns.

Differences between family members such as parents, partners and siblings of those who have died in the disaster are, unfortunately, not uncommon in our experience. These differences may spill over into the group.

If the group elects one or more individuals to act on behalf of the group, or to make statements on the group's behalf, it is important to ensure that any messages conveyed to those outside the group – such as the media or government departments – reflect the overall interests of the wider group. Contact with the media can be difficult and it may be that they refer to members as 'spokespeople' when in fact they are commenting on their own behalf.

Will you be able to cope with working for the group?

A potential difficulty for those who take on more responsibility in the group is that the workload is tiring and a source of additional stress, given that the aftermath of any disaster is bound to be hard. You may be struggling to cope with day-to-day commitments in addition to the needs of the group. One possible way of dealing with this is to accept offers of help from friends and relatives. You may be able to get their assistance in the more practical aspects of running the group. Another way is as suggested above, to rotate roles within the committee.

SETTING UP AND RUNNING AN E-FORUM DISCUSSION GROUP

This leaflet offers guidance to those directly affected by a disaster on how to set up a secure discussion forum. It is not intended to be a comprehensive guide to the subject, but the links below offer further useful information. Increasingly, those affected by the same or a similar disaster but scattered around the country wish to find ways to be in touch with each other.

How to start

Getting started is one of the biggest hurdles, but there are plenty of people out there who have already done this and can offer help and advice. Setting up and running a successful forum requires time and patience, particularly in becoming familiar with the management aspects, so be prepared to put in several hours of work to preparing your forum.

Before you dive in

The first step is to check whether or not a forum along the lines you have planned already exists. If it does, you may end up splitting the audience and so weakening both forums. Consider instead becoming a regular contributor and then moderator to the existing forum. Then, as and when the opportunity arises, launch your own more specialist forum.

Creating your forum

Having decided to start an online forum you now need to work out how to 'deliver' it. This usually comes down either to having someone provide you with a 'ready to go' forum service – a hosted service – or opting for the DIY approach, which involves providing the web site and forum system yourself.

If you are setting up your first forum, the hosted service is where you should start. DIY hosted forums are really for those who want the highest level of control over the look, feel and operation of the forum as well as its branding. With a hosted forum, these aspects are set already and so you can concentrate on the actual business of the forum itself.

Yahoo! offers one of the most widely used hosted forum services, through its 'Yahoo! Groups'. Google and MSN also offer their own hosted forums or groups and all are free, easy to set up and to use. In almost all cases you and your contributors will need an 'ID' or email account associated with the provider, which again are free.

Setting up a forum or 'group'

Creating a hosted forum or 'group' is a straightforward process and the following points describe the basic steps using the Yahoo! Groups service. (Please note that plenty of guidance is available at each stage.)

Go to http://groups.yahoo.com.

Click the 'Start your group' today link.

Sign-in using your Yahoo! ID (or create your own Yahoo! ID if you haven't already got one).

Find, either by browsing or searching, a suitable category that best describes your group.

Click the 'Place my group here' button – this categorises your group.

Next, choose a name for your group, a group email address and then provide a short description of its purpose.

Click 'Continue' to move to the next step. Don't be surprised if you are returned to this page and advised that the email address or Group name is already in use. Keep choosing names and addresses until you find one that works for you.

Finally, confirm your Yahoo! Profile (used when other members of the group want to learn more about you), enter the security code and finally click 'Continue'.

That's it! Your group has been created and you are given its web and email addresses to advertise.

Although you now have an online forum to use, there still are a few important tasks to do.

Customising the Group

Once you have created your group you will be given the option of customising it, including setting the joining and posting rules, which are matters that should be given very careful consideration.

The first thing you need to do is to decide how people join the group. For a Yahoo! Group you have a choice:

1. Anyone can join (initial setting); or
2. People can join only with your approval.

If your forum is discussing sensitive and personal matters, which a forum for survivors and bereaved from disasters may well be, you should go for option 2 and be sure to vet (via a separate email or phone conversation) the individuals who request to join. The onus will be on you as the 'owner' to ensure that those who join are suitable – other participants will be relying on you to protect their conversations.

Next you need to decide who can post messages to your group:

1. Only group members – making it a private discussion group (the initial setting).
2. Anyone – making it an open discussion group.
3. Only you – making it a newsletter.

The initial setting is recommended as this ensures that group members can discuss matters whilst knowing those who are 'listening'.

As the group owner, you can change these options at any time, but do make sure you think things through beforehand and discuss any prospective changes with others.

The finishing touches

There are numerous ways to customise the look, feel and operation of your group. Take your time to look through and consider what is available and whether or not it will improve your forum. For example, when someone new joins, you can have the system send them a Welcome message that may contain some background to the group, who it comprises and any instructions for posting, etc. Doing this helps to answer common queries about the group (so you don't have to answer them) and makes your new member feel welcome.

Be sure also to spend plenty of time getting used to the forum system, how it operates, and the management of posts and members. Ask a few friends to join the group, add posts, etc. and come to you with any queries they might have. This will help you become more familiar with the day-to-day management tasks.

Before you launch your Forum

Before you launch your forum, be sure to delete any of your test messages and posts – these look untidy and may confuse new members. You should also have a few core people join the forum and start several discussions off so that when potential members visit they can see there is some activity and so will be more inclined to join in.

Launching your Forum

There are many factors that go into making a forum successful. It is vital that you have enough visitors and posts to sustain existing discussions and start new ones. Therefore make sure you advertise your forum at every opportunity and ensure that members do likewise. You may be able to advertise the existence of the forum to others affected by a specific disaster, for example, through the police family liaison officer service. If activity on the forum is tailing off, it is up to you to step in and add a few posts and send an email to existing and potential members reminding them of the forum and its purpose and perhaps outlining some of its recent activity.

Launching a forum is much like getting a spinning top going – it requires a lot of initial effort but once it is going, a gentle push now and again is all that is needed to keep it on track.

Forum Rules

Setting out some basic rules of behaviour is essential for any forum, as is the enforcement of these rules. Your rules should be clear and prominent on your website, but can be kept very simple. For example, here are the rules from Just Chat:

We do not permit:

- Sexual or offensive language or content
- Harassment of other users
- Abuse or disruption of our services
- The impersonation of Just Chat staff
- Advertising of third party services or websites, unless authorised by us in advance and in writing.

Legal aspects

The legal aspects of running a forum are straightforward, the only important issues being copyright and privacy.

- Copyright: the copyright in any user's contribution remains with the user

- Privacy: you must ensure that personal information provided by users on registration is secure. If you are using a hosted forum, this will always be the case.

Moderation

Who or what is a 'Moderator'?

An online forum is a powerful tool for allowing people from geographically different places to contribute easily to a discussion. However, like any form of discussion or debate, it is vital that it stays on the topic being discussed, and that people follow the forum rules and behave in an appropriate manner. To ensure this is the case a forum can have one or more moderators.

Unlike the owner of a forum, who is responsible for its operation, a moderator performs a similar role to that of the chairperson and is essential to the success of any forum. He or she is responsible for ensuring that the discussion remains on topic and that everyone has the chance to voice their opinions. They are also responsible for ensuring that contributors behave themselves and in extreme situations may remove people from the forum or have their comments amended or removed. Finally, a moderator should take the time to make new contributors welcome and act where necessary to promote discussion and keep the forum active.

Being a moderator is not an easy job – it requires tact and patience as well as the ability to anticipate problems and deal with them before they arise. A moderator also receives little or no reward for their work, yet there is a great deal of satisfaction to be had in helping start, grow and steer an online community of people with a related interest.

Challenges for the moderator

Online forums also introduce a number of challenges for moderators. With some forum systems, moderators must approve each and every item that is posted. This is fine if you have a small community of people in the same time zone, but if your forums are drawing together people from all over the world or you get a particularly 'hot topic', it may become difficult to keep an eye on all of the activity that is going on. As a result either something may slip through or the forum cannot be sustained.

It is therefore important that as a forum grows, so too does the number of people who are available to moderate it. Recruitment of moderators can be a difficult task, although often the forum itself can offer individuals who already have experience of the topic and the tact and skill needed to share the load.

Forum 'Jargon'

This is a small selection of terms or jargon that you will come across when working with or contributing to online forums:

Blog The online diary of an individual or group in which postings are categorised and can be commented on by readers.

Flame The act of posting a hostile comment towards an individual or group and usually the result of frustration.

IP A forum system may keep a record of the IP address or 'telephone number' of the computer that was used to make a post. This is usually used where forums permit anonymous posts, but you need to ensure any posts found to have legal or criminal implications can be traced back to the originator if required.

Link A connection within a posting to another topic or word, picture, page elsewhere on the Web. Some forum systems prevent linking from within postings.

Newbie An individual who is new to a forum and so is unfamiliar with either its etiquette or the act of posting contributions.

Post A single contribution made by an individual to a topic in a forum.

Thread A 'topic' of discussion to which individuals post contributions and replies. As time goes on, the thread may create other topics or come to an end.

Useful Links

Community Spark – This web site offers a wealth of tips and advice for building successful online communities and is worth spending plenty of time reading.
http://www.communityspark.com/

Hosted Groups – The following are a selection of the most popular online-hosted forum providers. These are not recommendations and each will typically require contributors to have an email account with the provider, but they all offer high quality services that will meet most needs at little or no cost:

Google Groups – http://groups.google.com

Yahoo! Groups – http://groups.yahoo.com

MSN Groups – http://groups.msn.com

ManagingCommunities.com – A website written by Patrick O'Keefe who has been managing online communities since 2000. There are a number of useful articles and links on the site including a link to an online forum dedicated to those tasked with managing online communities.

http://www.managingcommunities.com

http://www.communityadmins.com

Security

As noted previously, the subject matter of some forums may be very personal and not to be shared with those outside of the group. Therefore the security of the forum and its information it contains is vital.

In setting up an online forum using Yahoo! Groups there are various security options. Firstly, all potential contributors need to have a Yahoo! ID, which is required whenever you want to join or post anything to a forum. Next, membership of the forum can be controlled so that only known and vetted individuals may join. Finally, contributing and access to the content of the forum can be limited to its members only.

Providing that IDs are kept private and that members are properly identified and known, then the security of the forum can be maintained. However, such stringent security may also put people off and makes it difficult to show potential members how the forum might help them.

It may therefore be worth considering having a 'public' and a 'private' forum with different security requirements. In doing so though, bear in mind that you may need to balance the needs of both and that it will add to the time needed for managing the forums.

INTERVIEWS ABOUT DISASTER EXPERIENCE: PERSONAL REFLECTIONS AND GUIDELINES FOR INTERVIEWERS

These notes are based on the personal views and experience of Disaster Action members concerning being approached and interviewed about disasters. They are relevant for journalists, researchers including university students, and for those from organisations reviewing services or protocols for survivors and bereaved. We appreciate that many requests for interviews are based on a desire to understand the first-hand experience of a disaster from the perspective of survivors and the bereaved.

The reflections in Part One give an insight into what it feels like to be contacted and interviewed. Part Two provides practical guidelines for those undertaking research for academic, policy-based and/or media presentations that draw on the experiences of those directly affected by disasters.

Part One: Personal Reflections on Being Interviewed

On Being Interviewed: Pros

- It was nice to feel I could **make a difference** by helping to learn lessons. I tell myself this is one way to try to reduce some of my guilt at surviving
- By listening to my story I felt someone was at least **acknowledging** the importance of my brother's life and death
- It's good to have the **chance to talk** about what happened. Feeling valued by people who wish to hear your story and who are willing to listen can be helpful
- We really wanted the **system changed** so that others could benefit from our experience
- We wanted people to know the **truth** about what had happened.

On Being Interviewed: Cons

- Having **no control** over how what I say will be interpreted or used can be a big drawback. This matters because what may be mere detail to a researcher is part of a sensitive, significant and emotionally loaded account for me
- I have been upset on occasions when journalists **rewrite my words** for their own agenda or put words in my mouth/make up quotes. Sometimes they do this without asking and so it is no longer my experience. I feel used. Even the best journalists can misquote you. I am also taken back to what it was like not to be in control in the disaster
- Some researchers do not seem to understand the difference between **anonymity and confidentiality**. With the media I have learnt that there is almost no such thing as confidentiality – nothing is ever 'off the record'
- Some researchers do not understand the meaning of **'representativeness'** in relation to their research. They might draw on the personal experiences of one or two interviewees and use these to make general statements about everyone affected. It is annoying to find that my personal experiences/ views have been turned into a statement relating to others, as I know that even in one disaster everyone involved will have experiences and feelings unique to them. So I am always wary

about papers or articles that make generalised claims about 'the bereaved' or 'the survivors'

- **Structured questionnaires** are not necessarily appropriate for finding out detailed experiences, feelings and emotions. They can feel anonymous and filling them in on your own can make you feel vulnerable. The researcher wants the ease and speed of quantifying measurable data, but for me as the one being researched, experience and emotion may not fit into these neat boxes. My experiences and feelings to this day cannot be 'tick-boxed' and controlled in this way

- Some researchers assume that because the disaster was some time ago you must be **'over'** it. They may also assume that because you seem less raw in the way you present yourself you will not be affected by 'opening the box'

- Some are not interested in seeing me as more than **just a 'victim'** and don't want to hear about positive recovery. Or sometimes it is the other way round – they only want to hear an 'inspirational story'. The bad researcher/journalist has already written the story before they meet you. The good one wants to reflect what is really there. So how far should questions be determined in advance? An open agenda is more likely to allow a real picture to emerge

- Researchers/journalists normally wish **to use my experience for their own ends** – whether in pursuit of a personal qualification or an article. While this is understandable, it can be annoying when they suggest that I should feel grateful for the chance to donate my time, emotion and experiences without any acknowledgement of the costs (emotional and financial) to me

- There is **no guarantee** that the interview will be used – you could be the lead story at 12 noon and at 12.30 not covered due to other news

- Don't release pictures or give comments **unless you are really sure** about them.

Part Two: Guidelines for Interviewers

Being interviewed can be a positive, negative or mixed experience for those being asked the questions. The following tips are for those conducting research and/or media interviews. The purpose is to better inform interviewers in the hope of minimising the risk of interviewees feeling unprepared, exploited or abused.

Preparation

- Approach potential interviewees with **care and respect**. If contacting them by telephone ask if the timing of the call is convenient and offer to call back later if appropriate. Be clear in explaining who you are, why you are contacting them and how you got their contact details. Be sure that you have permission to proceed with the call and if the answer is negative, please respect that

- Remember that **recounting particular experiences** of disaster can be painful. Do not assume that the passing of time or the fact that an individual has spoken before to an interviewer means that it is necessarily easier or that they will be prepared to discuss some issues again

- In preparing for contact, ensure you have done **preliminary, advance research** into key facts and details about an event. Research these as fully as you can and remember that any account may not always be objective or accurate. If unsure about details, ask. Remember that it is important to **get details correct,** such as facts about numbers and the spellings of names of people who died or were injured. Check the **Internet** for what has already been written or said because interviewees will expect you to know

- An interviewer should have **good listening skills** and be prepared to spend time listening as part of this kind of interview. Allow for this in planning the timing of meetings. Listening is a mark of respect and courtesy, even if the detail is beyond the primary remit and purpose of your interview

- If conducting a research project, consider the **choice of your research methods** carefully. As well as considering what is easiest and most appropriate for *you* as a researcher, consider the advantages and disadvantages for your interviewees in terms of what might feel more appropriate or user-friendly for them. Be prepared to explain and justify your methods to research participants

- If conducting an interview for a newspaper or magazine, take time to explain the **nature, readership and style** of the publication to a potential interviewee and where your article will appear. If possible, send them a copy in advance so they may be aware of the typical style and content

- Consider with care the **number and choice of questions** to be asked. Have a reason for asking particular questions and remember that a lengthy list of questions may have disadvantages. Be particularly mindful of **intrusive questions** and be honest with yourself and the interviewee about why such questions are important and how answers will be used

- The **choice of location** for an interview is important. Interviewees may feel more comfortable in places that are familiar (e.g. they may prefer for an interview to be conducted at or away from home), and may prefer either a more private or public location. Noisy public places will make tape-recording (if appropriate) harder. **Telephone interviews** have advantages and disadvantages in relation to meeting face-to-face; you may find it helpful to discuss these with potential interviewees.
- Are you prepared to let the interviewee have sight of a **draft paper/report or transcript** of your interview? Whether or not this is so, let them know in advance of the interview
- Be clear and transparent about any **payment available** for interviewees, including, for example, travel and accommodation costs. Be clear about any **terms or conditions** relating to the use of personal photographs or other material owned or loaned by an interviewee
- Be prepared for **potentially powerful emotion**, such as tears, anger and frustration.

Conducting Interviews
- Expect interviews to **take time**. As stated above, people may wish to talk about their experiences and issues beyond your agenda and questions. This may be important for the interviewee, so do not miscalculate the time needed or rush the conversation
- Never use **a tape-recorder or other recording material** without advance permission
- Take time at the start of an interview to remind the interviewee about the **aims of the research and use of interview material**. Interviews tend to go better if both parties feel prepared and relaxed
- State again at the start the parameters around **anonymity and confidentiality** (see Disaster Action's leaflet: 'Working with Disaster Survivors and the Bereaved: Code of Practice on Privacy, Anonymity and Confidentiality')
- At the end of an interview **check key points and summarise** what has been covered. Ask if the interviewee feels OK and,

perhaps, what it felt like to be interviewed). Let them know **how/when they may have access** to interview transcripts or the final article/paper produced and inform them of any deadlines/key dates for this. If you make any promises in this regard, keep them

- Some family members may be around, but will **not wish to contribute** – this should be respected
- Explain that there are **no guarantees** that the interview will be used
- Ensure that you **thank** the interviewees for their time.

Use of material

'Material' here includes observational accounts, transcripts and quotes as well as images, headings and captions accompanying articles and/or the presentation of research material. Be clear about any terms or conditions relating to the use of personal material owned or loaned by an interviewee.

- The use of insensitive material such as **photos relating to and/or depicting an event** may be distressing and offensive either to interviewees and/or others affected by that event. While editors/research supervisors may have the final say over the use of content, headings and/or images used to accompany an article, interviewers have a moral responsibility to liaise between interviewees and editors/supervisors about the use and appropriateness of selected material
- Photographs and other **personal mementoes** associated with individuals involved in a disaster are likely to have a **special significance** for their owners and should always be handled with care and respect. If borrowed and taken away they should be returned quickly and with care. Under no circumstances should irreplaceable items be passed to third parties with the danger of their being lost or misplaced. Remember that in such circumstances an apology is never enough.

THE RETURN OF PERSONAL PROPERTY

The purpose of this guide is to take you through what may happen to the personal property that someone killed or injured in the disaster may have had with them. While there will normally be a system for dealing with personal property after a disaster, there is potential for misunderstanding, confusion and additional upset. Make sure your wishes are known, understood and recorded. As time goes by, you may have to check on the current status of the policy concerning personal property in your case.

Those responding to a disaster may make judgements about what property they believe has significance to families and survivors. Our purpose is to assist you in making whatever choices are *possible* about what is important to *you* in terms of recovery of personal property. Some of the language used by officials to describe items that may be precious to you can seem impersonal and insensitive; in order to explain the process, we have used some of these terms within this guide.

This process may seem like a further invasion of you and your family's privacy at a very difficult time, but from our experience, the return of personal property is very significant to those affected.

Part One: Introduction

What happens to property after a disaster?
After a disaster many items of personal property may have become separated from their owners or found at or near to the site. Other items will be found on or with those who have died. Items recovered may belong to people who have been killed, to survivors or to companies and corporations. Such property may be referred to as 'belongings' or 'personal effects' and it can include a huge variety of items that have been caught up in the disaster.

Initially the police will aim to gather these items as part of their search and carefully store them. Other organisations and agencies, such as funeral directors, may also have a role in handling the items found. All property should be kept secure and in conditions that prevent any deterioration of its condition.

The role of personal property
Property may be needed as evidence in investigations by different agencies. It may become what is referred to as 'exhibits' and required in any future court cases. Such cases may take some time to complete. Property can assist in establishing the identities of those involved in the disaster if there is difficulty in identifying them by other means. Unfortunately, you may therefore have to wait for some time before property is returned, but you are entitled to know how long you should expect to wait, and why.

Access to property
The careful recovery and storage of personal property is unlikely to be the initial priority for the emergency services, as their first priority

will be to save life and then to recover the dead. If you have chosen to visit the disaster site, you will not normally be permitted to collect any of this property from there yourself. (The only circumstance where you may not be able to visit the site at this time is where safety may be an issue.) As the site is potentially a crime scene, the police and others investigating will want to ensure that nothing is done that may have an impact on the investigation and its outcome.

You should also be aware that property may become available at different stages in the weeks, months and even years after a disaster. Throughout this time a police family liaison officer may be your contact, but others such as funeral directors may also have a role to play.

In some circumstances there may be public health reasons that mean items of property cannot be returned and for safety reasons these will need to be securely destroyed. You are entitled to information as to why this decision has been taken, which should only be as a last resort. Decisions may also be taken – on the basis of the scale of the disaster or the level of damage to the property – to dispose of items rather than to seek to identify and return them all.

The role of family liaison officers

You may have had support from a police family liaison officer and others after the disaster. Information about property should be given to you by your family liaison officer, and ideally they will also carry the process through to discussing your options relating to property and returning it according to your wishes. If the property is retained and then returned to you some time after the disaster, other police officers may take on this responsibility.

Choosing whether to retrieve the property

Choosing whether to retrieve the property is an individual decision. You may feel that to do so would only distress you further, or you may feel that however difficult the process, you wish to go through it. Property may be very badly damaged, burned or contaminated and the first instinct of the police and others may be to protect you, and in so doing they may try to make decisions for you. This is OK if it feels right, but you can choose whether or not to take decisions yourself. Not everyone may understand your need to see the items and have them back, but what may seem morbid or unacceptable to those not directly affected can be a natural thing to do. If you are unsure about receiving items of property you can look at photographs first. You may want to make these choices with the assistance of friends, family, the police or an experienced counsellor.

If you don't feel able to deal with the return of property right away, you have the right to delay any decision making until you are able to. You should ask how long the property is being retained for and how/when you may revisit this decision.

If you are a survivor of a disaster you may feel that the property you have lost does not need to be returned or is a difficult reminder of your experiences. If, however, you would prefer to have property returned to you, you should make this known to the authorities, though it may be that you will not be able to exercise this choice.

Part Two: Returning the Property

Who will the property be returned to?

The authorities will usually only be able to release items of property to the next of kin. This may add extra time to the process, as the agencies involved will wish to minimise the possibility of making a mistake.

Identification of property

In order to establish who it belongs to, property may need to be sorted, photographed and recorded. It is reasonable to ask about this and how any information or photographs will be used.

You may also be asked for information that can help with this process, including:

- Descriptions of any property lost
- Clear, recent photographs of the property if possible
- Details of items that family and friends may have had with them.

Throughout the process you have the legally protected right to expect that information about you and your family members is kept secure and confidential.

There may be circumstances in which it is necessary to clean or launder items in order to identify them (see paragraph below on **Cleaning, laundering and repairs** for more on this).

Generally, property can be divided into categories defined technically as 'associated' and 'unassociated'.

Associated items such as passports, bank cards, cheque books and other documents may have a very clear name on them, although the agencies will still need to ensure that they have the right owner. There may also be identifiable items such as some jewellery, images within a photograph or video recording and data within a mobile phone or laptop memory. These items may be returned much earlier than unassociated items if the investigation allows.

Unassociated items tend to be much harder to place with an individual and may include items such as suitcases, clothing, toys, books, paperwork, etc. There may also be items that do not belong to an individual, such as a company's cargo.

In both cases identifying the property may need to wait while other investigations such as inquests, health and safety inquiries, civil prosecutions and criminal trials are undertaken.

The unassociated property process
The agencies involved will then try to match the unassociated property with an owner. Whether and how this process is carried out will depend on factors such as the amount of property recovered and its condition. This process should be explained to you and you should feel free to ask any questions you wish about what is happening. You should be given the option to opt-in to any unassociated property process by giving your written consent.

A catalogue of photographs may be shown to those who have agreed to participate in order to make claims on property. Although this process should be carried out sensitively, it is still likely to be stressful. If you choose to do this, you may consider involving other family members, an experienced counsellor, or police officer. The catalogue will not usually include bank notes and coins, as these are dealt with separately. Whoever is guiding you through the process should be able to advise you on how this has been done. The police or other agencies involved may ask for assistance from external companies who specialise in this work, but you have the right to be informed of the way in which this process will be conducted.

Personal property overseas
Where a disaster affects victims from more than one country, investigative procedures involving agencies such as embassies, consular departments and the Foreign & Commonwealth Office can be complicated by differing international systems. The return of personal property may be handled very differently in other countries and there may also be logistical reasons why this is more difficult than after a disaster in the UK. Your family liaison officer or other officials should keep you informed and up-to-date with ongoing developments and procedures.

There may be occasions where the return of unassociated items of property is contracted to recognised international couriers. In these cases, where the property has been requested to be returned, the recipients of the property may have to pay for the repatriation.

Multiple claims

Circumstances may arise where multiple claims will be made for an item of property in the catalogue and in this case agencies involved may ask for additional information such as receipts or photographs and will then make a decision on ownership.

Non-identification

You need to prepare for the possibility that none of the property that you wish to have returned will be found or identified. It may take many months, or even longer, before the agencies involved can be certain that this is the case.

Cleaning, laundering and repairs

Once property is ready to be returned you should be asked if you would like the items cleaned, laundered or repaired. It is your choice whether to have these done – except if such cleaning is necessary in order to identify an item – and agencies should not make assumptions about what you want. Property should also have been kept secure, to ensure that no well meaning agency or individual can clean or repair items before you have decided. There may be certain restrictions, depending on the nature of the disaster, and insurance companies may also impose restrictions on the amount of repair and renovation that can be done.

Standard cleaning products are likely to be used, although occasionally specialist products will have to be used for soiled items. Some of the chemicals used in this process may leave a strong residual smell, which may be upsetting. If you have a concern about this issue, you can raise it with the police or others involved.

Where possible, you should be offered the option of having property returned 'as is', which is the term used to describe as little intervention to the property as possible. Items returned cleaned or repaired when you have cherished them as slightly worn or damaged before the disaster may be distressing. The property will normally be dried out first if this is necessary and there may be very basic cleaning in circumstances where public health may be an issue, but little else will be done. During the investigations the property may have been labelled and kept in evidence bags, but these should be removed before you receive the property, unless you specifically ask to see them.

To decide on the process that you wish to have undertaken, it may be helpful to look at photographs first. You should feel free to ask for all the information that you need in order to make your decision.

Returning property to you

The property should be returned to you in a sensitive and professional manner. You can discuss the timing and how the property will be given to you, in order to make arrangements that best suit you. Depending on the circumstances of the disaster, there may be issues about the transportation of items that have been contaminated. The police or any other agency involved with the process should discuss this with you.

What happens to unclaimed property?

The process of property return may take many months, but even if a quicker conclusion is reached you have the right to expect unclaimed property to be securely stored for a further period of time. This is so that you can decide to revisit the process when you feel able. The time-scale should be explained to you, and you should be given information about how the process will be concluded. Eventually unclaimed property will usually be securely destroyed (this will also be the case when property cannot be returned for public health reasons).

What happens now?

The circumstances of the disaster will determine how the property process is run and how complicated it will be. It may happen quickly or in some cases take years. This will mean that the way in which it unfolds can differ and you may find that you need help facing it. If you are the next of kin, consulting with family and friends, if possible, can be a great help at a time of such intense anxiety, as well as helping others who may wish to be involved in the process.

REFLECTIONS ON PERSONAL EXPERIENCE OF DISASTER

Some of this may be painful to read, but our intention is to help those who may go through similar reactions after other disasters. We hope it may also help friends and family members to understand the feelings of those they care for. Those who helped us most did not try to categorise us or dictate how we should feel.

We have prepared this based on our own personal experiences of the effects of disaster and focus here on what it was like for us in the first days and months. While we wish to give an idea of how we felt emotionally there is a huge range of reactions and you may or may not feel something similar, either now or later.

Reflections from some survivors

Soon after the event

'The total shock of the event carried us through as did the deeper shock from euphoria at surviving. The "survivor guilt" you hear about started early and was overwhelming at times. I felt guilt about everything and everyone, but once I could label it as such it started to become easier to deal with. I often wished I had died and reading about funerals and obituaries was like observing my own. A part of me had died and I needed to grieve.'

'Obsession with reading every account and watching every video clip of the disaster which comes on the news, etc. Having to record every programme and keep all the newspapers and articles (I have them to this day and they are very precious). I think this is about trying to make it "real" when the feeling of utter disbelief is so strong and trying to get control back when everything has been out of control and all "routine" matters of life are gone. Nothing felt normal anymore.'

'I noticed how people's faces had changed from before the disaster – the young people I was travelling and survived with looked so much older, haggard, their childhood had gone.'

After a month or so

'Reports of having a "glazed" look came up however within a month and the panic attacks and for some people (but not all) flashbacks were so bad as to be crippling and preventing travel, work, or concentration. What was needed was someone to talk to who had been in the accident. Feeling isolated, for some, added to the trauma.'

After a few months

'Into the "recovery" survival, people "froze", not able to move arms or legs. This was shocking and unexpected in itself. It would have been helpful to have understanding GPs, but in some cases they had to learn from us as we went through our journeys.'

'We needed information on what the time scales might be to getting some financial support if people had lost jobs or were off work and injuries had led to serious financial hardship.'

'Survivors often felt their families and friends had no idea how to deal with these strange people who had returned to live with them. There was no understanding or information available at the time and no support for the families. Survivors also didn't always see that their families were victims of the disaster too, albeit in a different way.'

'Collecting belongings was a horrible experience with no understanding of the effect it might have on us. For us there was no information on what would happen and no attempt to single out belongings for individuals was made.'

Reflections from some of the bereaved

Soon after the event

'Feeling at times devastated, howling with pain, at times numb with shock, still not quite believing it. Constantly going from one emotion to another, sometimes I am feeling crazy, it is almost a kind of euphoria, like I am free from fear, as the worst thing I could ever have imagined has happened, so now I fear nothing.'

'Unable to concentrate on daily routine, I am taking an hour to remember to boil a kettle. I find most foods really hard to contemplate eating, especially meat.'

'I am obsessing about how he died. Where was he exactly, did he suffer, did he know he was dying, what was it like for him? Going through it over and over in my mind. Reading every single newspaper every day – they have different stories about how it all happened. I can't work out where he was. I need to find someone who was there, but I daren't ask. Wishing I could have died instead.'

'B is coping by working out the statistical probability of him having been there at that time. Tells me it's so close to zero as to be a non-probability. Makes no sense to me, but it is his "mathematical" blokey way of coping.'

'Getting his belongings back, everything smelled of soot and ash. Got us closer to him somehow, which sounds really crazy.'

'Finding everything I read or watch on TV meaningless. Can't stand soppy sad movies in particular. I went to the library and started reading my way through every book with "death" in the title. Only things linked with him, it, or death mean anything.'

'For the first few months we only wanted to be with people who knew him. Felt angry and impatient with people who are wasting time doing really trivial stuff, like arguing or getting upset with tiny unimportant details. This was not what life was about. We felt such amazing clarity about that.'

'Some friends are good and supportive, others run away. I know it must be boring for them to have me wanting to talk about him, and it, all the time. But it's my way of keeping him alive.'

'The ongoing trauma seems not to lessen, only change from anger to sadness to numbness and back almost daily.'

Some months later

'I found it increasingly hard to relate to anyone who hadn't shared my experience. Friends thought they were doing the right thing by trying to "make me feel better", which really wasn't helpful. I wanted to talk about my brother's death – where his body was found, who found him, and exactly how he had died. My brothers didn't want to talk about these things at all.'

'All of us in the family were dealing with it in different ways – the dynamics between us had changed completely. The gap in the family seemed so big and the sadness was in knowing it couldn't be filled again.'

'People continued to ask me how my parents were, but I felt increasingly – why don't they ask about me? As "only" a sister, I felt I was pushed down the so-called hierarchy of grief. It did help a bit when people I met from other disasters said the same thing had happened to them.'

DISASTER VICTIM IDENTIFICATION: RELATIVES' EXPERIENCES

Many DA members have had experience of the death of close family and friends and their identification through odontology, finger printing, DNA, visual means, jewellery and other associated items. The impact of the often impersonal and invasive processes that lead to an identification can be profound and long-lasting on those left behind. The personal stories here illustrate the depth of that impact and suggest ways in which that impact can be alleviated. The experiences and views expressed here – which at times seem contradictory – show the need for flexibility and the importance of, wherever possible, treating each set of bereaved individually.

Need for well managed and direct communication with families

Polish Air Force Tu-154, Russia, 2010

'In our case, naming of the victims as well as many other aspects was not managed or controlled. Families would find out very intimate details about their loved ones from the press most of the time.'

Saudia Air Crash, Saudi Arabia, 1980

'My husband's body was sent back to the UK, along with the other British bodies from the Saudia disaster. I was asked if I wanted to see the body (not to identify him – I presumed someone from the British Embassy did. I never established who), but in light of the fact that he had been burnt to death, I was not too keen on the idea.'

Need for clear explanation and informed choice and sensitivity

Hillsborough Football Stadium Disaster, Liverpool, England, 1989

'This subject is of importance to every parent or next of kin in that the coroner should explain your legal rights before a post mortem takes place. Families were not advised as to what is involved with a post mortem or their rights. Everybody is now aware that the body becomes the property of the Coroner; however, not one family was advised that if they were unhappy with the result of the first post mortem you could ask for a second post mortem.'

11 September Attacks, New York, 2001

'It took ten months for my brother to be identified. The samples taken from me and my parents got damaged in the post, and so we went back to New York. The process was then carried out respectfully. The medical examiners were a fine example of good practice, explaining what they were doing, holding meetings, explaining the science. They asked every family member how they wished to be kept informed, ignoring the "next of kin" concept.'

Value in seeing the body

King's Cross, London Underground Fire, London, England, 1987

'If DNA testing had been available to identify the dead in 1987 it is likely that I would have been denied the chance to identify my brother myself, visually, which I did as he lay on a trolley in the corridor of a mortuary. I found that seeing him was psychologically extremely bene-ficial as it helped me to understand with certainty what had happened to him, and to grasp that he was no longer there. It was also good to have a last moment to spend with him before he was buried.

Moreover, it was important to me that I had been involved and alongside him, as it were, in the last part of my brother's journey, even after he died. It felt like other people whom he didn't know were "dealing with him" and just "processing" him otherwise. What might have been helpful was a degree of preparation before I saw him. I felt terrified not knowing at all what kind of state he was going to be in.'

Significance of information, timing, sensitivity and respect

Al Khobar Terrorist Attack, Saudi Arabia 2004

'I was informed that it would be difficult and traumatic for me to identify my husband in the morgue of a Saudi hospital, particularly given the damage done to his body after death by the terrorists, and the chaotic conditions in the hospital. Identification was carried out by the British Ambassador, a friend in whom I had complete trust. I never had any doubts about the identification. I was not able to see my husband's body until about ten days after his death, once his body had been repatriated to the United Kingdom and after a post mortem had been carried out by a Home Office pathologist. I would have liked to have spent a few moments with him and to see him at peace. But the time lapse and damage, particularly to his face, meant that his body was almost unrecognizable to me and seeing him in this state even for a few seconds has left a lasting and horrifying impression. But I would like to stress that all the advice I received at the time was not only correct but was given to me with consideration, empathy and respect. And being given the choice about whether or not to see Michael was appropriate.'

Need for positive confirmation and correct identification

Saudia Air Crash

'My husband was buried. A few months later, I was told that the parents of one of the British air hostesses had been given some of her jewellery that had been on the body, only it wasn't that of their daughter; in other words, they had buried the wrong body! I was asked if I wanted to take this further. I refused as I felt I did not want to go down a very painful route.'

King's Cross, London Underground Fire

'These days there is a worrying fear of misidentification. The desire for certainty means that there is now a total reliance on scientific methods of identification, the use of which (and the delays) must surely sometimes fly in the face of common sense and compassion, in circumstances when people *can* be visually identified.

On the other hand, one person remained unidentified after King's Cross, but, in 2004, he was exhumed and his identity restored to him through the use of DNA. This was made possible because of the fore-thought of those who had handled the process.'

Lockerbie Air Crash, Scotland, 1988

'DNA was not in use for Lockerbie – many were identified by finger prints and dental records even when they were fully recognisable, as in my brother's case, when he was travelling with his US Green Card in his pocket (which has a full face photo, social security number and fingerprint on it).

Seventeen people remained unidentified even though there were three intact male bodies and a certain number of missing men. Six weeks after the crash all the unidentified remains were cremated and buried. It would not have occurred to us then that this meant their identifications would never be possible. The loss is all the more acute for the lack of physical certainty, but in any case it takes years for the feeling that one day you might see him at the door, or in the street, to fade away.'

RAF Nimrod Crash, Afghanistan, 2006

'Body parts of British soldiers who died on operations in Afghanistan have been mixed up and placed in the wrong coffins. The government has admitted that the remains of at least one serviceman, who died in Britain's worst military disaster in the war, ended up inside another victim's coffin.' (Guardian newspaper, 29 April 2007)

'When I had to speak to the pathologist he said the mix up happened when they swabbed a finger with a wedding ring which had been covered in someone else's blood. They had failed to take a tissue sample. We are both grateful that DNA identification was avail-able and that we got some of "our" son back, but it must be done thoroughly.'

Polish Air Force Tu-154

'The fact that the investigation is being carried out by a foreign state has meant that mistakes have been made in identifications and exhumations have been necessary. For example president in exile Kaczorowski was mistakenly identified by someone who thought he recognised him from TV appearances. I believe that there was political pressure to have identifications completed as quickly as possible at the sacrifice of carrying out DNA in majority of cases. This led to great distress and the need to exhume victims.'

UT 772 Air Crash, Niger, 1989

'My brother was never identified. Nor was it made clear that a body which might have been his was buried at Père La Chaise cemetery in Paris, at the foot of the UTA memorial, quite a big piece of ground probably some 30 yards by 15.... There was a small chance that he was not buried there though his body was recovered. I think the odds were against that. I was offered a body as his in November 1989 and rejected it on the grounds that the shoe size was too small and the body was wearing heavy metal jewellery, such as I'd never seen my brother wear.'

The difference DNA can make

Manchester Air Disaster, Manchester, England, 1985

'When I think of the difference the use of DNA would have made to families in the spate of disasters in the 1980s – there would have been a huge saving in unnecessary pain and suffering. We had to wait five days before our daughter was formally identified because they had to have a minimum number of criteria to agree before they would confirm a death.

Because they refused to release the names of victims until all had been identified (the result of bodies being identified with the wrong name), we had to wait an extra three days for the dentist to come back from holiday to confirm the dental records of another victim.

So, the advent of DNA testing is a significant breakthrough in being able to accurately identify victims swiftly and to put their families out of their misery.

It is still a very emotional subject for me to discuss even after 27 years and I hope that new practices will help to alleviate the anguish we and others suffered in all those disasters of the 1980s and since.'

The importance of identification for making sense of loss and grieving

11 September Attacks

'"Ambiguous loss" affects all those waiting for an identification of a loved one, whether for a week, a month, a year or forever. The missing are physically absent but psychologically present. There is incredible stress associated with living with this. Normal rituals are not possible.

The waiting is incredibly difficult because it messes up the natural processes. It is not that our reaction is complicated, but that the *death itself* is complicated. Accepting this takes the pressure off the families. It is like living with a chronic illness – eventually we find ways of living with it.'

Need for compassion and the impact of insensitivity

11 September Attacks

'For our first funeral we buried ashes from Ground Zero, which were given to every family by the Mayor. A second funeral was possible years later, but my brother's remains were posted like a cargo parcel to Europe after seven years of fighting. "Normal" bereavement could then start.'

Polish Air Force Tu-154

'Recently pictures of bodies from the crash site have been leaked on the Internet. The pictures were taken by someone officially at the site and cover bodies at the site, bodies in coffins before they were sealed and bodies at the morgue. These pictures identify the persons photographed. Such things should never have been allowed to occur.

Aside from naming individuals we have experienced their voices being played at press conferences. In our case there seems to be little understanding as to the trauma events such as this cause.

I feel sometimes that no public disclosures should be made at all until the investigation is closed and permission from affected families has been obtained. In our case the press is the medium for disseminating all the information.'

London Bombings, England, 2005

'This is a painful subject but one of great importance. For us, being asked for DNA samples by our police family liaison officer was an acknowledgment that our concerns about our son's involvement were real ones and being taken seriously. This was in marked contrast to the initial attitude of the Help Line and the three days we had to endure of remarks like "Oh, he'll turn up" and questions like "Does he often go off without telling you?"

... Taking DNA samples was handled very sensitively. More problematic for me were other aspects of the identification process – for example, our family dentist was contacted without consulting us and this was very upsetting for staff there who had known my son since he was four years old but had not realised his involvement in 7/7 at that stage. With hindsight, it seems increasingly important to me for the complete implications of "naming the dead" to be explained to the bereaved in as sensitive way as possible and more than once given the state of shock and incomprehension sudden, violent bereavement involves.'

South East Asian Tsunami, 2004

'There were two different stages, in Thailand it was very confused and then when we went back to England it was very difficult. We got a police family liaison officer who requested personal items – we were unsure about the process. It was very upsetting. To us it felt like it was a crime scene.'

Reminder of Key Principles

- Medical care
- Access to information
- Practical and financial help
- Openness, transparency, sensitivity
- Empowerment
- Informed choices
- Emotional first aid/psychosocial support
- Respect for individual difference/privacy/dignity
- Acknowledgment and recognition

GUIDANCE FOR RESPONDERS

The following series of leaflets was written for emergency planners and responders and all those in the statutory and voluntary services whose role brings them into contact with survivors and bereaved. The purpose of the leaflets is to highlight issues for those on the receiving end, and suggest ways in which these might best be approached. As with the 'When Disaster Strikes' leaflets, the links and Useful Contacts in the originally published versions have been taken out.

> *Working with Disaster Survivors and the Bereaved: Code of Practice on Privacy, Anonymity & Confidentiality*
>
> *Disaster Victim Identification: Issues for Families and Implications for Police Family Liaison Officers and Coroners' Officers*
>
> *Longer-term Support for Survivors and Bereaved after Disaster*
>
> *Bringing People Together and Enabling the Development of Support Groups after Disaster*
>
> *Young People and Disasters*
>
> *Guidance on Management and Distribution of Disaster Trust Funds*
>
> *Notes on Family Viewing*

WORKING WITH DISASTER SURVIVORS AND THE BEREAVED: CODE OF PRACTICE ON PRIVACY, ANONYMITY & CONFIDENTIALITY

This code has been developed by Disaster Action with a view to protecting the rights and interests of those affected by disaster, specifically survivors and the bereaved. It is designed to govern the attitudes and behaviour of all those who may work directly or indirectly with all those affected by disaster. It includes, but is not limited to, local authorities, coroners and all those involved in identification processes, members of the emergency services and investigation teams, National Health trusts and voluntary agencies.

General Principles
- It is incumbent upon responders to be aware of the possible consequences – direct and indirect – of their work with survivors and the bereaved. Wherever possible they should attempt to **anticipate, and to guard against, consequences that** can be predicted to be harmful
- All responders should be aware that **legislation such as the Data Protection Act, the Freedom of Information Act, Human Rights Act, copyright and libel law** may affect the rights of survivors and the bereaved and thus should positively influence their conduct, inquiries, data dissemination, relations with the media and storage and publication of information
- Responders should strike a balance between enabling access and preventing intrusion in working with survivors and the bereaved. This is particularly relevant when considering issues such as information sharing and seeking and obtaining consent.

Confidentiality

Personal information
All personal information about survivors and the bereaved should be treated as confidential and used only for the purposes for which it was given, unless essential to their welfare and/or an investigation. In some cases it may be necessary for a responder to decide whether it is proper or appropriate **even to record** certain kinds of sensitive information.

Personal or identifying data should be **rendered anonymous** before information is given for the purposes of research, teaching, audits or administration. Responders should respect the anonymity of survivors and the bereaved at all times.

Sharing information within a team

In **sharing information** with other team members about the identity, welfare, status and decisions affecting individual survivors and the bereaved, responders should respect confidentiality as far as possible. Survivors and the bereaved should, however, be made aware that information about them may be shared within the team unless they object. Responders must ensure that anyone with whom information is shared understands that it is given to them **in confidence**, which they must respect.

Disclosing information to third parties

Sensitive information regarding the personal circumstances of survivors and the bereaved **should not be divulged to third parties** unless essential to their welfare and/or an investigation, or unless consent has been obtained. This is particularly pertinent in multi-agency responses, meetings and discussions (formal and informal).

Disclosure of information to other bereaved or survivors should be made only when specific consent to do so has been obtained.

Disclosing information to an individual's family or friends

The wishes of survivors and the bereaved should also be established and followed regarding the sharing of any information with their family or others known to them.

Legal Privilege

Information given in confidence does not enjoy legal privilege; that is, it may be liable to subpoena by a court and **survivors and the bereaved should be informed of this.**

Unintentional disclosures

Responders should avoid making unintentional disclosures by **not discussing individuals' details where they can be overheard.** Written records should not be left where they can be seen by third parties.

Consent

Consent **must** be obtained from survivors and the bereaved **where it is considered desirable** to disclose information to third parties. Such disclosure may be desirable in particular where survivors or bereaved could benefit from contacting each other. In this case, only basic information should be disclosed. Responding agencies may also wish to ensure that they have consent for basic information to be disclosed to other agencies providing potentially appropriate services. Consent should be sought specifically for the purpose for which it is required and the implications of giving consent explained fully.

In some situations access to individuals is gained via a 'gatekeeper' or 'intermediary'. In these situations responders should adhere to the **principle of obtaining informed consent** directly from those to whom access is required, while at the same time taking account of the gate-keeper's interests.

Special care should be taken **where survivors and the bereaved are particularly vulnerable** by virtue of factors such as age, disability and their physical or mental health. Responders will need to take into account the legal and ethical complexities involved in those circumstances where there are particular difficulties in eliciting fully informed consent. Specialist advice and expertise should be sought where relevant.

Anonymity

Responders should not, unless it is necessary to their welfare and/ or an investigation, permit communication of personal or identifying details of individuals to audiences other than those to which **survivors and the bereaved have agreed**.

Personal or identifying data should be **rendered anonymous** before information is given for the purposes of research, teaching, audits or administration. Responders should respect the anonymity of survivors and the bereaved at all times.

Data Protection

Appropriate measures should be taken to **store data on survivors and the bereaved in a secure manner**. Responders should have regard to their obligations under the Data Protection Acts. They should also take care to prevent data being published or released in a form which would permit the actual or potential identification of individuals without their **prior written consent**. **Guarantees of confidentiality and anonymity given to survivors and the bereaved must be honoured,** unless there are clear and overriding reasons to do otherwise, for example in relation to the abuse of children. Other people, such as colleagues, researchers or others who are given access to data must also be made aware of their obligations in this respect.

DISASTER VICTIM IDENTIFICATION: ISSUES FOR FAMILIES AND IMPLICATIONS FOR POLICE FAMILY LIAISON OFFICERS AND CORONERS' OFFICERS

The aim of this guide is not to describe the identification methods that may be used after a disaster. It highlights the issues around identification that, based on our common experience, are important to families, whatever the origin of the disaster, and the implications of these issues for police family liaison officers (FLOs) and coroners' officers (COs).

Differences within the Family

Although our definition of 'family' has become much broader than it used to be, in our experience differences between family members such as parents, partners and siblings of those who have died in a disaster are, unfortunately, not uncommon. One person may feel entitled (perhaps as next of kin) to have information about the manner of death or the progress of any criminal investigation, without sharing this information with others. In some past disasters, the next of kin was permitted to decide on key matters concerning the dead, including whether other family members should be 'allowed' to see photographs of the dead person. Giving such powers – which have no basis in law – to next of kin can create additional distress for the wider family.

Implications for FLOs and COs

FLOs and COs should be aware of the possibility of differences of opinion and potential conflict within families. Such cases may require careful discussion with the family by FLOs/COs, who should seek advice from line management to ensure that the most appropriate and effective response is provided.

Knowing the Cause of Death

Many relatives and friends of those killed in a disaster ask searching and detailed questions about exactly how the person died. If a decision is taken not to hold a post mortem, this may leave more open the question of establishing the exact cause of death. While families may appreciate the least amount of disruption to the body, many will ask questions that perhaps can only be answered by post mortem.

If a single cause of death is given for all those killed in a disaster, this is unlikely to satisfy the need to know how an individual met their death. People may feel that all was not done that should have been in order to satisfy their need for information, or that they were being denied information that was available. (At the Fatal Accident Inquiry two years after the Pan Am 103 bombing, for example, the cause of death was given in the public forum as 'multiple injuries resulting from a fatal air crash'. This level of information merely fuelled many families' desire to know more. In that instance, it was possible to learn more, given that post mortems were required for evidence purposes.)

Implications for FLOs and COs
FLOs and other responders may be asked questions about the cause of death, such as why there is/isn't a post mortem, what (more) information is/may be available once a victim has been identified, or at or after an inquest. FLOs should have a basic understanding of the general processes and the specific procedures in place for the event they are dealing with. They should also make sure they are aware of who they and/or the family members can liaise with for further information/explanation. Regular updates should be given to families about post mortem and inquest arrangements.

Viewing of Bodies/Remains
Disaster Action stresses the importance of creating a facility whereby family members can see and be with the person/people after death. After a disaster, regardless of the state of the body, family members may wish to have the opportunity to see that person before the remains are returned home or to the place of burial or cremation. Others may not wish to do this, but we believe it is vital that facilities are created to make this possible and that all effort is made to facilitate opportunities to view.

Lord Justice Clarke's *Inquiry Report into the Identification of Victims following Major Transport Accidents* spelt out that families should have a right to view bodies if they wish to do so. Sometimes, with the best of intentions, it might be felt that viewing bodies should be denied for the sake of protecting people. However, it is now understood that exercising the right to view is important for the future psychological wellbeing of families, as well as in some instances for identification purposes. Being prevented from exercising this choice can have a long-term detrimental effect.

The following research may also be of assistance. '**Viewing the body after bereavement due to a traumatic death: qualitative study in the UK**' by A. Chapple and S. Ziebland was published in the *British Medical Journal* on 30 April 2010 and is available on the BMJ website http://www.bmj.com/cgi/content/full/340/apr30_2/c2032.

Implications for FLOs and COs

Those liaising with families should never advise whether or not to view; rather they should enable *informed choice* by family members. FLOs should be prepared to answer questions and give information about what to expect in terms of the state of the body, which may require them to view the body or photographs of the deceased in advance in order to inform families. They should also explain how the process of viewing would work for families (how long they can be with the body, whether or not they wish to be accompanied/left alone, whether they can touch the body, etc.).

While the natural instinct of FLOs may be to protect families, in the experience of Disaster Action members it can be counterproductive to over-protect. Equally, FLOs should understand that different members of the same family might make different choices as to whether to see the body. It is important to facilitate these choices as far as possible and not to make any judgement about the decisions taken.

Return of Remains after Disaster

Issues may arise over who has the right to have the remains returned to them. There may be conflict within families as to who has this right and disagreement as to what should be done with the remains. Although this may seem unlikely, as it has happened in the past it should be anticipated as a possibility. (After the 11 September attacks in the United States, the medical examiner in New York decided to allow a court to make a decision in the event of such unresolved conflict.)

Implications for FLOs and COs

FLOs should be clear that it is not their role to make such decisions for families. Where possible a solution should not be imposed upon families, but they should be facilitated in their need to resolve such conflict themselves, with outside help if necessary.

Partial Recovery of Remains/Recovery over a Long Period

There may be circumstances where only partial remains of those killed in a disaster are recovered and/or where remains may be found over a long period. Depending on where and how the disaster occurs, social, political and cultural approaches to dealing with death and the treatment of bodies may have an impact on the ways in which recovery, identification and repatriation are dealt with. Dealing with these issues may be highly sensitive and also give rise to differences of opinion within families about the choices they may face, or be denied.

Implications for FLOs and COs

Wherever possible, at an appropriate stage in the process families should be offered the choice as to whether or not they wish to be kept informed of the recovery of any further remains, however long this may take. Some will wish to bury or cremate further remains recovered over time and others will choose not to be kept informed after an initial identification has been made.

As far as possible, the opportunity should be offered to families to re-visit this decision if they wish to. Written records detailing the decision should be retained, and copies also given to families.

If constraints prevent the identification and return of further remains, then the reasons should be explained to families in a sensitive manner, at an appropriate time and place and always on a face-to-face basis.

Missing People

When people remain missing and are unaccounted for, friends and family members may go to great lengths to find them themselves, regardless of other efforts or advice by the authorities. This may include travelling to disaster sites/zones, temporary mortuaries, hospitals, etc.

It is important that their families feel reassured that all that could be done is being or has been done to find, recover and establish the identity of all the victims.

Even if a body is not found, any documents/personal effects that are recovered will be of enormous value to families (see 'When Disaster Strikes' *The Return of Personal Property*, for more on this issue).

There are important legal and social implications of having a loved one still missing. Under usual circumstances without identification, a death certificate is not issued for seven years, thus meaning financial affairs such as mortgages, selling property or inheriting assets cannot be settled. Following disasters where people remain unaccounted for but are considered highly likely to have been killed, measures may be introduced to speed up this process such as after the 2004 South East Asian tsunami.

Implications for FLOs and COs

FLOs and COs should be mindful of the need for great sensitivity around when people are thought of as likely to be dead. Families will differ in the way they deal with this. However, it is likely that families will want as much information as possible on an ongoing basis (even if there is no news as such), in order to reach a stage when an identification is accepted as unlikely to happen. After all, there will be those who will be found alive and well, so it is important not to make judgements too soon.

In overseas disasters, where protocols for recovery and identification might be complex and change over the duration of the disaster response, updates to waiting families may need to occur over a protracted period of time. Many families will wish to be kept updated about how the general identification process is going, even if there is no specific progress on the identification of their loved one(s) as yet.

Information and updates on procedures may need to be given many times and over subsequent visits in order to be fully understood and taken in. This is partly because when people are grieving such complicated deaths it can be difficult to absorb information. Families are also unlikely to be be familiar with the complex procedures and processes involved.

With regard to the legal status of missing persons and the practical implications for families, FLOs should source and pass on details of support organisations, which may be able to assist with financial and legal advice. These include organisations listed below.

Trust and Confidentiality

Losing a loved one in a disaster can mean private grief and decision-making around sensitive personal matters needs to be discussed and shared with outsiders. For families this can reinforce a sense of vulnerability and intrusiveness, especially when others regard this as being in the public interest and worthy of media and other exposure.

Implications for FLOs and COs

While it may be necessary to share some aspects of a family's private affairs with individuals and other organisations outside the family, it is important always to be aware of the importance of trust and confidentiality. Information should be shared with fellow professionals strictly on a need-to-know basis.

Even where a family has given sensitive personal information to an FLO or CO where possible and appropriate permission should be sought from family members for disclosure of such information to others.

LONGER-TERM SUPPORT FOR SURVIVORS AND BEREAVED AFTER DISASTER

How long do individuals need support for following a disaster (both bereaved and survivors)?

People's response to a disaster depends on the individual. There are some whose need for support (from others affected and/or from support services) is primarily or even exclusively in the immediate aftermath. For others, this need may arise some time after the event (six months, a year or even considerably longer) when the impact on their lives is such that they may turn to external support, or to others directly affected.

It should be borne in mind that those affected by less high profile and/or smaller incidents have felt that their needs are less well recognised and catered for than those affected by larger scale disasters.

In terms of organised services, any transition from full-time provision to part time and then the closure of a service should be managed with considerable care. Good and sensitive communication is vital and consulting users on what they would wish for, and when, may also be valuable. Any such consultation process must have real substance, however.

In previous disasters, maintaining contact with a key worker through a telephone support service, after the closure of a drop-in centre (such as provided by Camden following the 1987 King's Cross underground fire) has been of considerable value. This service remained in place for three years after King's Cross so that those affected could continue to discuss issues of importance to them and receive information and signposting to other services (see below).

Our comments should be read in terms of a general need for services, within which there may be a centre such as the 7 July Assistance Centre, which developed following the closure of the Family Assistance Centre in London in August 2005, but not exclusively so.

What type of support is most useful in the long-term?

Organised service provision

Disaster Action promotes a needs-driven, user-led approach to organised service provision. This is not a substitute for self-support but an addition to it. The ideal is to enable people to help themselves, while facilitating access to ongoing practical/medical/financial/legal help for survivors and bereaved, including those whose disaster-related needs may not become apparent until some time after the disaster. This could include, for example, longer-term health consequences or support needs that may arise out of life-changing physical injury. The need for practical/medical/financial/legal help to be available may continue for a considerable period of time.

The most effective support is a practical, signposting (or gateway) service that enables people to access the services they may require including psychological intervention if needed. In the past, such services have been provided through drop-in centres, outreach services, telephone helplines and virtual (Internet-based) support networks.

Clear information on the roles and responsibilities of the different agencies involved should be made available, as well as clear sign-posting on accessing available support services. Support should be offered on a non-judgemental basis and those providing services should be appropriately trained, experienced and supported. It is useful if those involved in running such support services are in contact with other agencies and bodies that are involved in aspects of the aftermath such as the police.

Independent action/support groups

Many people find the mutual support of others affected by their own, and sometimes other, disaster(s) to be helpful and in some cases even the most valuable form of support. An important implication of this is that those providing services should make available, at the earliest opportunity, the means for those directly affected to be in contact with and meet each other if they wish to. This may include the provision of meeting spaces and other practical assistance such as help with travel arrangements and providing refreshments. Anything more organised may be controlling, and unhelpfully stifle the emergence of the independent qualities that make such self-help and self-determining support groups so beneficial for those who choose to join them.

It should be for the individuals affected to decide for themselves whether, when and why they wish to form a group, as well as how any such group might be run (see Disaster Action leaflets *Setting up Survivor and Family Support Groups* and *Setting up an E-forum Discussion Group*).

The desire to meet and join with others affected by a disaster may emerge very soon after the incident, or not for some months or even years afterwards.

Smaller/facilitated support groups

Following disasters some people have found it helpful to participate in smaller groups with a focus on emotional support and an opportunity to talk about their personal experiences. The ways in which these groups have been organised and their relationship to the type of independent action/support groups mentioned above can vary. For example, following the 11 September attacks in 2001, such smaller groups were organised some months after the formation of the main group and initiated by members of that group themselves. By contrast, after the 2004 South East Asia Tsunami, those formally providing the Tsunami Support Network before the independent group was formed facilitated the smaller groups.

The need for, nature and way in which such facilitated support groups may work will vary considerably. Sensitive and appropriate management is required for them to be effective. In our experience they work best when organised and facilitated by those with appropriate expertise, experience and knowledge of trauma and disasters (as opposed to general bereavement and counselling). A solid professional grounding in ethical issues is also needed. Facilitators should understand the dynamics of such groups (such as the fact that in some cases survivor only and/or bereaved only membership works best), and be fully aware of the role and relationship between these groups and other recovery-related strategies and services.

At the same time, responders should understand that many people will not find this approach appropriate for their needs as individuals.

Memorial services/acts of remembrance

As well as memorial services soon after a disaster, it is to be expected that a disaster should be marked on future anniversaries. This is the case for disasters of whatever origin. In the shorter term, those affected will wish to know that their suffering and that of their loved ones continues to be recognised and acknowledged by the wider community, and by government. Involving the bereaved in arrangements for the events is important. In the longer term, families and survivors may wish to make arrangements themselves for such events.

A key service is financial support to attend memorial services for those who need to travel. Those affected are likely to expect central and local government support for the creation of a permanent memorial to those who died.

Criminal Inquiries/inquest process

Many of those affected will wish to have continuing information through informed sources (the police, the coroner, etc.) concerning the judicial processes. In addition, families and friends may benefit from support during and at any relevant hearings, which may not take place for a considerable time after the disaster. Many will wish to have detailed answers to their questions about why and how a disaster occurred and what happened in the aftermath. Others may choose not to ask for/have such information.

There are a number of examples of support services that have been of benefit to families through the inquest and any criminal trial. In the case of the Lockerbie disaster, funding and support services were made available through the United States Office for Victims of Crime for live video links to the trial of the accused (12 years after the bombing). The services included financial support to travel to the video links and travel and accommodation costs for those who wished to attend the trial for a period. A secure website was made available to families, with detailed information about the conduct of the trial. This support had a highly practical focus, but psychological support was also made available.

BRINGING PEOPLE TOGETHER AND ENABLING THE DEVELOPMENT OF SUPPORT GROUPS AFTER DISASTER

Disaster Support Groups

After disaster, as well as the kind of practical, financial and legal assistance that may be provided through organised support services, many people find the opportunity to be in touch with others who have had similar experiences a source of unique understanding and mutual support.

Communities spontaneously come together for support and there may be a natural impulse to convene and provide mutual support in times of crisis. Psychosocial support – in the form of family, group and/or community support – is fundamental to people's recovery after disaster.

For this reason disaster support groups, consisting of bereaved people and/or survivors with similar experiences and interests, are often formed after disasters. It has long been recognised that psychosocial support strategies that facilitate, support and enable such opportunities are an important way of enhancing self-help, community resilience and longer-term recovery.

Some of those directly affected by disaster will not wish to join a support group while others may seek the chance to meet, stay in touch with others and even lead a group. The reasons people wish to join groups vary, but include the desire for mutual support, to share information and/or work together in the pursuit of common goals such as the prevention of similar incidents and/or legal outcomes.

Disaster Response and Recovery

Under the Civil Contingencies Act 2004, disaster response and recovery is the responsibility of responders such as the local authority, health authorities and police service. Personnel such as police family liaison officers, telephone support line operators, those managing reception and assistance centres may have direct contact with families and others affected very soon after a disaster.

It is sometimes wrongly assumed that providing information about opportunities for those affected to be in touch with each other may be harmful for them and/or for any investigation. On the contrary, it is important that at the earliest opportunity people are given information and choices about how, where and when they may come together and meet in a safe, comfortable and appropriate place. Those responsible for developing humanitarian assistance strategies should recognise and facilitate options for people to come together in this way.

Our experience is that people also benefit from meeting people from other disasters even where the actual disaster experience has been different. With collective experience of 28 disasters DA members offer common understanding and support in the early aftermath and later, when the decision to meet others comes sometimes even years after a disaster.

Helping to Bring People Together

In the days and weeks following a disaster many people will wish for and seek out opportunities to be in touch with others affected. As well as the growing use of social networking media, opportunities should be offered for those directly affected to meet face-to-face.

Depending on the circumstances there may be a natural or existing community or group of people already known to and in contact with each other, for example where tragedy strikes a school or workplace. In other circumstances, opportunities should be provided early on for contact between people who wish to meet each other because of the experience of the disaster itself.

Those responsible for emergency response and recovery (for example local and health authorities, the police and psychosocial service providers), can offer practical assistance to enable the formation of independent disaster support groups. They can do this by:

- Collating and sharing of names and contact details of those affected by a disaster, in line with the principles and protocols incorporated in government guidance on information sharing (see below)
- Informing those affected about opportunities to meet, including for example preparing a written invitation to a first meeting, which may be circulated privately through police family liaison officers or, if appropriate, publicly through the media
- Identifying and/or providing early opportunities and appropriate places where meetings can be held, for example in humanitarian assistance centres or other community centres
- Carefully planning, preparing and thinking through arrangements for meetings in view of the sensitivities associated with the disaster; certain venues, dates and times may be more or less appropriate, and there may be differing needs and issues for bereaved people and for survivors
- Coordinating and taking care of practical arrangements for an initial meeting, such as refreshments and exclusion of unwanted media presence and, as appropriate, arranging for official representatives to attend the meeting
- Working on the key principle that the best way to promote self help and independence is to enable attendees to maintain control of decisions about the development, direction and running of any support group they choose to set up
- Contacting DA for information, assistance, advice and support in relation to these principles and processes.

YOUNG PEOPLE AND DISASTERS

Many disasters will involve children and young people to a greater or lesser extent depending on the circumstances. Their particular needs should be taken into account as part of the humanitarian response.

This guide contains links to resources that should enable adults to support young people as well as to resources written for young people themselves.

The immediate aftermath

A disaster takes away the sense that we are in control of our lives. The feeling of disempowerment that can follow may feel especially bewildering for children if the adults around them are – through good intention – trying to make decisions on their behalf. Involving children in decisions on whether to visit a disaster site, for example, may seem too difficult for those caught up in the trauma. However, they should be given the same opportunities as adults to make informed choices to prevent them from feeling excluded.

Children and young people should be encouraged to speak about what has happened, if they wish to, but without being forced to do so. Providing children, in particular, with as 'normal' and ordinary a routine as possible can feel particularly difficult at a time when adults are finding it hard to cope with a trauma themselves, but this may also help.

Police family liaison officers may be working with families where there are children and young people. Their role and purpose with the family should be explained in ways appropriate to the young person's level of understanding. Given the often intense pressure and emotional strain in the aftermath of disaster, such information will probably need to be repeated. Each person is unique and should be treated as such, without being judged.

Seeking appropriately qualified advice and support If the disaster involves children and young people in particular, certain agencies may be directly involved in offering practical and emotional support. These may include, for example, school-based personnel and educational psychologists. Some organisations are more experienced than others in responding to traumatic incidents and specialise in addressing the needs of children and young people at this time – see below.

Trust and confidentiality

A disaster often makes adults question the world in which they live and the same is likely to be true for children and young people. Their sense of security may have taken a heavy blow. Restoring their trust in the world may be difficult and it is essential that those around them are 'super-trustworthy'. Children may be embarrassed about how they feel, so they need to know that they can speak to adults in confidence; at the same time, adults around young people should be aware that there may be circumstances in which such confidentiality can be broken, for example if they believe a young person's welfare is at risk.

Longer-term aftermath

Adults affected by disaster respond in different ways. Some seem to cope well at the outset and then react badly later on; others have the opposite reaction. There is no right or wrong way to recover and deal with the experience as time passes. This will also be the case for children and young people. It is important for young people to feel that they have 'permission' to talk about their feelings even some considerable time after the event; they should be made aware of how to get help if they need it.

Books

Jupiter's Children (Mary Campion, Liverpool University Press, 1998) Mary Campion, a teacher leading a school cruise trip on the Jupiter that sank off Athens in October 1988, compiled this book from the first-person accounts of those affected, including teenagers who survived the disaster.

Literature and Best Practice Review and Assessment: Identifying People's Needs in Major Emergencies and Best Practice in Humanitarian Response (Dr Anne Eyre Department for Culture Media and Sport, 2006). See pages 18–19, which refer to the needs of children and young people following disasters.

https://www.gov.uk/government/uploads/system/uploads/attachment_data/file/86357/ha_literature_review.pdf

---

GUIDANCE ON MANAGEMENT AND DISTRIBUTION OF DISASTER TRUST FUNDS

Members of Disaster Action, who are survivors and bereaved people from 28 disasters of different origin, have written this leaflet. Its purpose is to offer the benefit of our experience of disaster trust funds to those responsible for setting up and managing a fund. It is one of the outcomes from a piece of research undertaken by Disaster Action, resulting in a report entitled Disaster Funds: Lessons & Guidance on the Management & Distribution of Disaster Funds. Effective, efficient and sensitive approaches to the establishment, administration and distribution of such funds will help avoid the sort of difficulties that can worsen rather than alleviate distress in those whom they are supposed to help.

Disaster trust funds are intended as a recognition and acknowledgement by society of the experience of being involved in a disaster. They are neither a substitute for insurance nor compensation for injury or loss, but the giving and receiving of funds aimed at relieving suffering and distress after disaster can make a difference. As one of our bereaved colleagues in Disaster Action has commented, 'money won't bring a loved one back, but not having it won't either'.

Launching an appeal

Where a number of appeals are launched in relation to the same disaster, there can be advantages in a combined partnership or coordinated approach. It is advisable to identify and communicate with other appeals early on and look to combine or coordinate appeals where possible. See the links below for guidance on sources of help in setting up an appeal, different forms of appeal, suggested wording, and the pros and cons of using different types of trusts, with links to guidance on the tax treatment of funds.

Decide early and communicate clearly the type of trust or appeal fund, with reference to guidance. Be clear and consistent about objectives from the outset; ensure that the terms that are used in public announcements about the purpose of the Fund correspond exactly with the form of the Trust Deed.

Appointing trustees, fund managers and steering committees

A disaster trust fund will require the selection and appointment of a range of personnel. If the appeal is set up through an existing organisation, such as a community foundation, the appeal may operate under its existing charity status and board of trustees. If the appeal is set up as a new charity, it will require the appointment of trustees. It can take time to appoint a board of trustees with the appropriate authority to take action and establish systems and procedures for fund administration. This could lead to long delays in financial assistance reaching beneficiaries. For this reason it may be valuable to appoint temporary trustees, but seek to ensure this does not cause unnecessary administrative delays.

In the past, as well as referring to published guidelines, new disaster fund trustees have found it especially helpful to speak with administrators of previous funds and access their advice, particularly in the early stages and in relation to key areas of decision-making

Where trustees bring skills such as accountancy this can be an advantage. Most importantly, the chair of the trustees should, wherever possible, have had previous experience in this area. The sums of money involved can be very large, the decisions that have to be made sometimes difficult, and there can be close scrutiny by the media of how the trust is managing its affairs after a disaster. A good rapport between trustees also makes a difference.

Type of trust or appeal fund

An important decision at the outset is whether or not the appeal will be a charitable one. This decision will affect the uses to which donations can be made and the decisions available to trustees about the distribution of any fund(s).

The Attorney General's guidelines advise that a charitable fund has the advantage of tax relief but its aims must be limited to: the relief of poverty, the advancement of education or religion, and the benefit of the community. Being essentially public funds, distributing sizeable amounts from this kind of fund is constrained by the requirement not to benefit individuals over and above their needs.

A non-charitable discretionary trust on the other hand, though taxable, is not so limited. Trustees remain free to determine how the money ought to be spent and there is no limit on the amount that can be paid to individual beneficiaries if none has been imposed by the appeal.

Many disaster appeals have opted to set up two kinds of fund in parallel to make use of the advantages of both types.

Trust aims

There have been cases where the stated, and binding, aims of a trust have been set out, in great haste, in such a way that they prevent flexibility on the part of the trustees in deciding how monies received can be allocated. This can cause subsequent difficulties when unusual situations arise. The wording of the 'aims' of the fund should therefore be clear, but flexible.

Whatever the objectives of an appeal, experienced trustees have advised making the purpose very clear so that donors and potential beneficiaries neither misunderstand nor are misled about how the money will be used. In raising and distributing money the aim and objectives of any appeal should be clear and consistent from the start.

Naming the Fund

Naming a fund may seem straightforward, for example after a place (such as the 'Hillsborough Disaster Fund'), type of disaster ('xxx flood appeal'), or significant date ('7 July'). The appropriateness and implications of associating a disaster with a particular name, date or place, should be considered, however, bearing in mind that this association may endure for a long time.

Duration and Residue

Establish plans for duration of the appeal and the spending of residue from the beginning and make these clear to all concerned; consult as much as possible with relatives and survivors. Many relatives experience their greatest financial need years after the event, because of the potential long-term consequences on their physical and emotional health.

The Immediate Aftermath: Early Payments

Prompt contact with beneficiaries and emergency payments can relieve many anxieties and may be followed by further, supplementary payments to address longer-term needs. Seek to make rapid disbursement of early, interim payments to address emergency needs. Initial payments should not be means tested.

Some relatives or next of kin may find themselves in difficulty with paying for funeral expenses, a gathering for family and friends, and a headstone or other memorial. If a fund is sufficient at this point, consideration should be given to making an immediate ex-gratia payment to cover funeral expenses

Application Methods

Ensure application procedures include clear eligibility criteria at the outset, transparent explanation of the distribution criteria and are sensitive and straightforward. Application forms should be adapted to address the needs and diversity of those affected. This may include translating forms and accompanying information into different languages and providing appropriately skilled and briefed interpreters.

Distribution of the Fund

Trustees should bear in mind at all times that those who donate money to funds do so because they wish to show their sympathy to people affected, the bereaved and survivors. The funds raised should therefore never be seen as 'compensation' (which may be available in law, in any case), but as that expression of sympathy by the society at large, for all those adversely affected by the disaster. Trustees are not personal injury lawyers, on the whole, and should avoid trying to apply compensation principles to the distribution of the monies.

Where multiple funds exist, take account of other assistance available to those affected. Appeal eligibility conditions should aim to include insured, non-insured and underinsured applicants. Consider the overall outcomes of distribution decisions with a view to ensuring that serious unintended consequences are minimized.

Be clear about the benefit and tax implications of receiving payments by liaising with the DWP (Department for Work and Pensions) before starting the distribution process, and advise applicants accordingly.

If the fund is to be used to help pay for a permanent memorial, consultation and participation by those directly affected by the disaster should form a key part of the design and development process.

Assessing 'need'

Arguably the most difficult challenge facing those administering disaster appeals is sensitively assessing and addressing needs after disaster. Aspects of 'injury', 'loss' and 'need' are notoriously difficult to measure and quantify and having large sums of money available to distribute does not mitigate this. Administrators should always bear in mind, especially in their communications about their decisions, that although their task may require such quantification, understanding and responding to disaster-related needs cannot simply be reduced to mathematical formulas.

Means testing

It will, normally, not be necessary to means test potential beneficiaries, provided that the applications for funds are found to be genuine, from those closely connected to the deceased, or from those injured in the disaster.

Trustees should bear in mind that means testing has, in our experience, been perceived as intrusive and humiliating for potential beneficiaries who, often, have never received – or applied for – financial support in the past.

Broadly speaking, the bereaved should be treated equally, irrespective of means, since the money represents not compensation, but a gift from society at large to send a message of sympathy for their loss.

The most difficult aspect of assessment will be in respect of injured survivors, since levels of injury and incapacity will inevitably vary greatly, depending on the nature of the disaster. Trustees in the past have drawn on expert advice where appropriate and developed broad categories for the injured based, for example, on length of time spent in hospital, awarding greater or lesser sums according to the seriousness of the injury.

Openness and Transparency

There is likely to be a range of expectations on the part of donors, potential beneficiaries and the wider public as to how the money accumulated will be managed and distributed. Past experience has shown how a mismatch in expectations and outcomes can cause conflict and frustration.

Avoiding this may be achieved through openness and transparency about:

- How trustees and fund managers have been chosen
- Whether trustees, administrators, consultants or anyone else associated with the fund are to be paid for their services
- General criteria and methods for assessing disaster impacts
- The percentage of the fund to be paid directly to bereaved/ survivors
- Whether any payment is one-off, interim or final
- The anticipated life of the fund and how decisions to close it will be made.

Bearing in mind individual confidentiality, the general public should be able to review in broad terms the distribution of funds and how any surplus over and above the objectives of the fund is to be disbursed.

Attention should be paid to details such as the wording of forms and letters. With one fund, beneficiaries especially appreciated the trustees' decision that letters sent with payments should be individually addressed and signed.

Communications and Media Strategy

Trustees should be aware that there is sometimes the need to be proactive in inviting relatives/survivors to make applications. It may be appropriate to give examples of what sort of applications can be made (for example travel to inquests/inquiries), as many of the people will never have applied for anything in their lives before. A good number will simply think that they do not deserve any money, or that they do not feel they should make a 'profit' from the death of a loved one.

Good, clear lines of communication are therefore essential. To facilitate this, it may be necessary to:

- Set up a website, where visitors can read about the fund, download application forms and see updates on progress and activities
- Provide a single, named, administrator who beneficiaries can contact and get to know
- Be in touch with several individuals from each bereaved

family. It cannot be assumed that communicating with one member of a bereaved family will ensure that everyone else will get the information, in view of complex family relationships and the fact that bereavement can exacerbate difficulties between some family members. The next of kin may also be overwhelmed by the tragedy and unable to take in or pass on information

- Send regular updates once lines of contact have been established. As much general information about the contents of the fund, its objectives, even – without breaching confidentiality in terms of names and amounts – what sorts of awards are being made. It is not uncommon for families to feel they might be the only ones asking for money, and therefore deciding not to make an application

- Ensure that information is kept up-to-date. If people move home after a disaster, for example, they can easily fall out of the system.

It is also important to ensure that as many potential beneficiaries as possible are made aware not only of the existence of the fund, but the fact that the fund will welcome applications from all those directly affected.

Media coverage can have a significant influence on levels of donations to a fund. It can be used to highlight ways of donating, as well as being a means of communicating with potential beneficiaries. Regular press releases can highlight both the immediate and continuing needs of those affected by disasters. It may also be useful for those managing donations to publicise a facility for responding to queries and offering advice about specific gifts before they are sent in.

We recommend that trustees use the services of a public relations/media expert in developing their communications and media strategy.

Confidentiality and Anonymity

Fund managers and trustees should be mindful of issues concerning confidentiality and anonymity in relation to beneficiaries. See Disaster Action's Guidance for Responders: 'Code of Practice on Privacy, Anonymity and Confidentiality', which highlights areas such as the sharing and disclosing of personal information, unintentional disclosures, consent and data protection.

While the criteria for assessment and distribution should be clear and well publicised, details of individual beneficiaries and what they individually receive must remain confidential. When a fund is wound up, all working papers should be shredded and personal details and records removed from computers in order to safeguard confidentiality.

Evaluating the Fund

We recommend that feedback on a fund should be sought from those responsible for establishing the fund and its distribution, in addition to beneficiaries, and all lessons learned recorded, discussed and disseminated widely.

Advice from a Trustee

'We recognized that we were not in the honour and glory business – we knew what we were to do might well be unpopular. We said if we could look ourselves in the eyes and say we had done our best to be fair at the end of the day, then that was going to be sufficient satisfaction.'

Comments from Beneficiaries

These comments reflect the meaning and significance of disaster funds:

'It doesn't take the memories of that day away, but it helps to know that you don't have to go through anything like this alone, and that is why I am so grateful.'

'I am overwhelmed by the kindness and compassion that has been shown to me. Believe it or not, it is not just the money – the letters that accompany it are a model of genuineness.'

'We have lost so much and it has been very difficult over the last six months; this payment has been a big help to us all, you have restored my faith in humanity.'

'Many, many thanks for everything. Without your generosity things would have been unbearable.'

NOTES ON FAMILY VIEWING

Many of our members have had experience of the death of close family and friends and their identification through odontology, finger printing, DNA, visual means, jewellery and other associated items. Some members have been able to see those who have died and others have not, depending on the circumstances of the disaster and the way in which responders have dealt with this matter. Our experience underlines the need for flexibility and the importance of, wherever possible, offering informed choice as well as treating each set of bereaved individually.

These notes should not be considered exhaustive, but are an effort to outline the most pressing considerations. Families will have the same objective as the responding services: **speedy, accurate identification and release of the dead**. The following notes are written with this objective in mind.

Family Viewing

Every effort should be made to enable people to see a body as soon as possible whatever the event. Seeing a body at a later stage, perhaps at a funeral director's to whom the body has been released – sometimes following a lengthy identification process – is quite a different matter. By this time family members may feel unnerved and daunted by the prospect of seeing the person. We strongly recommend that viewing facilities should therefore be made available when a temporary mortuary is set up following a major emergency. While it is understood that this may depend on the circumstances of the disaster, this intention should be the starting point for a temporary mortuary plan.

Offering **informed choices** to families, including whether to view disrupted bodies and remains should be the norm. It is in the immediate and long-term best interests of all concerned if the timeliness of the human elements of an emergency are understood and integrated into the planning at appropriate stages, and not postponed as 'too difficult' to resolve. Consideration of the potential benefits as well as risks of this approach should be taken into account.

Issues to consider:
- Families may move quickly from understanding the constraints on responders to distrust and resentment if their needs (including the need for speedy, accurate identification, viewing and release) are not being addressed. This will cause more problems, such as: losing trust and cooperation from families; the risk of an adverse psychosocial impact on the bereaved, responders and wider community; adverse publicity; pressure from the media; and political pressure
- Families will not consider logistical difficulties an acceptable reason for delaying viewing
- Viewing at a funeral director's facility some time later after release of the body **is not the same as the opportunity to see the body as soon as possible after identification** (see Chapple and Ziebland research below)
- If viewing facilities are not made available, local funeral directors will have to take responsibility for issues around viewing.

While we appreciate that appropriate training is available to funeral directors on this issue, many (if not most) will not have dealt with the dead from a major disaster. The experience of our members and others whom we have been in contact with have illustrated the difficulties that can arise with attempting to view a body at a later stage

- Despite the best efforts of those responding, a consistent service to families will be difficult if not impossible to guarantee if viewing of individuals is cascaded in this way to funeral directors around the country
- The assumption (or misconception) that work around DVI should stop on a mortuary site because families may be visiting a part of the facility dedicated to viewing should be challenged. It should be possible to develop an appropriate and respectful protocol, which will include careful consideration of **where viewing facilities should be sited** in relation to the mortuary without delaying or interfering with the ongoing vital work of identifying all those who have been killed
- Police family liaison officers can explain what activities are taking place on the site, and its purpose, **prior** to any visit by a family
- Some families may visit the site whether or not viewing facilities have been set up, which should be taken into account. Families have done this in the past. Making people feel like unwelcome intruders can add greatly to their already considerable distress
- We recognise that it is not possible to plan for all eventualities. If circumstances of an emergency make it impossible for viewing facilities to be set up, this can be explained but this **must not be considered the default option.**

Viewing the body after bereavement due to traumatic death: qualitative study in the UK

See http://www.primarycare.ox.ac.uk/pc-bibliography/
ChappleZiebland 2010
Alison Chapple and Sue Ziebland (BMJ, 2010)
Conclusion from this research:
'Even after a traumatic death, relatives should have the opportunity to view the body, and time to decide which family member, if any, should identify remains. Officials should prepare relatives for what they might see, and explain any legal reasons why the body cannot be touched. Guidelines for professional practice must be sensitive to the needs and preferences of people bereaved by traumatic death.'

BIBLIOGRAPHY

BBC News Online Saturday, 17 November 2007 'The King's Cross fire 20 years on' http://news.bbc.co.uk/1/hi/england/london/7096481.stm.

Bergman, D. *The Case for Corporate Responsibility: Corporate Violence and the Criminal Justice System* (Disaster Action, London 2000).

Bergman, D. *Disasters: Where the Law Fails: A New Agenda for Dealing with Corporate Violence* (Herald Families Association/Herald Charitable Trust, London 1993).

Brewin, C. R., Fuchkan, N., Huntley, Z., Robertson, M., Thompson, M., Scragg, P., d'Ardenne, P. and Ehlers, A. 'Outreach and Screening Following the 2005 London Bombings: Usage and Outcomes', in *Psychological Medicine,* 40, 2049–2057 (2010).

Campion, M. *Jupiter's Children* (Liverpool University Press, Liverpool 1998).

Crainer, S. *Zeebrugge: Learning from Disaster: Lessons in Corporate Responsibility* (Herald Families Association/Herald Charitable Trust, London 1993).

Deppa J., et al. *The Media and Disasters: Pan Am 103* (David Fulton Publishers, London 1993).

Disaster Action 'Guidance for Responders' leaflet series.

Disaster Action Newsletters 1992–1995

Disaster Action 'When Disaster Strikes' leaflet series.

Dix P. 'Access to the Dead: The Role of Relatives in the Aftermath of Disaster', in *The Lancet,* 352 (26 September 1998).

Emergency Planning Society *Responding to Disaster: The Human Aspects* (1998).

Eyre, A. *Community Support after Disasters.* Report of Winston Churchill

Travelling Fellowship (2006). http://www.wcmt.org.uk/fellowships/fellows-reports.html.

Eyre, A. *Disaster Funds: Lessons & Guidance on the Management & Distribution of Disaster Funds* (Disaster Action, London 2010).

Eyre, A. *Identifying People's Needs in Major Emergencies and Best Practice in Humanitarian Response.* Independent report commissioned by the Department for Culture, Media & Sport, Contract Number: D3/621 (October 2006). http://webarchive.nationalarchives.gov.uk/+/http://www.cabinetoffice.gov.uk/media/132790/ha_literature_review.pdf.

Eyre, A. 'In Remembrance: Post Disaster Rituals and Symbols', in the *Australian Journal of Emergency Management* (Spring 1999). http://www.em.gov.au/Documents/AJEM_Vol14_Issue3.pdf.

Eyre, A. 'More than PTSD: Proactive Responses among Disaster Survivors', in *The Australasian Journal of Disaster and Trauma Studies*, Volume: 1998-2 (1998) http://www.massey.ac.nz/~trauma/issues/1998-2/eyre.htm.

Eyre, A. 'Psychosocial Aspects of Disaster Recovery: Practical Implications for Disaster Managers', in the *Australian Journal of Emergency Management*, 19 (4) (November 2004) http://www.em.gov.au/Documents/AJEM_Vol19_Issue4.pdf.

Eyre, A. 'Public Information and Disasters: A Report of Consultation with People Directly Affected by Disasters and the Implications for the Crisis Support Team for Essex (CSTE)' (unpublished, 1998).

Eyre, A. 'Public Information and Support after Disasters: A Research Project', in the *Journal of Public Mental Health*, 7 (2) (November 2008).

Guide to Coroners and Inquests and Charter for Coroners Services (Ministry of Justice, 2012).

Homewood, S. *Zeebrugge: A Hero's Story* (Bloomsbury Publishing, London 1989).

Madgwick, G. *Aberfan: Struggling out of the Darkness: A Survivor's Story* (Valley and Vale/Zenith Media, Cardiff 1996).

McLean, I. and Johnes, M. *Aberfan: Government and Disasters* (Welsh Academic Press, Cardiff 2000).

Mosey, J. 'A Life Less Ordinary', BBC Radio 4. http://www.bbc.co.uk/programmes/b011j303.

Nicholson, J. *A Song for Jenny: A Mother's Story of Love and Loss* (Harper Collins, London 2010).

People Management/Chartered Institute for Personnel and Development, 'Corporate manslaughter cases increase' (12 April 2013). http://www.cipd.co.uk/pm/peoplemanagement/b/weblog/archive/2013/04/12/rise-in-corporate-manslaughter-cases.aspx.

Petrig, A. *The War Dead and Their Gravesites*, International Committee of the Red Cross, *International Review of the Red Cross*, 91 (874) (June 2009) http://www.icrc.org/eng/assets/files/other/irrc-874-petrig.pdf.

Quarantelli, E. L. and Dynes, R. 'Introduction: Special Issue on Organizational and Group Behavior in Disaster', in *American Behavioral Scientist*, 13 (3) (January/February 1970) 325–330.

Quinton, A. 'You don't always have to be brave', the *Sunday Express* (23 August 1998).

Scottish TV News, 'Lessons not learnt from Piper Alpha disaster, says HSE'. http://www.stv.tv/content/news/local/north/display.html?id=opencms:/news/north_scotland/newArticle5282191 (Scottish TV News 1998).

Smith, G. 'Oil industry "cannot rule out another Piper Alpha disaster"', in *The Herald* (30 May 2008). http://www.heraldscotland.com/oil-industry-cannot-rule-out-another-piper-alpha-disaster-1.881511.

STV (Scottish Television) 'Piper Alpha Twenty Years On' (video made with families http://www.stv.tv/news/specialReports/piper_alpha/Piper_Alpha_The_families_030708) (2008).

Sweeney, C. 'Twenty years on, Piper Alpha survivor tells of fleeing fireball' in *The Times* (4 July 2008). http://www.thetimes.co.uk/tto/news/uk/scotland/article2630821.ece.

Taylor, M. 'The real story of body 115' in the *Guardian* (22 January 2004) http://www.theguardian.com/world/2004/jan/22/transport.uk.

Taylor, R., Ward A. and Newburn, T. *The Day of the Hillsborough Disaster: A Narrative Account* (Liverpool University Press, Liverpool 1995).

Watkins, J. 'How I Became a Therapist', in *Therapy Today*, 24 (10) (December 2013). http://therapytoday.net/article/show/4035/.

Young, P. *Disasters: Focusing on Management Responsibility* (Herald Families Association/Herald Charitable Trust, London 1993).

INDEX